Ireland and the Popish Plot

Ireland and the Popish Plot

John Gibney
Government of Ireland Postdoctoral Fellow,
National University of Ireland, Galway

© John Gibney 2009

All rights reserved. No reproduction, copy or transmission of this publication may be made without written permission.

No portion of this publication may be reproduced, copied or transmitted save with written permission or in accordance with the provisions of the Copyright, Designs and Patents Act 1988, or under the terms of any licence permitting limited copying issued by the Copyright Licensing Agency, Saffron House, 6-10 Kirby Street, London EC1N 8TS.

Any person who does any unauthorized act in relation to this publication may be liable to criminal prosecution and civil claims for damages.

The author has asserted his right to be identified as the author of this work in accordance with the Copyright, Designs and Patents Act 1988.

First published 2009 by
PALGRAVE MACMILLAN

Palgrave Macmillan in the UK is an imprint of Macmillan Publishers Limited, registered in England, company number 785998, of Houndmills, Basingstoke, Hampshire RG21 6XS.

Palgrave Macmillan in the US is a division of St Martin's Press LLC, 175 Fifth Avenue, New York, NY 10010.

Palgrave Macmillan is the global academic imprint of the above companies and has companies and representatives throughout the world.

Palgrave® and Macmillan® are registered trademarks in the United States, the United Kingdom, Europe and other countries.

ISBN-13: 978–0–230–20365–5 hardback
ISBN-10: 0–230–20365–5 hardback

This book is printed on paper suitable for recycling and made from fully managed and sustained forest sources. Logging, pulping and manufacturing processes are expected to conform to the environmental regulations of the country of origin.

A catalogue record for this book is available from the British Library.

Library of Congress Cataloging-in-Publication Data
Gibney, John, 1976–
  Ireland and the Popish Plot / John Gibney.
    p. cm.
  Includes bibliographical references.
  ISBN-13: 978-0-230-20365-5 (alk. paper)
  ISBN-10: 0-230-20365-5 (alk. paper)
  1. Popish Plot, 1678. 2. Ireland—History—1660–1688.
  3. Catholics—Ireland—History—17th century. 4. Ireland—Politics and government—17th century. 5. Great Britain—History—Restoration, 1660–1688. 6. Ormonde, James Butler, Duke of, 1610–1688.
  I. Title.
DA944.5.G53 2009
941.06′6—dc22   2008029942

10 9 8 7 6 5 4 3 2 1
18 17 16 15 14 13 12 11 10 09

Printed and bound in Great Britain by
CPI Antony Rowe, Chippenham and Eastbourne

For my parents

Contents

Preface	viii
Acknowledgements and Conventions	x
Introduction	1
1 Restoration Ireland: Structural Problems and Structural Prejudice	5
2 The Popish Plot in Ireland, September 1678–May 1679	28
3 Institutions and the 'Irish Plot', May 1679–November 1680	66
4 Irish Evidence, November 1680	99
5 The Decline of the Irish Plot and the Road to the 'Tory Revenge', November 1680–July 1681	115
Conclusion	151
Aftermath, 1681–1691	156
Abbreviations	166
Notes	168
Index	200

Preface

This book is the product of two institutions. It began life as a doctoral thesis in the Department of Modern History, Trinity College, Dublin. I would like to acknowledge the financial assistance provided by a postgraduate award and studentship from Trinity College, Dublin. Research in British archives was facilitated by funding from the Grace Lawless Lee fund, the Trinity Trust, and the T.W. Moody fund, all of Trinity College, Dublin. I also wish to thank the Northside Partnership for additional financial assistance. The thesis was turned into a book under the generous auspices of a National Endowment for the Humanities fellowship at the Keough-Naughton Institute for Irish Studies at the University of Notre Dame: that too should be recorded. Finally, I would like to record my thanks to the staff of the various archives and libraries in which this book was slowly shaped.

In personal terms, numerous people have helped me to complete this thesis over the past few years, in both major and minor ways: from providing sage advice to letting me sleep on the couch. Such assistance has taken a variety of forms, direct, indirect, and in some cases quite possibly forgotten by those who provided it. To record the precise details of each debt would result in a list of inordinate length, so I will confine myself to a list of names, to each of whom I am grateful for something: Guy Beiner, Ciaran Brady, Michael Brown, Coleman Dennehy, Sean Duffy, Aoife Duignan, David Edwards, Fiona Fitzsimons, Kevin Forkan, Ciara Hogan, Tara Keenan-Thomson, Breandán Mac Suibhne, Mairead McAuley, Kevin Murphy, Jason McHugh, Edward Madigan, Dave Murphy, Jill Northridge, Kate O'Malley, Micheál Ó Siochrú, Jane Ohlmeyer, Helga Robinson-Hammerstein, Jennifer Scholtz, Freya Verstraten, and Darina Wade. In addition, James McGuire and Éamonn Ó Ciardha deserve to be singled out for particular thanks for helping me out in far too many ways as I muddled my way through the process of writing the original thesis.

The thesis was written under the supervision of Aidan Clarke, and it would not have been written without him. More than anyone else at Trinity College, I would particularly like to thank him for his advice, assistance, encouragement, and eagle eye over the past few years. I also wish to thank Robert Armstrong, Tim Harris, and Jim Smyth for extended commentaries on the thesis that proved invaluable in helping to turn it into a book. At Notre Dame, Aedin Clements and Christopher Fox did everything possible to facilitate that process, while Breandán Ó Buachalla generously let me avail of his expertise with sources in Irish. Aidan Clarke and Éamonn Ó Ciardha generously commented on an earlier draft of the manuscript: any mistakes in the final version will be mine, and mine alone. Finally, I would like to thank my family, especially my parents, Charlie and Joan, for their encouragement, patience, and support.

I could easily construct a rogues gallery of friends and colleagues outside academia who, in their own various ways, helped me to complete this thesis (or in some cases, inadvertently did their utmost to prevent me from doing so). But they should know who they are.

Acknowledgements and Conventions

Dates have been given according to the old style calendar, but the year is taken to begin on 1 January rather than 25 March. Quotations in the text have been modernized, with the exception of archaic words, and instances where spelling has dictated phonetic purpose. There have been occasional (and silent) minor grammatical alterations for the sake of clarity. Interpolations, and unclear or illegible words, have been indicated in square brackets. In the text itself, the names of individuals have been standardized wherever possible. Unless otherwise indicated, biographical details are taken from the *Oxford Dictionary of National Biography* (60 vols, Oxford, 2004) and the Royal Irish Academy's forthcoming *Dictionary of Irish Biography* (Cambridge).

I would like to thank the following institutions for permission to reproduce material retained in their possession: the Board of the National Library of Ireland; Dublin Public Libraries; the National Archives of the United Kingdom; the Council of King's Inn's, Dublin; the Bodleian Library, University of Oxford; and the Royal Irish Academy. Earlier versions of parts of the text have been published as 'An Irish Informer in Restoration England: David Fitzgerald and the "Irish Plot" in the Exclusion Crisis', in *Éire-Ireland: A Journal of Irish Studies*, vol. 42: 3 & 4 (Fall/Winter 2007), pp. 249–76, and 'The memory of 1641 and Protestant identity in Restoration and Jacobite Ireland' in Mervyn Busteed, Frank Neal and Jonathan Tonge (eds) *Irish Protestant Identities* (Manchester University Press, 2008), pp. 13–27. I would like to thank both the Irish American Cultural Institute and Manchester University Press for permission to reproduce this material.

Introduction

The Popish Plot was the outburst of anti-Catholic hysteria in England prompted by allegations made in the autumn of 1678 of a Catholic conspiracy to wipe out Protestantism in the three Stuart kingdoms. Over time it gave way to the so-called 'Exclusion Crisis', the intense political struggle that arose in England between 1679 and 1681 over the vexing question of who would succeed Charles II as king. As matters stood in 1678, the heir was a Catholic: Charles's younger brother James, duke of York. In an atmosphere of intense anti-Catholicism, this was bound to prove contentious, and over the next two years a campaign to exclude York from the succession would be conducted both inside and outside the English parliament. The exclusion campaign rested upon fears of a Catholic monarch which stemmed from a fear of Catholics. And hence the issue that ensured the relevance of the crisis to Ireland, and vice versa: many of these Catholics were Irish, for most of the Irish were Catholics.

But historians usually pass over Ireland's links to the Popish Plot on the reasonable grounds that little or nothing actually happened there. The only Irish aspect of the Popish Plot to garner any significant attention is the execution in London of the Catholic primate and Archbishop of Armagh, Oliver Plunkett, in July 1681.[1] According to one scholar, it would be 'repetitive and largely purposeless' to write 'an elaborate description of a phenomenon which was, in any event, far more influential and pervasive in England than in Ireland'.[2] And it is not just the Popish Plot that remains neglected, for the period in which it fell – that of the Restoration and the reign of Charles II (1660–1685) – is traditionally seen as little more than an 'interim between upheavals'.³ J.C. Beckett eloquently described Restoration Ireland as

> A period of transition, in a more direct and genuine sense than that overworked phrase commonly implies. By the 1660s the basis of the 'Protestant Ascendancy' that was to dominate the eighteenth century had already been laid; but it was not until after the wars of the Revolution that Irish Protestants acquired the arrogant self-confidence that became one of their main characteristics. In the interval, they still felt insecure; they still feared that the dispossessed Roman Catholics might strike a blow to recover their estates and their power; and they watched anxiously the course of events in England, lest some change of policy there should weaken or destroy their position.⁴

Ireland's role and relevance in the crisis of 1678–1681 has recently attracted attention from English historians.⁵ But in Irish historiography, the Popish Plot is usually interpreted in terms set by Thomas Carte almost 300 years ago: that it is essentially unimportant because the incumbent viceroy James Butler, duke of Ormond, kept Ireland under control and thus guaranteed its stability. It is a view reflected (and perhaps even shaped) by the contemporary assessment of Sir Robert Southwell, who wrote in May 1682 that

> You will find in Ireland a profound quiet, as it has lately been, when Scotland had instead actual rebellion and England been filled and disquieted about the plot. I cannot impute this under God to anything but the conduct of the duke of Ormond. For he, having by long experience, knowledge of the kingdom and all men in it, having a large fortune and consequently many dependents scattered into its several parts, and being also related in blood to great numbers of the Irish Papists, the discontented had either dreaded to begin, or he presently knew and suppressed whatever was contriving. Thus knowing what security the kingdom was in, he had the courage to undergo all those calumnies and accusations thrown upon him in the heat of the plot. Whereas if a stranger had there governed who must have been influenced by the general outcry, the Irish had certainly been driven into desperation.⁶

Consequently, thanks to the role ascribed to Ormond, the crisis had few *overt* consequences with regards to Ireland. In terms of events, this is true. But in terms of expectations it is another matter entirely. Allegations of Catholic plotting were bound to have a resonance in a country with an overwhelmingly Catholic population, and they did. The crisis was deemed by many to have the potential to replicate the events of the early 1640s in Ireland, most particularly the 1641 rebellion and the atrocities committed against Protestants during it: after all, it was supposedly a *Popish* plot. The fear of being wiped out *en masse* was naturally of particular concern to Irish Protestants, who were broadly of the opinion that in 1641, this is precisely what Irish Catholics had attempted to do. The impact of the crisis of 1678–1681 stretched the fragile fabric of a post-war society, revealing the latent tensions that underpinned the Restoration settlement in Ireland. War, conquest, and colonization in the 1640s and 1650s had radically altered Irish society in ways that were maintained beyond the Restoration at the expense of a diverse, disgruntled, and dispossessed Catholic community. What had also persisted was a lingering uncertainty as to whether the changes wrought in the 1650s would be permanent, or might yet be reversed. Therein lies the fundamental nature of Beckett's 'transition'. The events of 1689–1691 – the 'wars of the Revolution', as he called them – would guarantee the eventual outcome.

This book is about a part of that transition. The Popish Plot offers a window into the ostensibly unruffled world of Restoration Ireland. To write the history of the Popish Plot in relation to Ireland is to write the history of what did not happen, but of what was believed to be imminent. As events transpired, the Popish Plot in Ireland was indeed a non-event. But to those contemporaries who lived through the crisis, the fears, expectations, and possibilities that it consisted of assumed a significance and relevance that was very real indeed.

There are two intertwined strands to this study. One is the impact of the Popish Plot and Exclusion Crisis upon Ireland. The other is the role played by Ireland within the Popish Plot and Exclusion Crisis. While these are interrelated, they are not automatically the same. This is first and foremost a work of Irish history: its focus is on Ireland, not England. It is not intended to be a self-conscious addition to the increasingly tiresome debates about the so-called 'New British' history. The Stuart kingdoms of England, Ireland, and

Scotland had distinct yet interrelated historical experiences. That is no great insight: it is an obvious fact that does not need to be proclaimed. The significance of the crisis in England, its origins, and its events, are outlined at the outset in order to liberate the Irish dimensions of the story from the weight of other histories. True, the impact of the Popish Plot on Ireland has to be understood against a British backdrop: the currents of the crisis in the larger island shaped its course in Ireland. But the crisis also has to be understood against the backdrop of war and sectarian conflict in Europe, and in the light of the colonial history of early modern Ireland. This is a story within stories, and it takes the form of an interpretive narrative, a tentative attempt at a history intended to illustrate both the mounting impact of the Popish Plot – the rumour and innuendo that is the subject matter of this book – on the structure of a colonial society, and thereby to illustrate the perceived and actual fragility of its foundations. The first chapter is intended to set the stage by glancing back in time to outline why the revelations of a Popish Plot in August 1678 would have had the impact that they did both in Ireland, and in relation to it. The remaining chapters attempt to illustrate and explain what this consisted of, while the final chapter looks forward in time to offer a suggestion about its significance.

The sources for this study revolve around two sets of material. The first is the vast archive of the first duke of Ormond, scattered between Dublin, London, and Oxford: the unavoidable substitute for the vast corpus of documentation that has been lost through the centuries, the destruction of which renders so much of Irish history – including the local implications of the Popish Plot – permanently obscure. The second set consists of the various testimonies of Irish informers that were generally revealed to be falsehoods. This hardly inspires confidence: one type of source material is incomplete and the other is untrue. But between these two poles more can be gathered; enough to try to make sense of the subject at hand. The history of what did not happen is also the history of what might have happened, or what was believed could happen. And to make sense of the Popish Plot in relation to Ireland, the stage has to be set across the Irish Sea.

1
Restoration Ireland
Structural Problems and Structural Prejudice

To understand the Popish Plot and Exclusion Crisis in relation to Ireland, it is necessary to first explain these events, the beliefs that underpinned them, and the structural faults within Irish society that ensured they would have an impact there. This chapter is intended to provide an introduction to the Popish Plot in England, and an interpretive introduction to the unsettled condition of Restoration Ireland.

I

The London cleric Israel Tonge first met Titus Oates in 1677. Tonge's fanatical anti-Catholicism was unquestionable, and in Oates he seemed to find confirmation to match his conviction. For Oates himself, a pivotal moment in a dubious career came after his expulsion from the Catholic seminary of St Omer in June 1678, for when he returned to London in July, he furnished Tonge with an elaborate account of a Catholic conspiracy against Protestant England that both men recounted to Charles II and the Privy Council in the autumn of 1678. This was the genesis of the Popish Plot.

It came at a particular juncture in English affairs. The 1670s had been characterized by emerging fears that the Stuart regime was drifting towards Catholicism and authoritarian government. Of particular concern was the fact that thanks to Charles II's habit of fathering children only with his mistresses, the legitimate heir to the throne was his younger brother James, duke of York, and it was an open secret that he had converted to Catholicism in 1673. The prospect of a Catholic king in the near future was therefore very real. Nor had the reality of events helped matters. After negotiating a treaty with the French in 1670 containing a secret (though ultimately unfulfilled) commitment by Charles II to publicly convert to Catholicism, Charles joined Louis XIV in embarking upon a disastrous war with the Dutch in 1672. A succession of failures combined with public discontent forced Charles to abandon the French and negotiate peace with the Dutch in February 1674. But there could be no avoiding the fact that the king of Protestant England had allied himself with Catholic France to make war on the even more Protestant Dutch.

However, by 1678 the rift with the Dutch had been healed (in part by the marriage of York's daughter Mary to William of Orange), and England prepared itself to re-enter the conflict, this time on the side of the Dutch. Against this backdrop, the possibility that the French were conspiring to subvert Protestant England (not to mention Ireland and Scotland) was bound to assume a greater significance. While some credence was given to Oates' claims, the authorities became increasingly sceptical in the absence of concrete evidence. Then, on 17 October 1678, the body of Sir Edmund Bury Godfrey was found in London. He was the magistrate before whom Titus Oates had sworn his original claims; he had now been murdered. Arguably, he was a man who knew too much, and the obvious conclusion to draw was that he met his death at Catholic hands. Oates had also implicated Edward Coleman, York's former secretary, who in the early 1670s had embarked on a tentative and unofficial correspondence with the French that even they had disregarded. After he was implicated by Oates, evidence of these negotiations fortuitously came to light. Irrespective of what they had actually consisted of, between Coleman's machinations and Godfrey's murder the Popish Plot had received enough credibility to be sustained.

Oates' claims were presented to the English House of Lords on 31 October 1678.[1] The subsequent development of the plot was intimately linked to proceedings in the English parliament, as it became both the venue for Oates' testimony and the forum for the investigation of what he had alleged. While this would not be fully publicized until April 1679, in the meantime rumours and fragments of information contributed to a growing climate of public fear and paranoia. Parliament demanded that the king take measures against Catholics, and by December the succession of trials that would characterize the

Popish Plot began in earnest with that of Edward Coleman. These would continue in a climate fed by further allegations, ending with the acquittal of Sir George Wakeman on charges of attempting to poison the king in July 1679.

It is perhaps misleading to draw distinctions, implicitly or explicitly, between the Popish Plot and the Exclusion Crisis, for one had built upon the other. It had been obvious that York's Catholicism, and the question of the succession, would attract attention from the outset: his removal from the Privy Council, and even from England itself, was being demanded in parliament as early as November 1678. After the Cavalier parliament was dissolved in December 1678, the first elections since 1661 were fought in February and March 1679. In the new parliament, the implications of a Catholic succession were openly being discussed. Consequently, it was suggested that York could simply have limitations placed upon his future rule, or, eventually and more significantly, that he could be completely excluded from the succession. The momentum created by the Popish Plot was such that, in May 1679, legislation to provide for the latter was introduced to parliament.

This was anathema to Charles, who prorogued and then dissolved the English parliament towards the end of the month. Consequently, when a second set of elections was held in the summer of 1679, divisions began to emerge across England between the opponents of York's succession and its supporters. Charles would postpone the meeting of this new parliament until October 1680, but in the meantime, political mobilization began to take place on a large scale, as the popular fears of Catholics that had so characterized 1678–1679 were now harnessed by the nascent opposition to the purpose of both calling a parliament and exerting pressure upon it to exclude York from the succession. Huge anti-Catholic rallies, often involving the burning of an effigy of the Pope, and mass-petitioning campaigns demanding the meeting of parliament were two obvious aspects of this. Another was the burgeoning propaganda war facilitated by the lapse of the Licensing Act in 1679 that opened the door to the proliferation of printed news and propaganda that became another characteristic of the crisis. Both sides of the debate over the succession engaged in this propaganda war, but it was not all orchestrated. Whether on paper or on the streets, spontaneous interjections into this raucous world of public debate happened on a regular basis, for the Popish Plot had both tapped into and reflected a deep-seated and very real fear and hatred of Catholicism. The exclusion campaign may have fed upon fears and activities of this kind. But it did not create them.

Throughout the winter of 1680 the 'Whig' grouping in the English parliament remained committed to excluding York from the succession, and parliament was dissolved for its pains the following spring. While 'exclusion' had never received wholly unanimous backing, the attempted reintroduction of legislation to this effect in a new parliament summoned in March 1681 prompted Charles to dissolve it within a week, and to justify his actions via a declaration read from pulpits across the land. He blamed the crisis on the activities of malcontents driven by a concealed republicanism and committed himself to a number of policies, such as suppressing Catholicism and calling regular parliaments. But Charles acted from a position of strength underpinned by a massive financial subsidy from the French that removed the awkward necessity whereby English monarchs were obliged to expose themselves to their parliaments in exchange for the money they needed to govern. Charles II no longer had this problem. He would never again call a parliament, and over the next few years he and his government would exact their revenge upon their opponents. The Popish Plot and Exclusion Crisis had ended in 1681. By 1685 it was obvious that they had failed when York succeeded his brother as James II, thereby becoming the first Catholic king of England, Ireland, and Scotland in over a century, and the last they would ever have.

II

The Popish Plot and the Exclusion Crisis were connected and sustained by one common thread: a visceral English anti-Catholicism. There may have been a Popish Plot; but there was a widespread belief that there had always been a Popish Plot. The crisis of 1678–1681 was simply the latest manifestation of a particular tradition, for anti-Catholicism had long been a vital element of the mental world of Protestants in early modern Britain and Ireland.[2]

After the break with Rome in the 1530s, much English theological discussion had dwelt upon the iniquities of the Catholic Church, depicted as at best a corrupt and sinful institution that had strayed from the true path, or at worst as the Whore of Babylon foretold in Revelation, led by the Antichrist in the form of the Pope. Arguably, this was understandable at a time when an alternative English church was being created, but key themes were formulated at this time that would survive for centuries. Sinister interpretations could be derived from Roman Catholic doctrine: the hierarchical nature of the Catholic Church was deemed to be inherently tyrannical, being dedicated to the oppression of its laity and the exaltation of the charmed circle of its clergy. Where Protestantism sought to redeem, Popery sought to enslave.

This was the ideological framework within which English anti-Popery was cast, but another crucial layer of anti-Catholic discourse came with the persecution (most especially the burning) of Protestants in the reign of Queen Mary (1553–1558). While her regime was short-lived and its excesses were exaggerated (most notably in John Foxe's *Acts and Monuments*[3]), it nonetheless seemed to offer visceral proof of the evils of Popery. Theological underpinnings were now overlaid with a distinctively English experience, and this proved to be the starting point for a martyrological tradition that, over time, would assimilate events in other countries, such as the St Bartholomew's Day Massacre in Paris in 1572, or the atrocities of the Irish rebellion of 1641. Protestantism was seen to be engaged in a cosmic struggle that cut across national boundaries – after all, Mary had been married to Philip II of Spain – and paradoxically, this notion developed in tandem with the perception of Protestant England's individuality before God; England was an 'elect nation', providentially chosen for God's purpose. This reached particular heights in the reign of Elizabeth I (1558–1603), as England was part of an increasingly embattled Protestant island off the coast of Catholic Europe, as illustrated by the dispatch of the Spanish Armada by Philip II in 1588. But God's providence, and His willingness to save people who were obviously His people, was deemed to be equally evident when the same armada was scattered across the ocean by the elements. After the belief system of English Protestantism was set in place during the first half of the sixteenth century, the second half saw English anti-Popery take on political connotations in the face of the conflict with Spain that England became embroiled in. The fact that Pope Pius V had committed the Papacy to reconverting England, denouncing Elizabeth as a heretic in 1570 and absolving English Catholics from their obedience to her, raised the fear of subversion being fostered from within by Catholic emissaries who would, in time, become the most feared of enemies: Jesuits. English Protestantism may have been diverse and factious, but all were Protestants in the face of a Catholic threat deemed to be both external and internal. Anti-Catholic sentiment was often at odds with the reality of an increasingly small and weak English Catholic community, but the increasing politicized fear of Catholicism found expression in the brutal and draconian Elizabethan penal code. Popery was treasonous: as such it warranted the utmost vigilance and the most severe penalties.

By 1600 all bar one of the themes that defined English anti-Popery throughout the seventeenth century were in place. The final one stemmed from the discovery of the Gunpowder Plot in 1605. Again, this was perceived as another example of God's providence, when a plot to blow up King James I and parliament was uncovered on 5 November 1605. Along with the accession of Elizabeth on 17 November, this became part of an English Protestant calendar that served as a locus for anti-Catholic sentiment in future generations (both dates were utilized extensively for public and politicized commemorations during the Exclusion Crisis). But it also provided the paradigm of a Catholic conspiracy, of a secret and hidden plot bent to a horrendous purpose. If the activities of Jesuit missionaries had initially given rise to this trope in the reign of Elizabeth, it was perfected by the Gunpowder Plot in the reign of her successor.

Peter Lake has contended that English Protestantism defined itself in terms of a binary opposition: that Catholicism, and its works and attributions, were the polar opposite – the 'others' – of their English Protestant counterparts.[4] Anthony Milton qualified this, suggesting that the English had not fully shaken off their Catholic past, and that both domestic and international realities forced uneasy attempts at accommodation with Catholicism both within and without England (though this did not imply compromise in the spiritual struggle). But paradoxically, as the English Catholic community decreased in size and thus in visibility, a belief in Catholic conspiracy seemed to grow. After all, recusants were at least recognizable; in the 1630s and 1640s fears of the hidden danger of Popery flourished.

But English Catholics were not the only Catholics. If, as Lake suggested, anti-Catholicism required an 'other', and if English Protestant identity had acquired specifically national connotations, then foreign

Catholics became a more pronounced bugbear. After the restoration of Charles II in 1660 English anti-Popery retained its visceral edge. Protestant England had to survive, for by the 1670s there had been unsettling developments as European Protestantism was weakened after the Thirty Years War. Within England, Catholics were believed to be at work for subversive purposes: the Jesuits were blamed for the Great Fire of London in 1666. And across the English Channel was potentially a more real danger in the shape of the reinvigorated Catholic superpower that was Louis XIV's France.

There was also a common view that there was another Catholic threat to England's west. Arguably, Ireland had always played a role in English anti-Catholicism; from the rebellion of James Fitzmaurice Fitzgerald in 1579 and the Nine Years War (1594–1603) to the events of the 1641 rebellion, fears of Catholic Ireland had become part of the mental world of English Protestants. Combined with Ireland's overwhelmingly Catholic population, often assumed of being capable of collective treachery, these perceptions guaranteed that anti-Popery retained a particular potency with regards to Ireland. However, it would be equally, if not more potent, within Ireland itself.

III

In October 1641 Catholics in Ulster embarked upon a rebellion against Protestant colonists in the province that rapidly escalated across the island. On 22 October 1641 Sir Phelim O'Neill, MP for Dungannon (amongst other things), called to Charlemont Fort in Armagh under the pretext of dining with its governor, and proceeded to take over the fort. Similar events happened across Armagh and Tyrone over the next two days, as members of the Catholic landed gentry captured various key positions by force and guile. These seem to have been part of a larger scheme for a rebellion, as on 22 October the government in Dublin were informed of a plan to capture Dublin Castle and appropriate its arsenal. Having been duly warned, the government imprisoned all those who were accused or suspected of involvement. However, the failure of this did nothing to impede the widespread revolt that soon followed.

These events were essentially a reaction to the plantation of Ulster by British settlers in the first decades of the seventeenth century. The nature and rhetoric of much of what happened in the weeks that followed illustrates that Catholic Irish insurgents sought to exact a price upon many of those settlers.[5] The original purpose of the conspiracy headed by O'Neill was straightforward enough. The Catholic gentry of Ulster sought a position of security and strength from which to negotiate with Charles I on the principal issues of concern to them at a time of great uncertainty, namely, the security of their lands and religion. However, the limited capture of key positions in Ulster for specific purposes gave way to a popular rebellion directed at the English Protestant colonists who had settled there under the plantation. There was a deep groundswell of resentment on the part of the Irish at those who were accurately perceived to have supplanted them. As the rebellion fanned out from its core in Armagh and the authority of the colonial government collapsed, Protestant settlers were explicitly targeted for attack. Some of these attacks stemmed from little more than banditry and robbery. Some arose from ubiquitous socio-economic tensions. But alongside such short-term considerations were deeper resentments. A visceral anti-Englishness was evident as settlers were attacked and stripped before being sent out into the winter. It was also illustrated by such macabre events as the occasional mock trials of English cattle, and in the concern with the eradication of the culture of the English colonists. What also became evident was naked sectarianism as the symbols of Protestantism were also attacked. Taken as a whole, the winter of 1641–1642 saw almost ritualized attempts to wipe out the physical, cultural, and religious presence of the colonists in Ireland. The subsequent wars of the 1640s became a parallel theatre to the British Civil Wars as well as an internecine conflict, and would only be ended by the Parliamentarian reconquest of Ireland in 1649–1653. However, the initial months of the rebellion could be (and were) seen as markedly distinct from the remainder of the conflict. Fears of a repeat of the 1641 rebellion would prey on the minds of Irish Protestants in the later seventeenth century. The reason was simple: it was perceived as having been a concerted attempt to wipe out the Protestant presence in Ireland. The events of 1641 came to be seen as the ultimate proof of the barbarity of the Catholic Irish, a perception that played a role in political discourse in both islands.

Traumatic experiences have often proved crucial in defining collective identities in the face of threats.[6] Despite the diversity of Ireland's Protestant communities, in subsequent decades 1641 became a touchstone for that aspect of their developing identity that perceived their position in Ireland as besieged and under threat. Consequently, there developed a specifically Irish tradition of anti-Popery, which, while undoubtedly influenced by the stock imagery and rhetoric of British anti-Popery, derived its potency from the structural reality that Protestants in Ireland remained a minority in a country that had been wracked by warfare in the 1640s and 1650s. The blunt reality was that in 1641 the Catholic Irish embarked upon what eventually became a nationwide rebellion that was essentially directed at Protestant – and in the early phases of the rebellion, primarily English – colonists.

The rebellion was rightly assumed to be a defining moment in Irish history. But what actually happened during it? The perception was that the colonists had narrowly escaped extermination in an unmitigated and brutal sectarian onslaught. The most recent and substantive study readily identifies the basis for such Protestant fears, outlining the extent of violence against the settlers, and its politicized and ritualistic nature.[7] But the sheer extent of the assault across the country was undoubtedly exaggerated. Lurid accounts of the torture and massacre of British Protestant settlers became stock perceptions of the rebellion, and atrocity stories published in the aftermath, and decades later, emphasized the supposed lack of provocation for the attacks upon Protestants. Allegations of planned and actual massacres in Ireland were immediately evident in books and pamphlets published in the immediate aftermath of the rebellion, as intention was conflated with reality.[8] Many of the same types of atrocity would be reiterated in the pamphlets: the drowning of prisoners, the brutal murder of children, the disembowelling of pregnant women. Such depictions drew upon long-established tropes of Catholic atrocities stemming back to the Reformation that had been shaped by works such as Foxe's *Acts and Monuments*: the Marian persecutions in England, the St Bartholomew's Day Massacre in France, and the excesses of the Spanish in both the Americas and the Netherlands automatically provided a paradigm of Catholic perfidy and brutality into which the 1641 rebellion was itself integrated over time. Amidst a welter of printed works that dwelt on the exaggerated atrocities of the rebellion, there were others that strengthened such perceptions by providing specifically Protestant interpretations of the rebellion, along with the testimony of Protestants who had survived it. One of these was Henry Jones' *A Remonstrance of Divers Remarkable Passages Concerning the Church and Kingdom of Ireland* (1642).

Henry Jones was the Church of Ireland dean of Kilmore, straddling a number of counties in the north-west of Ireland. The *Remonstrance* arose from the commission he had headed that was appointed to enquire into the losses endured by the Protestant survivors of the rebellion; it was presented to the English parliament in March 1642 and was subsequently published. The vast bulk of the text consisted of printed depositions that had been recorded by Jones and his colleagues. Within these testimonies, as taken down in the chaotic aftermath of the rebellion, rumour and hearsay were reproduced alongside eyewitness accounts of the rebellions, which served to greatly exaggerate their cumulative effect. But the litany of horrors that these accounts purported to reveal were essentially appendices to an account of the rebellion that both prefaced them and had been derived from them. According to Jones and his colleagues

> There hath been beyond all parallel of former ages, a most bloody and Antichristian combination and plot hatched, by well-nigh the whole Romish sect, by way of combination from parts foreign, with those at home, against this our church and state; thereby intending the utter extirpation of the reformed religion, and the professors of it.[9]

It was immediately obvious that no distinction would be made between the various Catholic communities on the island. According to Jones, the rebels had expected assistance from France and Spain, the two great Catholic powers of Europe, and had received the blessing of the Pope for the enterprise. This Irish rebellion had been planned for a long time, perhaps decades, and was to be linked to uprisings in both England and Scotland. This interpretation would prove potent: it was essentially reiterated during the Popish Plot almost 40 years later, and was malleable enough to misrepresent events to suit its purpose. Within popular discourse (insofar it can be discerned), the dominant view of the rebellion was that articulated by figures such as Jones. The atrocious nature and purpose of the rebellion were revealed in the ample testimony presented to the English parliament and reproduced in the *Remonstrance*. 'But what pen can set forth, what tongue express, whose eye can read, ear hear, or heart, without melting, consider the cruelties, more than barbarous, daily exercised upon us by those inhuman, blood-sucking tigers!'[10] Despite such hyperbole, this view of the rebellion as an attempt at sectarian genocide would be stoutly restated by another canonical account of 1641: Sir John Temple's *The Irish Rebellion*.

Temple had been the Irish master of the rolls, who had ultimately taken the side of parliament during the wars of the 1640s. Oft cited, his history rarely seems to receive adequate scholarly attention.[11] Toby Barnard pithily defined the enduring relevance of *The Irish Rebellion* in providing the 'circumstantial detail and explanatory framework' to perpetuate a Protestant perspective on 1641.[12] Its purpose was set out in its preface: to reveal to readers 'the sad story of our miseries'.[13] Temple had placed great emphasis on the veracity and variety of the evidence that he sought to present, and readily cast himself in the role of 'public informer':[14]

> With a resolution most clearly to declare the truth.... All that I aim at is, that there may remain for the benefit of this present age, as well as of posterity, some certain records and monuments of the first beginnings and fatal progress of this rebellion, together with the horrid cruelties most unmercifully exercised by the Irish rebels upon the British, and Protestants within this kingdom of Ireland.[15]

It is debatable to what extent Temple himself set an agenda for future Protestant analyses of Ireland and the Irish, or whether he was simply reiterating a point of view that would itself be repeated over time. Certainly, he provided 'the raw material from which Protestant memories were shaped and reshaped over generations'[16] by printing large numbers of extracts from witness accounts of the rebellion, and thus provided raw material for future generations of polemicists; though equally, his account would be viewed with scepticism by many. Temple was no advocate of persuasion or conciliation with regard to the Catholic Irish; rather, in a manner redolent of the 'penal laws' of the eighteenth century, he proposed 'a wall of separation betwixt the English and the Irish'[17] as a preventative measure to ensure that future generations of Protestants in Ireland might be saved from a recurrence of the events of the rebellion. He referred to the basis of his work in the testimony provided by the witness depositions collected in the aftermath, correctly observing that the testimonies were 'most commonly decried, and held by the Irish as very injurious to their countrymen'.[18] Their polemical value was not lost on contemporaries. But Temple's own definition of their purpose was revealing: 'to provide some general account of the losses suffered by the British', which accurately reflected their original purpose, but also to authoritatively describe 'the cruelties exercised by the Irish'.[19] His claim that many of the deponents died soon after presenting their testimony seemed to intensify their veracity; the depositions stood as their final testament, and as a valediction. There were good reasons to be adamant about this. Any doctoring of the record, to remove awkward realities, would inevitably have implications for the future, as the rebels would seek to 'palliate their rebellion... under the name of a holy and just war'.[20] In explaining the evident hostility of the Irish towards the English, he emphasized religion, intertwined with ethnicity; civility and religion were in this way inextricably linked.[21] The suffering of the Irish was due to the wrath of God, in punishment for their sinfulness; and in such a reading the English were the instruments of God's wrath, being punished for their sins by the rebellion but gaining given a chance to redeem themselves by their survival.[22] The savage and barbarous nature of the Irish, and their unremitting hostility to the English, was a running theme in his narrative as it approached its terminal date of 1641, and he seemed to implicitly concede that this loathing was mutual.[23] However, he painted a rosy picture of 40 years of relative peace and harmony prior to the outbreak of the rebellion, that on the one hand eroded any basis for claiming that the rebellion had its origins in anything other than the savagery of the Irish, while on the other set the scene for the brutality he sought to describe, as presented in the evidence of the rebellion's Protestant victims.

Like Jones' *Remonstrance*, the ideological and physical core of *The Irish Rebellion* was to be found in the depositions printed within it, and he emphasized that the basis of his work lay in these testimonies.[24] Over time such visceral depictions would gain a cumulative effect. When stripped of the complexity of its background, the technical reality of a Catholic rebellion against Protestant colonists was that the battle lines inevitably adopted a religious tinge. In time then 1641 could be depicted as a purely religious war, and its events would retain a resonance. Protestant political argument in the decades after the event became predicated on the fact that they remained an embattled minority, endangered in Ireland and aware that they had come under attack in the past. But by the end of the 1640s, the interpretation of the rebellion articulated by writers such as Jones and Temple had influenced both the English Parliament's decisive re-intervention in Irish affairs and the fact that many of Ireland's Protestants would align themselves with it. Alongside these was the welter of ephemeral tracts and accounts that seemed to offer further confirmation of what had happened. The rebels had 'shed abundance of English blood, and have vowed to destroy all the Protestants now living in Ireland'.[25] The Pope had ordered Catholics to massacre 'heretics', and Catholics were instructed to 'study your brains daily, to invent instruments of torture'.[26] 'The rebels' tyranny is great, that they put both man, woman and child (that are Protestants) to the sword, not sparing either age, degree, sex or their reputation.'[27] In the immediate aftermath of the rebellion, the perception of the rebellion that was being presented to English audiences was of an untrammelled and horrific attempt at sectarian genocide in Ireland. This perception of Irish events would have a role to play in England throughout the decade, most especially when England eventually turned its attention back to Ireland in 1649.

IV

One of the principal reasons for the parliamentarian invasion of Ireland was the strategic necessity to defeat royalist forces there, especially after the 1649 treaty between the incumbent viceroy, Ormond, and the Confederate Catholics that seemed to presage an alliance between them. In these circumstances, Oliver Cromwell had argued that 'they will in a very short time be able to land forces in England, and put us to trouble here', and furthermore, 'I had rather be overrun with a Cavalierish interest than a Scotch interest; I had rather be overrun with a Scotch interest, than an Irish interest; and I think of all this is most dangerous... for all the world knows their barbarism.'[28]

It is reasonable to presume that 1641 was part of the latter consideration. After all, much of the atrocity propaganda generated by the rebellion had been printed in England for an English audience. But the rebellion had a more immediate and visceral relevance to Protestants in Ireland, many of whom perceived parliament as being the best guarantor of their interests, and who consequently transferred their allegiance to it; Henry Jones, for example, became scoutmaster-general of the Cromwellian army in Ireland. If, as Toby Barnard has argued, the period between 1641 and 1660 was decisive in ensuring the settler communities transition from viewing themselves in ethnic terms as an English interest to viewing themselves in religious terms as a Protestant interest, the sense of danger provided by the sectarian conflicts of the 1640s, and most especially the initial rebellion, was the catalyst that both created the change and cemented it.[29]

The Cromwellian land settlement that followed the prosecution of the war was intended to punish Irish Catholics for rebelling in 1641, whilst ensuring that the threat they seemed to pose was neutralized, and that the debts incurred by the prosecution of the war were repaid. The solution that collectively seemed to fulfil most of these objectives was the large-scale confiscation of Catholic land, and its transfer into Protestant hands. Despite the fact that this had been carried out by what was later deemed to be a regime that had usurped the rightful monarch, after the restoration of Charles II in 1660 the settlement was substantively preserved. The Irish Protestant interest successfully sought to maintain the gains that so many of them had made in the 1650s, for any restitution of the Catholic community could only come at the expense of those Protestants who had benefited from their dispossession.[30] The utility of scaremongering about a potential repeat of 1641 was not lost on those in the 1660s who sought to block the implications of the Restoration settlement.[31] Certainly, the Catholic cleric John Lynch took the view that the maintenance of the confiscations of the 1650s was the principal motivation for inciting hatred against Catholics.[32] But this is perhaps to underrate the extent to which the Protestant perception of 1641 was assimilated into genuine beliefs. Fears of a repeat of 1641 were useful, but they were also quite genuine in the 1660s and beyond, as it was assumed by some that 'less will not content the Irish than the rooting out all English interest here'.[33] Equally, opposing realities could differ: 'I suppose you have heard of a new Irish rebellion which has made a great noise here, and I guess a greater with you, but I do not find anything in it. It is said all was but a story, and therefore I shall say no more of it.'[34] Over 13 years later, the threat to Protestant Ireland (and England) perceived during the Popish Plot derived strength and credence from a belief in such perceptions, and the assumption that another Catholic rebellion along the lines of 1641 was imminent. Vigilance would be required to forestall this ever coming to pass. Indeed, in 1662 the Irish parliament codified the Protestant interpretation of the rebellion into law by passing an act for its outbreak to be commemorated. Each year, on 23 October, a sermon was to be preached at all Church of Ireland services to give thanks for Protestant Ireland's deliverance. No work was to be done on the day, and attendance at the sermons was mandatory: reminders were to be issued to the congregations on the preceding Sunday. If no sermon was prepared, the text of the act itself, and the interpretation of the rebellion that it contained, was to be read out in its stead: that such a 'conspiracy so generally inhumane, barbarous and cruel' had been permitted to proceed was deemed a judgement of God on Protestants, while its discovery and the assistance in suppressing it that eventually came from England provided a glimmer of 'redemption'; hence, the necessity for thanksgiving.[35] This seemed to provide a degree of ideological cohesion to the fractious Protestant interest that should not be underestimated: the commemoration would persist into the last quarter of the eighteenth century. But according to the Catholic bishop and polemicist Nicholas French, writing in 1674, 'it hath been a principal cause, and study of some statesmen near the king, to oppress and overthrow the Catholics of Ireland, and at the same time to persuade his Majesty, that we ought to be destroyed by justice and law'.[36] The basis for such efforts lay in a combination of genuine fear and naked self-interest that rested on the assumption that in 1641 Catholics had sought to wipe out Protestants in Ireland: thus, Catholics were to be punished in a manner that would safeguard both the nascent Protestant interest and, crucially, the gains that some of them had made. Ironically, the continued maintenance of the dispossession of a sizeable chunk of Catholic Ireland fuelled the fears of the Protestant interest that they remained in the shadow of a repeat of 1641.

In or around 1672 Sir William Petty, who had overseen the land surveys that facilitated the Cromwellian settlement, estimated the Irish population to consist of 200,000 English, 100,000 Scots (deemed Presbyterian) and 800,000 Irish (deemed Catholic).[37] His analysis went further: the Irish were inevitably linked to a foreign power in the form of the Catholic Church, and the land settlement was the key source of division on the island.[38] The Irish may well have had

valid grievances and thus were not inherently degenerate, but they
fully expected the restitution of what they had lost in the 1650s.[39]
What Petty had pointed out was the reality that in Ireland Catholics,
who had good reason to be aggrieved at their lot, vastly outnumbered
Protestants. However, other Irish Protestants could (and would) seek
to rationalize anti-Popery and its implications. In 1676 the ubiquitous Henry Jones, now bishop of Meath, preached a sermon at Christ
Church in Dublin that offered a salutary lesson to Ireland's Protestants, and warned them of the dangers they faced with Antichrist
abroad in the world. Published in Dublin in 1676, a London edition
was published without alteration in March 1679 during the Popish
Plot, in an edition dedicated to Arthur Capel, earl of Essex, a previous lord lieutenant of Ireland and by 1679 a leading member of the
'Whig' opposition in England. Jones proceeded from the assumption
that 'Ireland... is above all other nations in Europe, influenced by
the power of Rome... of this we have had memorials of former ages,
some of them fresh and bleeding': the implicit reference could only
be to 1641, especially in Jones' hands.[40] The text was a dense and
complex biblical exegesis that sought both to explore and to explain
the machinations of Antichrist who, in the form of the Papacy, had
sought to destroy Protestants across Europe.

> And can the bloody butcheries of poor Protestants by the cruel
> Irish in Ireland be in this forgotten, when about one hundred
> thousand perished anno 1641? Yet to that impudence is that now
> risen, as to disavow any such rebellion of the Irish, or such their
> murders of the innocent Protestants in Ireland; but daring to aver
> on the contrary, that they themselves were the sufferers, and that
> by the English and Protestants.[41]

Scepticism about the nature of a Catholic plot, not to mention the
events of 1641, would be notably absent in August 1678, when the
first allegations about the Popish Plot were presented to the English
government. One part of the plot was to be the securing of Ireland
'to the tyranny of the Pope... by a general rebellion and massacre
as formerly'.[42] The assumption was deemed to reflect the danger, for
Catholics were the enemy. For Irish Protestants, the most immediate
danger, as illustrated by their own historical experience, would be
from the Irish Catholics whom they lived amongst.

V

The substantive preservation of the Cromwellian settlement went hand-in-hand with the exclusion of Catholics from the power and influence they expected to regain after 1660. Consequently, throughout Charles' reign, Irish Catholics sought to redress this by attempting both to refute the allegations made against them with regard to 1641 and demonstrate their loyalty to the crown.[43] Under the aegis of the restoration, there had been a narrow settlement in Ireland legitimized under the auspices of the monarchy and established church, and underpinned by the anomaly of the land settlement. The problems that this presented were outlined by Sir John Temple's son William, in his unpublished 'essay on the present state and settlement of Ireland'.[44] Composed c.1668, it dealt with the settlement of the 1660s and its flaws. But it did so in order to best determine how 'to own and support that which is truly a loyal English Protestant interest, and to make it as comprehensive as can be'.[45] Despite the fact that the 'English' (according to Petty's formulation) were drastically outnumbered, they might not necessarily be the victims of another rebellion: they had a strategic and military advantage in Ireland, and could probably survive, especially as further support could come from England itself.[46] However, the Catholic Irish were inevitably linked to a foreign power in the form of the Catholic Church, the land settlement remained hugely divisive, and while the Irish may well have had valid grievances and were not inherently degenerate, and were therefore capable of reform, they fully expected the restitution of what they had lost in the 1650s.[47] The 'loyal English Protestant interest' was hardly oblivious to such matters. But the renewed Anglican ascendancy had weaknesses of its own. They were a colonial community who, despite occasional pretensions, remained aware that the basis of their safety and security lay across the Irish Sea, in England.[48] What they feared also had links across the sea. In Ulster there was a substantial Scottish dissenter population, whose potential for disaffection and rebellion after the restoration was grounded in both their activities during the 1640s and their relationship to their co-religionists in Scotland.[49] And above all there were the dispossessed Catholic Irish, who were rendered the more dangerous by the religion they shared with England's enemies in Catholic Europe and the links they had gradually forged with them, most especially with

Catholic France.⁵⁰ In January 1678 Sir Robert Southwell had observed that war with France seemed imminent, and 'it is manifest that our enemy will do his best to excite problems both in Scotland and Ireland... and in this latter especially where all places lie naked to his invasion... all who have their estates lying in that kingdom have reason to be alarmed'.⁵¹ The English Protestant interest had fallen between two stools, and they were acutely aware of it.

VI

Consequently, governments in Ireland throughout the 1670s sought to stabilize and secure Ireland after decades of warfare and instability, the consequences of which continued to linger.⁵² But they were in no position to comprehensively address any of the questions with which they were faced, or their implications; their slender financial and military resources were inadequate. The implementation of policies was thereby hamstrung, and two further issues emerged from this. First, the inability to implement such policies as were deemed appropriate ensured a degree of continual uncertainty about Irish affairs. Second, this reality ensured that the various viceroys of the period would be continually tasked with attempting to overhaul the branches of the administration that overlay and sought to manage the realities of Restoration Ireland.

The viceroyalty of Sir Arthur Capel, earl of Essex, exemplified this. From a royalist background in Hertfordshire, Essex is best known for the dubious circumstances in which he met his death in the Tower of London in 1683. But diligence and ability were evident in his tenure as lord lieutenant of Ireland (1672–1675). Fiscal and military reforms formed key elements of his instructions, but there was also a marked emphasis on religious matters. Essex had received private instructions from Charles II, authorizing him to determine 'what are the properest ways to give satisfaction to all our subjects in that our kingdom, in the point of liberty of conscience, without distinction of party, what numbers of several persuasions there are and by what proper means each party may best have its satisfaction': this naturally (and explicitly) extended to Catholics.⁵³ The fact that Catholics made up most of the population naturally ensured that this would have to be a consideration, but it was exacerbated by the fact that in the 1660s there had been attempts to rebuild the Catholic Church in Ireland after its decimation during the 1650s. This culminated in 1669 with the appointment of three Catholic bishops to Ireland. One of them was Oliver Plunkett.

Plunkett was a scion of a leading Old English family from Meath who had enjoyed a glittering career in Rome throughout the 1650s and 1660s before being appointed archbishop of Armagh. Having returned to Ireland, he rapidly asserted himself, forging a *de facto* accommodation with Essex's predecessor, the pro-Catholic John Berkeley, Baron Berkeley of Stratton. However, his reforming zeal and attempts at accommodation with both the government and various fractious groupings within Catholic Ireland began to alienate many as the decade wore on: some of these disputes would return to haunt him during the Popish Plot, when both he and Essex would have very different roles to play.

Essex was also prepared to reach unofficial accommodations with Plunkett and the Catholic Church through ostensibly severe but actually moderate policies. Disarming Catholics was problematic, given that 'the crown had other enemies in Ireland...who had been equally obnoxious', namely, militant Presbyterians, mainly of Scottish extraction. But there were important differences: Essex was advised that Irish Catholics, 'being poor and dispossessed of their estates were desperate and more likely therefore to take violent courses for the righting themselves'; Presbyterian loyalty, on the other hand, would be guaranteed by self-interest.[54] There were obvious concerns about their potential to cause unrest in Ulster, though Essex was inclined to permit them a limited degree of toleration.[55] Such problems as they presented were augmented in coastal areas by geography, for 'the seditious preachers of Scotland' often went on the run in Ulster.[56] A watching brief would be continually held on Presbyterians there, but ultimately, Catholics would always be deemed to be the greater danger.

It was also obvious that the security of Ireland was deemed significant to the security of England. In March 1673 the English House of Commons resolved to prepare an address to the King 'to represent to him the state and condition of the Kingdom of Ireland; and the danger of the English Protestant interest'.[57] When it was finally produced it outlined a variety of measures for 'the suppression of the insolencies and disorders of the Irish Papists'.[58] It was an implicit reminder that Essex was in Ireland to maintain the Protestant interest. He was aware that there were commonly held fears amongst Protestants regarding a breach of the land settlement.[59] This was based on both scepticism about the motives of Charles himself and the reality of Catholic discontent in Ireland.

> Though I have ever since my coming into this country made it my business to confirm all men in the belief that these acts would never be in the least measure violated, yet have I always found that the generality of the English who enjoy their estates upon these new titles could not shake off their apprehensions of losing them again.[60]

for 'the Irish do almost universally discourse that they will have their lands again'.[61]

The security of the Protestant interest might have been the government's priority, but it would also have to be paid for. The obvious solution was to call a parliament in Ireland in order to provide monies to do so, but the prevailing view was that the collection of the revenue was best left in private hands. Richard Jones, earl of Ranelagh, was a grandson of Richard Boyle, the first earl of Cork. He had sat as MP for Roscommon in the Irish parliament of 1661–1666, and held a number of financial appointments in the Irish administration thereafter. In March 1671 a consortium headed by Ranelagh had proposed to Charles II that they could pay the substantial royal debts incurred in the governance of Ireland between 20 December 1670 and 25 December 1675, whilst subsequently providing him with £80,000 directly into the Privy Purse over the next two years, on the condition that the consortium would pocket whatever proceeds remained. Charles was in no position to refuse a seemingly alluring offer. It may also have appealed to his authoritarian tendencies, as it enabled him to govern Ireland without recourse to a parliament in a manner that foreshadowed how he would govern England after 1681. The undertaking was, essentially, a license for corruption on a huge scale. Ranelagh and his partners were responsible for collecting revenue in Ireland. What they provided to the king bought them favour and political protection as they squeezed as much money out of the country as was possible in order to maximize their own profits, and covered up the traces of their activities by doctoring their records. This creative accounting, along with the ill-will engendered by their extortionate activities, would return to haunt both Essex and Ormond.

One consequence of this was that the army in Ireland was starved of funds, leaving it 'really in a worse condition than ever they were since his Majesties Restoration'; a want of money for the military had allegedly been an issue in permitting the spread of the rebellion in 1641.[62] The awareness of such vulnerability could be accentuated by fears of Catholic unrest. Copies of Nicholas French's *Bleeding Iphigenia* (another work from his pen that railed against the dispossession of the Irish) were reportedly circulating in Connacht, and 'the people are so taken with it that in my opinion if twenty thousand volumes had come over they would all have been bought up'; it presumably had a certain attraction to those who had been dispossessed.[63] At the other end of the confessional spectrum, Thomas Otway, the Church of Ireland bishop of Killala, was intent on dealing with Presbyterian preachers in his diocese who 'ride up and down the country like martial evangelists with sword and pistols, as if they came not to prate down; but storm our religion'.[64] The weakness of the state in Ireland ensured that such issues relating to the possibility of either Catholic or Presbyterian insurrection were, as yet, unresolved. Such institutional difficulties overlay more fundamental problems that were highlighted by the crisis of 1678–1681.

But that crisis would be dealt with by a different viceroy. Essex's constant inquiries into Ranelagh's activities irritated the king, and Ranelagh pressed for a more congenial replacement. Ormond was no friend of Ranelagh, but he had extracted a promise of reappointment from Charles and duly became lord lieutenant on 24 May 1677. He formally took over from Essex on 24 August 1677. Once again, Ormond was in control.

VII

James Butler, twelfth earl and first duke of Ormond, was born into one of the great Anglo-Norman families of Ireland, based in counties Kilkenny and Tipperary. He was brought up in England, and stood out amongst his Catholic kin by having been raised a Protestant. He succeeded to the earldom of Ormond in 1633, and came to prominence in Irish affairs in the 1630s under the patronage of the authoritarian viceroy Thomas Wentworth, later earl of Strafford. In the 1640s he fought against the Catholic forces that later coalesced into the Confederate Association, based in Kilkenny, for Ormond had alienated much of his family's traditional power base by his actions in the service of the government.

Ormond's record as a political and military leader was chequered. He was known for a ferocious if self-interested loyalty to the crown and an uncompromising attitude towards Catholics shot through with an occasional instinctive sympathy. He served as Charles I's lord lieutenant for much of the decade, but was unable to reconcile Charles's willingness to treat with the Confederates in exchange for assistance in the English Civil Wars with his own political and religious instincts; indeed, despite his allegiance to the king, Ormond surrendered Dublin to parliament in 1647. He spent most of the 1650s in exile, occasionally rueing his conduct in the 1640s, before returning to Ireland to serve as viceroy after the restoration of Charles II in 1660. Elevated to the title of duke in 1661, he oversaw much of the Restoration settlement in Ireland and was detested by some strands of Irish Catholic opinion for doing so; Nicholas French's *Unkinde Desertor* was basically an extensive attack upon Ormond, whom he characterized as 'a great bramble cruelly scratching and tormenting the Catholics of Ireland'.[65] Yet, despite slipping in and out of royal favour in the years after 1660, Ormond re-established himself. From his base in Kilkenny he was perceived by many as one of, if not, the wealthiest and most influential aristocrats in the three kingdoms. This was undoubtedly true of Ireland: Ormond was an obvious choice to govern it.

'After my Lord of Ormond had passed over 70 years in different fortunes, another surge of favour set him a fourth time in the government of Ireland.'[66] Soon after his reappointment, he set down his assessment of the condition of Ireland.[67] Within it, his traditional dislike of Presbyterians was obvious. But he was aware that realistically, they could not be subjected to the rigours of the law without a corresponding level of repression being applied to Catholics. The resources to do either were scarcely available, and the economic consequences of such a policy were potentially disastrous. On the other hand, inaction by the government might simply embolden prospective malcontents even further. He suggested instead a continuation of the policy of *de facto* indulgence, to defuse more radical and unacceptable activities, especially on the part of Presbyterians. Thus,

Ormond recommended that the parlous condition of the Irish armed forces be rectified with all available finances. He enquired as to when an Irish parliament might be called, and noticed certain irregularities in the Irish revenues.

These were the issues that Ormond was faced with at the outset of his tenure. They were essentially carried over from that of his predecessor. He was still dealing with them a year later when he was forced to deal with the additional difficulty of the Popish Plot.

2
The Popish Plot in Ireland, September 1678–May 1679

Ireland had a role to play in the Popish Plot from the outset. Amongst many other things, Titus Oates had claimed that the Catholic archbishop of Tuam, James Lynch intended 'to procure some Persons to dispatch the king'.[1] Furthermore, there were plans to facilitate 'the French king's landing in Ireland... the Irish Catholics were ready to rise, in order to which, there was forty thousand black bills provided, to furnish the Irish soldiers withal'.[2] The Jesuits were also implicated: Peter Talbot, the Catholic archbishop of Dublin, had supposedly claimed that 'the fathers of the society in Ireland were very vigilant to prepare the people to arise, for the defence of their liberty and religion, and to recover their estates'.[3] Emissaries were sent to Ireland to lay the ground for a rebellion, and within months the Irish were reportedly ready to rise. Ormond was supposedly 'in a great perplexity, to see Catholic religion thrive so well', and there were many who, at the behest of the Jesuits, 'resolve to cut the Protestants throats again, when once they rise'.[4]

Ormond was to be murdered by four Irish Jesuits, which would be the signal for the rebellion to begin. Should this attempt on the viceroy's life fail, 'Dr Fogarty' (who was alleged to have orchestrated the Southwark fire of 1676 and secured the services of four Irishmen to murder the king) would deal with him.[5] The Catholic Church had given permission to the Irish to swear the oaths of allegiance and supremacy, a Papal legate was now alleged to be in Ireland, and garrisons across the country had been infiltrated, all of which were intended to facilitate 'the design of the Jesuits; which was, to raise a rebellion in the three kingdoms, and to destroy the king'.[6]

The implication that the Protestants in those kingdoms were also to be destroyed hardly needed restating.

Oates tailored his account to suggest that he possessed inside knowledge. 'Its lack of originality was no disadvantage, for it told of the sort of Popish design which the anti-Catholic tradition had made all too familiar to English Protestants.'[7] It was crucial to the manner in which Oates had revealed this that he had apparently done so in the nick of time. His original allegations had been treated warily, but any chance that the plot might fade away would end in London on 17 October, when the body of Sir Edmund Bury Godfrey was found, run through with his own sword. The previous day, the concern of the English government about his allegations was made manifest in the report delivered to Charles II on the content of the papers of York's secretary Edward Coleman, which in itself would have given a further impetus to the investigation into the plot.[8] However, Godfrey's body was (and would become) an altogether more public matter, and its significance was lost on no-one: 'pray God it be not Sir Edmund Bury Godfrey', exclaimed one of its discoverers.[9] The political impact of Godfrey's sinister demise ensured that the plot was here to stay. It was bound to have repercussions throughout all three kingdoms.

I

There was an obvious Irish dimension to this 'self-consciously British' story.[10] First, there was to be an attempt by Irish assassins to kill the king. Second, there was to be a Franco-Irish rebellion that would involve the extermination of Protestants in both Ireland and Britain.

Allegations of this nature were nothing new. They had cropped up at intervals in both islands since at least the 1640s.[11] It was inevitable that Protestants in Ireland would pay attention to such rumours: after all, they would probably find themselves on the front line of any Anglo-French conflict. Despite the multifaceted political and religious identities that existed within Protestant Ireland, a pragmatic solidarity amongst otherwise diverse strands of Protestant opinion could be reformulated at moments of actual, or perceived, danger.[12] For example, the treaty signed in February 1674 that ended the second Anglo-Dutch War could be seen as a capitulation by the (Protestant) Dutch that conceded an advantage to the (Catholic)

French, and prompted one John O'Daly in Cork to claim that 'the king of France and the subduing of the Hollanders' had encouraged the lawlessness of the Irish.

> For no doubt the king of England will condescend to anything that shall be by the king of France demanded. And the curse of God light upon those that were in power for to own him for their sovereign, and that did not rather cut off his head as his father was, knowing him always inclinable and favourable to the Irish.[13]

Suspicions about the pro-French inclinations of Charles II were commonly held and entirely justified; his alignment with Catholic France became even more unpopular as the decade wore on.[14] Ireland naturally played a role in Protestant assessments of Catholic intentions in general, and French intentions in particular: as the most overwhelmingly Catholic of the Stuart kingdoms, it was an obvious place to attack. In January 1678 the Munster landowner and politician Sir Robert Southwell observed that war with France seemed imminent, and 'it is manifest that our enemy will do his best to excite problems both in Scotland and Ireland... and in this latter especially where all places lie naked to his invasion... all who have their estates lying in that kingdom have reason to be alarmed'.[15] Here was an acute awareness that the French might exploit Ireland's dispossessed Catholic majority, who in turn might themselves exploit the French in order to retrieve their lands at the expense of those, like Southwell, who now possessed them.

The contours of both the Catholic and Protestant communities of Restoration Ireland were shaped by factors common to both. Alongside the obvious distinctions of political and religious principle, class, ethnicity, affinity, familial links, personal history (especially with regards to the 1640s), residence, and regional origin all had a part in elaborating the complexities of confessional identity. Yet other common factors could be discerned. Just as the diversity of Protestant Ireland could be concealed beneath the carapace of common fears, so too could the diversity of Irish Catholic identity be concealed by a common rhetoric of dispossession and injustice articulated by most strands of Irish Catholic opinion. Just like its Protestant counterpart, the Catholic political interest was no monolith. If 'the ethos of restoration Ireland favoured individual self-help through networks of clientage and ingratiation rather than group action',[16] this characteristic was shared across the denominational divide; indeed, the nature of the restoration settlement had made it a necessity.[17] However, the precise 'political configuration of the Irish Catholic community' remains difficult to delineate.[18] The state that emerged in Ireland after 1660 was, *de facto*, a Protestant one. One of the few issues to shed light on the politics of Catholic Ireland is the abortive 'remonstrance' of 1661: an attempt to reconcile the perennial conflict between Catholic spiritual allegiance to the papacy with Catholic political allegiance to the crown.[19] The remonstrance was consistent with the tradition of constitutional allegiance that helped to define the 'Old English' prior to the 1640s, but proved disastrously divisive amongst both the Catholic clergy and laity. Traces of that division would continue to resonate during the Popish Plot.

II

On 28 September 1678 Sir Henry Coventry, the English secretary of state for the southern department, had written to Ormond telling him of the role Ireland had played in Oates's allegations. Ormond was ordered to arrest Peter Talbot and to monitor any suspicious Catholic activities, in order 'to provide such speedy remedies for the obstruction of those evils'.[20] He observed that 'if Oates tale be true, the Jesuits have found a short and sure way to put me out of the government'.[21] But he also conceded that there might well be 'an ill design one way or the other'.[22]

Prior to the disclosure of Oates's allegations, Ormond had been preoccupied with plans to call a parliament in Ireland. This had been his overriding priority since his reappointment as viceroy, primarily in order to provide money to provide for the otherwise neglected Irish military establishment, but permission to proceed with this had not yet been forthcoming when news of the plot arrived in Ireland.[23] Paradoxically, any delay in calling a parliament would delay the chance to bring Ireland's dilapidated army and fortifications up to scratch at a time when they might be needed most.[24]

Any attempt to provide for Ireland's security would have to confront two key issues. After the experience of Ranelagh's undertaking, the disgruntled representatives of the Protestant interest who would sit in any prospective parliament were unlikely to provide money to the government without something tangible to show for it. As a sweetener, Ormond intended to introduce legislation to confirm the holdings of all landowners in Ireland. But this would be seen automatically to favour Catholic landowners by confirming them in their holdings alongside Protestants, while closing the still contested land settlement to outstanding claims or future alterations. Such problems were compounded by Poyning's Law: any legislation proposed in Ireland had to be approved by the English Privy Council, who would not necessarily like what they saw. And even before it could raise money, the government still had to determine how much could be raised. An answer to this would necessitate a full accounting of the undertaking. For Ranelagh, who could potentially be endangered by what might be disclosed about his activities, an obvious means to defend himself was to discredit Ormond, who within days was bluntly informed that Ranelagh and his associates planned to smear him as being partial to Catholics, and that the implementation of his orders would be taken as the marker of his 'inclination'.[25] Ormond subsequently reassured Coventry (who like Ormond was known for his loyalty to the court) that he would act upon his orders, and so ordered Peter Talbot's arrest.[26] This was the first act of the Irish government as it sought to investigate the Popish Plot: it would remain the only one for some time.

Peter Talbot and his younger brother, Richard, were two of the most prominent Irish Catholic figures of the restoration period, for reasons that did not endear them to the Protestant interest. They were scions of a leading Old English family from the Pale; Peter had entered the priesthood, and Richard had embarked on a military career. Both were ardent royalists, and both had been heavily involved in the Irish Catholic émigré politics of the 1650s. Peter had assiduously sought to enlist the assistance of Catholic powers on the continent on the side of the royalist cause in general, and that of Irish Catholics in particular. Richard had fought in the Spanish service in the 1650s, where he became very close to York, and after 1660 he became a prominent agent at court for dispossessed Irish Catholics. Peter also rose to further prominence, being appointed archbishop of Dublin in 1669, in which capacity he proved a zealous opponent of the supporters of the 1661 remonstrance, and entered into an acrimonious and lengthy dispute with Oliver Plunkett – who had been appointed archbishop of Armagh at the same time as Talbot – over the primacy of their respective sees. As prominent Irish Catholics, the Talbot's fell foul of an increasingly anti-Catholic English parliament in 1673: Peter was banished from Ireland in 1673, and Richard, who had attracted particular abbrobrium for having sought a review of the Irish land settlement, left for France in the same year. But by 1678 both were back in Ireland; in Peter's case, he had essentially returned there to die.

Peter Talbot was staying with Richard in Luttrellstown, County Meath, when the Popish Plot came to light. Ormond was sceptical of reports of his ill-health, or at least he chose not to be troubled by them.[27] On 11 October Talbot was arrested and taken to Dublin Castle.[28] Ormond's antipathy towards Talbot was obvious, as he had stressed that while the rest of his orders were to be implemented warily, he intended to see Talbot arrested speedily.[29] 'Peter Talbot has undertaken or been assigned much the least wicked part of this tragedy, and that this is not the first time he has been said to have encouraged the acting of it.'[30] Politicking of various kinds had marked Talbot's career, including allegations that he had made threats against Ormond's life in 1664; presumably this was what the viceroy had in mind.

However, nothing could be proven against Talbot. Apart from one seemingly innocuous document ('this he took care should be found on him'), there was no material evidence.[31] But after the discovery of Godfrey's body in London Ormond could assume that he would soon be under increasing pressure to take measures to forestall the prospect of a Catholic rebellion. With regards to Catholics, Ormond's personal history and career had brought him to a point where he was neither 'transported with fury against them...because some of them, and perhaps too many are traitors and murderers; nor trusting too much to them, because I believe some of them are good subjects and honest men'. However, he was quite aware that 'it may be unseasonable to profess such a temper'.[32] In hindsight, it was perceived that 'to make Ormond a sacrifice, was a thing of highest merit. And nothing could do it more, than to shew how much Irish he was; what a favourer of Popish councils he had been; and how dangerous he still was to England in all these things'.[33] As the climate of fear generated by the Popish Plot intensified in England, it was perhaps inevitable that this would become an issue. Ormond manoeuvred as well as any, and survived better than most, but the Crown's enemies would inevitably be his, and there would always be room for those who were simply his enemies, and his alone. He was already concerned about 'what may be said in refutation of the suggestion of my being a favourer of the Papists'.³⁴

The examinations of those arrested, along with a report on the activities of the Irish government, were despatched to London to be presented to the House of Lords in late October.³⁵ Proclamations had been issued in Ireland on 14–16 October, just after Talbot's arrest: troops were ordered back to their garrisons, and it was ordered that the Catholic hierarchy be suppressed (pointedly, the latter referred to the lax enforcement of similar proclamations issued under Essex).³⁶ 20 November was set as the deadline for Catholic clergy to quit the kingdom. Or as Luke Wadding, the Catholic bishop of Ferns, later put it:

> For we have a proclamation,
> To banish wholly from this nation,
> All Popish prelates with their friars,
> And send them to attend their choirs,
> To say their masses in France and Spain,
> And never to return again.³⁷

This proclamation was the first public indication of how the Irish government intended to deal with the Popish Plot. When the English parliament met in London on 21 October, genuine fears about the existence of a plot were evident in its continual preoccupation with investigating it. But in Ireland, the lack of a parliament meant there was no institutional framework within which to coherently express the concerns of the Protestant elite. Consequently, sporadic and intermittent rumblings about the intentions of the Catholic Irish began to emerge elsewhere. Walter Harris of Dublin, for example, who owned lands in Wicklow, was advised against further investment in the county by two Catholic tenants who had previously recommended it as a good deal, but now changed their minds because of 'some fears...of the French king'. Reminding Harris of the 'late rebellion', they assured him that 'there were much sadder times at hand than ever'. Harris did not buy the land, but concluded 'that there might be some evil design of the Papists in hand'.³⁸ The assumption was automatic. Yet there was no overt reason to believe that anything was going to happen: Peter Talbot, the most significant Irish suspect, had admitted nothing, and no evidence had emerged against him.[39]

He was not the only suspect. Other figures had been implicated by Oates, most notably his brother Richard, and Ormond's elderly uncle Edmund Butler, Viscount Mountgarret.[40] Vague and sinister reports continued to emerge: of dubious contacts between members of the Connacht gentry and unknown figures in Germany and France, of the presence of a Jesuit in Sligo attempting to recruit to the French and Papal cause, and of questionable rumours that unusually large numbers of Catholics were suddenly attending mass in Athy.[41] The recorder of Galway was concerned about the possible murder of Martin French, an Augustinian Friar who had sworn treason some years earlier against James Lynch, the Catholic Archbishop of Tuam who was implicated by Oates.[42] And the gentry of Queen's County suspected the captain of their militia was a Catholic.[43] In the early phases of the Popish Plot, there were enough hints and suggestions of this kind to feed a burgeoning belief in the existence of its Irish dimensions.

III

These reports were rumours. Information circulated readily within the interlocking networks of trade, travel, and human interaction in early modern Ireland. This would later be evident in the accounts of Irish informers whose allegations often rested on the accumulation of information from person to person. However, while such personal networks were sufficient to facilitate the spread of information, they were unable to verify it properly. In early modern Ireland the infrastructure of transport and communication was far less developed than its English counterpart: it simply did not exist at a level sophisticated enough to offer proof or confirmation of what might be alleged or heard.[44] Rumour and news could travel a long way without necessarily being discredited, and were quite capable of crossing the Irish Sea without losing their assumed integrity. They were sufficiently self-contained to survive.

Oral culture and rumour were only partially removed from scribal and printed culture. Admittedly, the relative underdevelopment of print culture in Ireland rendered it a predominantly oral society that, by its nature, may have been more susceptible to rumour and suggestion. In Ireland, both the scribal and printed word could become vehicles for rumour: they could complement other forms of communication instead of simply being a substitute for them. News read and discussed in a coffee-house, for example, could easily begin to travel beyond its walls by word of mouth. Ballads, songs, and prayers facilitated the intersection between print and oral culture, and communal reading, along with rumour, gossip, and hearsay, would bring the written word to a greater audience.[45] The more circumscribed nature of print culture in Ireland as opposed to England may have imposed limits on this, but the written word in Ireland, whether in manuscript or print, undoubtedly influenced and reflected its spoken counterpart. For example, proclamations issued in Ireland during the Popish Plot dealt with issues such as the presence of Catholic clergy, Catholics within towns, and Catholic ownership of weapons.[46] These proclamations were inevitably seen, read, and heard in public, and thus could serve to remind onlookers of the potential danger posed by Catholics. Oral culture filled the gaps between the literate. It could easily bolster the awareness of a perceived Catholic danger.

All of which prompts reflection on the nature of rumours themselves.[47] Falsehood and exaggeration are part of their nature, but that does not make them irrational if couched within the appropriate framework. Their significance lay in their implications; their explanatory power derived from their malleability. They may have been bolstered by the absence of contradictory evidence, but rumours would have had at least some plausible basis. They could be sincerely believed, but also cynically manipulated. A belief in the malevolent intentions of Catholics was unlikely to be dispelled by a rumour that corresponded to expectations that went hand-in-hand with that belief. And such rumours were the lifeblood of the Popish Plot in both Britain and Ireland.

But the semi-secret nature of rumours dovetailed with the equally shady interpretive framework of a conspiracy. The idea that there was a Catholic conspiracy to destroy Protestants was not inherently irrational. On its own terms, it made perfect sense to those who believed it. Catholicism was often depicted in conspiratorial terms: Andrew Marvell's *An Account of the Growth of Popery and Arbitrary Government in England* (1677), while mainly concerned with Catholicism as a tool of French influence, was probably the best known example of this.[48]

A belief in a conspiracy was a means of making sense of the scattered fragments of information at ones disposal, and in a manner that was 'logically coherent with the prevailing interpretation patterns of a group, nation, culture, religion'.[49] Against the backdrop of what was expected of them, scattered reports of dubious activities might suggest that Irish Catholics were indeed up to something. Such rumours reflected a belief and had the capacity to nurture it still further.

IV

An obvious response to such reports came in the form of a number of proclamations issued in late October and early November. Catholics and certain categories of recusants (such as tradesmen) were to be expelled from towns, and the oaths of supremacy and allegiance were to be imposed on the latter. Catholics were also barred from owning weapons (and anyone from possessing more than a pound of gunpowder), and any weapons in Catholic hands were to be surrendered within 20 days.[50] However, the response to the first proclamation banishing Catholic clergy from Ireland had been poor; it was ignored by Oliver Plunkett, and had been openly defaced in Waterford.[51] Consequently, all ships in Irish ports were ordered to take Catholics on board, thereby removing any excuse for Catholic clergy to remain in Ireland.[52]

Ormond was already becoming sceptical about whether this plot actually existed. He accepted that an Irish rebellion was a possibility, for 'the alarums are many and great that we hear from all parts of the kingdom', but he was also aware that a rebellion could easily be provoked in a tense political climate, and that events in England would naturally have a bearing on Ireland: speeches in the Long Parliament almost 40 years previously regarding 'the extirpation of Popery were some cause or at least some pretence for the beginning of that rebellion in 1641'.[53]

Geography, an overwhelmingly Catholic population and weak military forces ensured that Ireland was easily perceived as the most vulnerable and potentially dangerous of the three kingdoms. From November 1678 onwards, with a new parliament in session, the English Privy Council began to take repressive measures against Catholics in England. It was inevitable that it would devote some time to the Irish component of that plot.[54] In November 1678 the English secretary of state, Joseph Williamson, congratulated the mayor of Chester for his assiduousness in apprehending Irish officers who, having been dismissed from the royal service, were now returning to Ireland, and instructed that records of such officers should be kept, regardless of whether they had been granted permission to go to Ireland.[55] Some had commissions to join a regiment to be commanded by Ormond's nephew Justin McCarthy, an Irish officer who had served in the French army during the 1670s.[56] Yet such officers were marked out by their religion and nationality. The fact that they had commissions caused consternation in parliament after it was revealed that Williamson had issued them, and had therefore exempted Irish Catholic officers from the oaths of allegiance and supremacy: both he and McCarthy were detained, while Colonel John Birch, MP for Weobley, claimed in the House of Commons that Ireland 'is not free from the plot'.[57] Allegations of an Irish dimension to the Popish Plot were plausible to an English Protestant audience, even if such credulity, as can be discerned, was confined to the English political elite. The assumption that there was likely to be an Irish Plot alongside (or within) the Popish Plot was perpetuated by other allegations of preparations for a rebellion in Ireland, along with Catholic plans for 'the king's death and the subversion of the Protestant religion'.[58] Irish Catholics were identified as potentially disloyal or dangerous, and concerns about them were voiced in both islands, but the most prominent, vocal, and consistent warnings issued forth from Munster, as Roger Boyle, earl of Orrery, began to make his opinions known.

Orrery was born into what was, in the first decades of the seventeenth century, the richest and most powerful family in Ireland: he was the son of Richard Boyle, first earl of Cork. Orrery had risen to prominence in the 1640s, as one of the political and military leaders of Munster's Protestants. Quite militantly Protestant, he had officially transferred his allegiances to parliament in 1644 in response to the truce Ormond had negotiated with the Confederate Catholics, and became a key Irish ally of the Commonwealth during the Cromwellian reconquest. He continued to serve the new regime, being briefly appointed lord president of Scotland and sitting in Westminster as MP for Cork. In 1657 he had encouraged Cromwell to adopt the title of king, and when Cromwell declined Orrery retired to Cork. He was drawn back into public affairs at the restoration, becoming a prominent advocate of the Irish Protestant interest and doing his utmost to preserve the gains of the 1650s. He retained this role for much of the rest of his life, but while his importance was reflected in the award of an earldom (his title only dated from 1660) and his appointment to the regional position of lord president of Munster, the distrust engendered by his personal history ensured that he would never be appointed viceroy. That role, both in the 1660s and later in the 1670s, went to a figure he seemed to have had little time for: Ormond.

By 1678 Orrery's long and protean career was winding down, as stricken by gout he continued to fulfil his personal interest in the safeguarding of Munster. The province had been heavily colonized in successive waves from the sixteenth century onwards, but it had been the brutal sectarian warfare of the 1640s that proved instrumental in forging the militant colonial identity of its Protestant community. Orrery exemplified this. However, the militancy of Munster Protestants was based on their contemporary circumstances as much as their history. They retained fears of Catholic subversion from within and invasion from without: the vulnerability of the southern coast was also the reason for the construction of the massive edifice of Charles Fort at Kinsale in the late 1670s. Low immigration to the province after 1660 had ensured the continued survival of the Catholic population as an economic necessity, and Munster's southern coastal location, hemmed in by the Atlantic Ocean and bisected by the river Shannon, made it an obvious place for a French landing.[59]

Vigilance was obligatory. By November 1678 Orrery had noted the large numbers of dispossessed Irish in the country, along with the impudence of Catholic clerics who were supposedly conducting synods.[60] Such concerns were rapidly magnified by the surprise arrival in Cork of Irish Catholic officers in the regiment of Thomas Dongan, a nephew of the Talbots (and future governor of New York). This arose from the same circumstances that had rebounded on Williamson and McCarthy: Dongan's unit had recently been recalled from the French service, and was allegedly responsible for unspecified 'disorders'. Ormond was inclined to discount this, but was also aware that the presence of such a force was bound to cause unease as it was 'wholly composed of Papists'. It was unclear what to do with them.[61] Orrery had instructed that these officers be detained on arrival at Kinsale, though some of them later explained their situation and assured him that no more were to arrive, despite rumours to the contrary.[62] Orrery seemed satisfied, but the episode illustrated his alertness where Catholics were concerned.[63] This was further illustrated by the attention he devoted to a letter circulating in Munster claiming that 'one Mr Fitzgerald of Connaught' had told Ormond that 'nothing could hinder the plot' which sought with the aid of numerous 'great persons' and the French to make the Catholics the 'masters of Ireland', though 'had any such thing been, I know I should have had notice of it from his Excellency my Lord Chancellor' (his kinsman Michael Boyle, archbishop of Dublin).[64] Such professed confidence in the government did not prevent Orrery from inquiring after such matters on his own behalf. Ormond himself conceded the circumstantial proof of 'some wicked designs ready to be put into execution', while emphasizing the existence of those 'honester Irish' who were warning their Protestant neighbours.[65]

Preventative measures continued. Two proclamations, on 19–20 November, exempted Catholic merchants and travellers from expulsion provided that they gave their names to the authorities, offered rewards of £20 for the apprehension of Jesuits, and ordered that Catholics of less than 12 month's residence were to be expelled from towns, barred from entry to fairs and markets, and banned from gathering in large numbers. These, like many others issued in Ireland, were all reprints of English proclamations.[66] But the issuing of such public warnings in the form of proclamations was not necessarily a vigorous and active policy. Ormond's analysis of the situation did not require one: he had not found any hard evidence of a plot, and was not inclined to take measures that might provoke substantial unrest. However, he was also aware that such a stance could pose a danger to him in the realm of English politics.

Ormond was well aware that in London, the 'frights' of Protestants would be blamed on him, despite his increasing conviction that there was actually little to fear. It had already been claimed in the English House of Lords that the Catholics of Waterford and Dublin were 'strangely insolent' and 'it is whispered' that Ormond had not seized Talbot's papers, an innuendo that could neither be proven nor disproven.[67] Indeed, the lack of any proof of a plot was becoming increasingly obvious: 'the real or pretended fears of some considerable men, have put the common sort of English and Protestants almost out of their wits, especially in Munster, from whence the terror is diffused throughout the whole kingdom, to the great disheartening of the English and encouragement of the disaffected Irish'. He almost certainly meant Orrery. The final point was the key: if no rebellion was stirring, stringent action was superfluous, but inactivity would leave him vulnerable to further accusations of favouring Catholics. If he was to take more severe measures purely to defend his own position, he ran the risk of provoking the very rebellion he sought to prevent. Ormond readily acknowledged the miserable state of Ireland's defences, and the capacity of the Irish to attack isolated Protestants, but this had to be tempered by the knowledge that retaliation would surely follow. However, the continual scaremongering did not help matters. The delicate equilibrium of restoration Ireland was amply revealed in this judgement.[68] Ormond's main fear was that his counsel might be requested in England, and if absent from Ireland, his control over events there would be automatically diminished.[69] This was becoming a very real concern, as 'the overtures from my lord Orrery were not directed to me but I have reason to believe they are sent into England'.[70]

Orrery's career had left him well connected in all three kingdoms, and given Ormond's view of the situation this could only compound his difficulties: his prudence might not be perceived as zeal. Since the beginning of the crisis, Ormond had sought to safeguard his own position, and keep himself as well informed as possible about affairs in London. In this he could depend upon a number of figures, most obviously his sons Thomas, earl of Ossory, and Richard, earl of Arran, along with Coventry and Sir Robert Southwell, the Cork-born clerk of the English Privy Council. And there were others: Francis Aungier, earl of Longford, a former Irish vice-treasurer to whom Ormond was related by marriage, and the Irish chief secretary Sir Cyril Wyche, who resided in London throughout this period. Indeed, it was to Wyche that Ormond outlined the reasoning behind his stance in the greatest detail. True, there were a disproportionate number of Catholics *vis-à-vis* Protestants in Ireland compared with England, 'yet despite this it cannot hence be infused that we are at their mercy; on the contrary, I think they are more at ours'. Harsher measures against them would be unrealistic and provocative: even a small insurrection, he argued, could attract the attention and involvement of the

French. He was highly critical of Orrery and his 'ensnaring overtures', the purpose of which was obviously 'to manifest his extraordinary vision and forecast'. Should nothing happen in Ireland Orrery was a loyal and diligent subject; should anything happen, he was also the correct one. Ormond was quite willing to state that Orrery was deliberately scaremongering to discredit the government (and thus the viceroy) in the eyes of Protestants, and for essentially cynical reasons, for 'I will not say that some private ill-will to some particular persons has a part in his propositions, or that he would be content there should be another rebellion that there may be another distribution of lands, but I am satisfied all he proposes looks very like it.'[71]

In this context Ormond had good reason to be concerned about ongoing rumours circulating in London that rapacious Catholic troops prowled the Irish countryside, poised to attack, or that Dublin swarmed with Catholics while the entire munitions store for the kingdom lay unguarded and thus for the taking; suggestions of unrest that were, with the exception of an attempted robbery at Naas, vigorously refuted.[72] After all, this was a time when anti-Catholic sentiment was running high in England, and it would be prudent for Ormond not to become embroiled in it, for even those close to the king could feel its effects. In late November the duchess of Portsmouth (Charles II's mistress) was obliged to dispense with her Irish servants, a suggestive indicator of the anti-Irish dimension of an anti-Catholic climate.[73] Yet Ormond was assured that his own actions to date were considered satisfactory.[74] Charles was not inclined to give too much credence to Orrery, for 'he knew him to be a rogue, and would ever continue so'.[75] It was undoubtedly a useful vote of confidence.

But Ormond was left in no doubt as to Orrery's opinion. Throughout November and December Orrery bombarded him with immensely detailed letters outlining the terror under which the locals suffered and his own vigilant attempts to safeguard the province of Munster.[76] All were prompted by the miserable condition of Munster defences, the alleged insolence of Munster Catholics and the prevailing fears of Munster Protestants. Orrery also bewailed the fact that anybody should claim that the government 'wanted zeal and care for the preservation of the Protestants', though such claims might not necessarily arise from malice. Perhaps revealingly, he claimed that 'honest men, who love the government, being frighted with the daily alarms, may have thought that the remedies not being so hasty as the danger seemed pressing'.[77] But Ormond remained sceptical, for

> if my lord of Orrery did mean fairly he would send his remarks to the king and the council, or even to the parliament, who are able to put us into a better condition than we are; and not scatter them to the terror of the English and Protestants and the defamation of the government.[78]

Nonetheless he acceded to some of Orrery's milder requests, or at least claimed to do so. He assured Orrery that he would order that the returning officers be temporarily deprived of their weapons, provided that they were returned to them eventually: such a token of mistrust was deemed more desirable than aggravating the fears of the locals, as he 'judged it better to commit some errors which might afterwards be rectified than leave the Protestants under the terrors they were in, and the government under a suspicion of want of zeal'.[79] In addition, anybody coming forward with information about plots was to be rewarded and pardoned.[80] These assurances flew in the face of Ormond's inclinations towards prudence, but may have been intended to mollify his old rival at a tense juncture; Orrery's call for the raising of the militia (which Ormond assured him he would consider) may have been prompted by the parallel demand of the English parliament that it be raised in England, and Ormond was wary of questioning his vigilance.[81]

Vigilance was evident elsewhere. On 29–30 November Dublin Corporation ordered that all freemen of the city arm themselves according to the law (lists were to be taken of those who did not do so) and offered rewards for information on Catholic officers and men in the army, hardly by its nature a reassuring suggestion; Arran, in Dublin at this time, found himself swamped by reports about caches of weapons and suspicious meetings.[82] But despite this, Ormond's opinion remained unchanged: that the real danger came not from the Irish but the French, for whom the Irish might admittedly be a useful, if incidental, tool; indeed, Ormond was concerned that the French threat was not sufficiently appreciated in London.[83] In the meantime his own security measures were meeting with grudging approval. Orrery observed that the government was putting the kingdom into 'a position of readiness', which would probably entail him commanding forces in Munster once again, but in a backhanded swipe at Ormond he wished for 'a better commander-in-chief, though I cannot wish them a commander who has more zeal for his religion, his king and his country'; though given Ormond's military and political track record during the 1640s, Orrery might have had a point.[84]

Ormond's growing impatience and mistrust of Orrery was increasingly obvious: he had been told of the similarities between certain dispatches sent from Ireland to England, and Orrery's missives to Michael Boyle.[85] It was reasonable to assume that any such attacks on the viceroy would eventually make their way to London. Ormond's Catholic familial network was one of the grounds on which he could be accused of favouring Catholics. His defensiveness on this point forced him to assure Southwell of his Protestant convictions, and that notwithstanding his family, he would, as in the 1640s, do his duty as required. 'Those that remain I hope have changed their principles as to rebellion, if they have not I am sure they will find I have not changed mine.'[86] For despite his professed scepticism, Ormond had not completely dismissed the possibility that an Irish Catholic plot might exist.

V

If there was indeed an Irish Plot, it was entirely up to Ormond and his government about how best to deal with it, and they were in the best position to do so. However, there was a degree of uncertainty in England as to whether the Irish administration was actually doing anything about it.

Malicious rumours were common currency. In a fearful political environment they could gain credence on the most slender of suggestions. Ormond was well aware of their potency, and of how easily they might gain credibility. He claimed to be in a no-win situation where he would be blamed for the disorders of the troops earmarked for the regiment in Cork (though the climate of the times ensured that this was never raised), while also having to fend off accusations of leniency towards Peter Talbot.[87] On 2 December the Irish council had ordered that searches were to begin around the country for any Catholic cleric who had defied the proclamations and remained in

Ireland: this was to be a recurring problem.[88] While the English Parliament could attempt to control or investigate the activities of the Irish in England, it had no automatic jurisdiction over Ireland. But this did not prevent information and allegations moving from one kingdom to the other.

Orrery had already told Ormond that he had advance notice of Oates's allegations from 'some friends in London'.[89] Such traffic went both ways. In December 1678 Orrery had informed his friend Sir John Malet, the zealously Protestant MP for Minehead in Somerset, that despite proclamations having been issued in Ireland banishing Catholic priests and demanding that Catholics surrender their weapons, few priests had departed and few weapons were recovered; the clear implication was that they were not being enforced.[90] There was subsequently a soothing report printed in London to counter rumours of Ireland's vulnerability by describing some of the measures taken by the Irish government, such as the arrests of both Peter and Richard Talbot, and the various proclamations that had been issued. Londoners were assured that 'although the Irish be in number very disproportionate to us, yet we are in perfect quiet, and in all probability like so to continue. For besides the army, our militia is raised, and in such a readiness that, with the blessing of God, we have nothing to fear'.[91] This uncannily – and perhaps deliberately – corresponded to Ormond's own assessment. But it also stood at odds to other perceptions of the condition of Ireland.

Occasionally these fears seemed to have a tangible basis. For example, in early November a scare about a ship bound for Ireland with weapons was defused when they proved to be no more than a handful of Dutch fowling pieces.[92] Ormond and Orrery continued to trade missives, with Ormond sharply telling Orrery of his own belief in the plot.[93] Despite this, Ormond soon told Orrery of his scepticism, given the time elapsed since the original allegations and the lack of actual evidence. He also felt that he should assure Orrery that he knew nothing of any plot until receiving Southwell's letter on 3 October.[94] But he also told Southwell that he simply did not believe there was any rebellion planned, or if there was, it was the work of a very few, which could be contained if need be.[95] In the meantime Orrery continued to provide Malet with copies of allegations made in Ireland about professions of loyalty being made to Louis XIV, rumours of the impending destruction of the English, and dark allegations that Louis and the Pope had a plan for the Irish to 'settle us in a better condition than ever we were yet'.⁹⁶ Presumably these did not go unnoticed in London: Wyche intimated his suspicions about Orrery to Ormond, suggesting that he should draw up a report of his proceedings to date, to present to the king with an eye to deflecting 'private whispers or insinuations'.⁹⁷

But if Ormond was being portrayed in an unduly bad light, events soon came to his aid when a plot to kill him was alleged to have been planned in Dublin. Orrery expressed his shock at the discovery of a 'hellish design of murdering your Grace', the discovery coming as a 'mercy' not only to Ormond's family and friends, but 'to all loyal subjects in this kingdom' (and to none more so than himself).⁹⁸ Letters telling of it had been scattered around Dublin, and while a reward of £200 was offered for information, Ormond himself took it manfully as one of the hazards of the job. At the very least it was useful in that it might alleviate the pressure on him.⁹⁹ Orrery produced a detailed account of this plot, claiming that four Irish priests had instigated it: two were arrested, one had gone to France, and the other had vanished. The examinations taken in the aftermath seemed to correspond with what Oates had earlier claimed about a plan to assassinate Ormond. The plot was traced back to a clothier's apprentice in Thomas Street, John Jephson, who admitted that for the previous year priests had implored him to convert to Catholicism, culminating in a reminder that Ormond had executed his father after Blood's Plot in 1663. Jephson was offered an opportunity for revenge that he ultimately declined. The examinations of those priests who were captured provided superficial circumstantial details that seemed to corroborate the allegation, but there were no more conclusive facts than these. However, the similarity to Oates's claim that Peter Talbot intended to kill Ormond in this manner was a strong implication that here was proof of what Oates had alleged, for, as Orrery put it, 'you will find them very agreeable'.¹⁰⁰

Assassination by Catholics hardly denoted sympathy towards them, and the news of this assassination plot was printed in London, thus driving the point home. In the account published in the official gazette, the attempt on Ormond's life was foiled by Jephson's guilt and repentance.¹⁰¹ An account of this plot published in early 1679 went further: the Jesuits in Ireland who had orchestrated it ('these sons of Satan') 'are carrying on the same design as those in England',

and Ormond's murder was to be, by implication, an integral part of this.[102] This was simply to reiterate one of Oate's original allegations, but it strongly implied that Ormond was perceived as an obstacle to sinister Catholic designs instead of being an integral part of them. It had been reported in the *London Gazette* in the aftermath that Ormond had prudently dealt with 'all those that were suspected to design troubles in that country', and was arresting priests and banning masses with gusto whilst leaving Ireland 'in a very good posture of defence'.[103] Whilst this could be seen as an effort to deflect criticism of the viceroy in England, it also suggested that such efforts were necessary.

But after this the dispute with Orrery continued.[104] Ormond gave up penning yet another riposte to him, 'because I saw no end of the contest'.[105]

VI

The alleged existence of an 'Irish Plot' was merely one element within the Popish Plot. But minor as it was, it remained a persistent concern. The suspicion that it actually existed was bolstered in December by the testimony before the English House of Lords of Thomas Shadwell, who implicated James Lynch once again in a scheme to kill the king, prompting the lords to demand the appearance before them of Martin French, an Augustinian from Galway whose life was previously alleged to be in danger for swearing to the same claim.[106] In May 1670 he had accused Lynch of, amongst other things, 'having said King James was in hell, and that his son Charles was justly beheaded'.[107] Lynch had been prosecuted for this, but was acquitted. In 1674 French made further allegations against Lynch, who was briefly imprisoned in Galway before going into exile in Madrid, where he was later appointed honorary chaplain to Charles II of Spain. Thus, these older allegations dovetailed with one significant detail mentioned by Oates: that Lynch spent time in Madrid. It was innuendo rather than evidence, but Oates repeated his allegations about the existence of an Irish Plot at Edward Coleman's trial in November.[108]

By now the concern of the English authorities with the existence or otherwise of an 'Irish Plot' had finally seemed to bear fruit. An informer, Edmund Everard (who may have been of Irish extraction), had provided fuller allegations to the lords of a conspiracy. He claimed to have been employed as an agent 'at the French court' in the 1670s. What he claimed to reveal resembled Oates's allegations in that a substantial role was accorded to both Ireland and Scotland in a plot spearheaded by the French. Charles was to be murdered, Catholicism was to be restored, and York was to be placed on the throne. Once again, key figures in these allegations were Peter and Richard Talbot, who had supposedly been negotiating with the French since 1670 about 'a business... which mightily concerns the welfare of the Catholics in England and especially in Ireland'.

It corresponded to a model already established. The plot was to involve an insurrection in Ireland to secure 'a seaport town' for the French. Peter Talbot apparently discussed the proposals in person with Louis XIV, 'and though his Majesty be of a morose temper yet he often smiled as at propositions that pleased him'. Everard also implicated Coventry and Justin McCarthy, and summed up his testimony by claiming that the imprisonment of the Talbots before he could give his evidence 'is an argument that long before these present times there were such matters spoken of by me in France, and that it came to the knowledge of many Irish'.[109] He claimed to have related this tale to one Sir Robert Walsh in 1673, who was himself apparently involved in this plot and had Everard imprisoned within a week, though Walsh himself later claimed that Everard was imprisoned for seeking to poison Monmouth.[110] However, there was no question but that Everard had been imprisoned: that alone might lend credence to his allegations.

Even the murder of Sir Edmund Bury Godfrey was alleged to have had an Irish connection; it was noted in the Commons on 26 December that as Charles was to have been murdered by 'four Irish ruffians', the same characters might have done for Godfrey.[111] The possibility of Irish involvement in the Popish Plot as it unfolded in England was an obvious corollary to the allegations that there was a plot in Ireland. This allegation was soon followed (and presumably strengthened) by those of Miles Prance, a Catholic who had been suspected of involvement in Godfrey's murder, and who had been arrested after a false accusation by a lodger who owed him money. Prance claimed that one 'Gerald' had offered him money to kill an unspecified man. 'He said it was no sin to kill him, because he was a wicked man, and had done the Queen and the Irish ill-service.'[112]

The alleged involvement of 'Fitzgerald' in the murder would still be mentioned in the Whig press a year later.[113] Prance claimed that Godfrey was murdered by 'one [Robert] Greene, an Irishman' and another unnamed Irishman in the royal residence of Somerset House.[114] Greene denied any involvement in the murder, but conceded the presence of 'Kelly, an Irish priest', who had departed before the proclamation banishing Catholic clerics had been issued.[115] The next day 'Dominick Kelley' was charged in the Lords to be guilty of the murder of Edmund Bury Godfrey.[116] All of the individuals implicated here were later named in the articles of impeachment directed at the unfortunate William Howard, Viscount Stafford.[117] As had been seen in the arrest of Peter Talbot in Ireland, the absence of evidence did not pose any problems in this climate, as an 'Irish Plot' began to become located more firmly within the political discourse of the Popish Plot.

VII

The informers in England who claimed to have knowledge of an Irish Plot continued to make their allegations. One Stephen Dugdale claimed that one 'Mr Evers', 'at several times, told me the Pope out [of] his revenues had granted sums of money towards the putting the Irish into a condition of opposing the now established government for it was his gracious pleasure to consider what a tyrannical government they lived under'.[118] Dugdale claimed to have seen proof that 'the Pope did still hold his good purpose for the speedy relieving [of] the poor Irish'.[119] Within days Coventry repeated these allegations to Ormond against the backdrop of ongoing French preparations for an unspecified purpose. Prudence was required in the light of this new information about Ireland, and 'what relation this may have to those French preparations may be worth inquiry'.[120] Further allegations soon followed. Another Irishman, James Netterville, was allegedly involved in dubious (if unspecified) transactions involving certain figures already named by Prance, and one Pierce Butler. They had sought to persuade an informant, William Brookes, into slandering Oates and his fellow informer William Bedloe for money.[121] Presumably such cross-referencing of English and Irish allegations would have suggested to interested parties that there was indeed a broader conspiracy extending across both islands. In an environment where there seemed to be a definite sense of the form any 'Irish Plot' would take, confirmation of one part of it could easily be assumed to be confirmation that it existed in its expected totality.

Then came the full allegations of Stephen Dugdale. He had been the steward of Walter Aston, third Lord Aston, on his estates at Tixell in Staffordshire, until he was sacked for embezzlement and theft. His subsequent career as an informer was seemingly prompted by a desire to avoid a prison sentence for debt. At Tixell, one 'Arthur', an Irish priest, had 'hoped it would appear in a short time which of the two nations would be found the best Christians, meaning Ireland would be found truest in that design, for the English would be false'. He stated that France would provide men and money (and that God would bless the enterprise).[122] The precise nature of the 'business of Ireland' was unclear, but in the light of his previous allegations, it was safe to assume that it meant that either an Irish rebellion or a French invasion was planned, with the inevitable assistance from the Pope.[123] This seems, on the face of it, to have arisen from little more than personal resentment against his employer, but it was couched in familiar terms, as providing yet more evidence of an Irish Catholic conspiracy. And there was a very specific implication within such claims that drew upon the perception of previous events to predict the precise nature of any such Irish rebellion, for Irish rebellions had happened before. According to Gilbert Burnet, Dugdale's claims carried a particular resonance, for 'the memory of the Irish massacre was yet so fresh, as [to] raise a particular horror at the very mention of this'.[124]

By this Burnet meant the 1641 rebellion. There was no shortage of pamphlets printed in early modern England depicting Catholic cruelties across Europe; it was a common trope that could be taken to almost pornographic levels.[125] On 23 December 1678 an anonymous pamphlet was licensed that took as its specific subject the events of 1641, or more particularly the atrocities against Protestants (English and Scottish) allegedly committed by the Irish during it.[126] It had originally been published in 1667, and essentially reprinted lurid accounts from Temple's *Irish Rebellion*. It depicted scenes of hanging, burning, burial alive, mutilation, starvation, exposure to the elements, and disembowelment, most especially of pregnant women. The Catholic clergy, especially the Jesuits, had supposedly encouraged their flocks to commit such atrocities. Children were fed to dogs, boiled alive and had their skulls smashed in, families were forced to kill one another, and 'such was their malice against the English, that they forced their children to kill English children'.[127] Wives and daughters were raped in front of their husbands and fathers, 'with the basest villains they could pick out',[128] and were usually murdered afterwards. 'These merciless Irish Papists, having set a castle on fire, wherein were many Protestants, they rejoicingly said, O how sweetly they do fry!'[129] Over 1500 Protestants were alleged to have been drowned in Portadown on a number of occasions, and their indignant ghosts returned seeking vengeance, vanishing once their message was understood by a passing English army. Nine hundred and fifty four Protestants in Antrim were supposedly murdered in one morning.[130] In Sligo, 40 Protestants were locked in a cellar to await the ministrations of a butcher and his axe, both of which arrived, appropriately, at midnight, and the bodies of men and women would be arranged into what the author delicately termed 'a most immodest posture'.[131] Given that the Irish had attacked Protestants irrespective of their ethnicity, they respected neither the sanctity of their persons nor the religion that marked them out; it too was attacked. Graves were desecrated and bibles set alight, for 'it was hell-fire they burnt'.[132] In Kilkenny the head of a minister was attached to a cross in the market place. The mouth was cut open to the ears, and the rebels 'laid a leaf of a Bible upon it, and bid him preach, for his mouth was wide enough'.[133] In a somewhat ignominious if no less cruel demise, a fat man was melted down to make candles for a mass. And by borrowing a passage from Temple's *Irish Rebellion* (republished twice in London in 1679), the obvious question was asked.

> All this wickedness they exercised upon the English, without any provocation given them. Alas! Who can comprehend the fears, terrors, anguish, bitterness and perplexity that seized upon the poor Protestants, finding themselves so suddenly surprised without remedy, and wrapped up in all kinds of outward miseries which could possibly by man be inflicted upon human kind?[134]

If the Popish Plot and subsequent Exclusion Crisis rested upon the assumption of an imminent Catholic attack on Protestants in the Stuart kingdoms, the perception of the 1641 rebellion as wholesale massacre meant that it became an obvious – and close – example of what this might entail. While English perspectives on 1641 and the Catholic Irish may have lacked the immediacy and pertinence of those held by Protestants in Ireland, this did not mean that such perceptions were purely abstract. Grafted as this was onto older English tropes of the Irish as being a barbarous, brutal, duplicitous, inferior, and stupid race, in the late seventeenth century the additional notion of their inherent savagary, as revealed in 1641, ensured that English fears of the Irish could easily be reconstituted during a crisis; they were not yet merely figures of fun.[135] Concerns about an 'Irish Plot' rested upon the assumption that a rebellion akin to 1641 was on the verge of happening again, and being transposed to England. This was a latent fear derived from memory that acquired a particular relevance at this juncture, for the fears of an Irish rebellion and a Catholic succession were interrelated, and over time the possibility of the first of these happening would be proclaimed imminent to prevent the second coming to pass.[136]

VIII

However, there does not seem to have been any Catholic plot in Ireland. Luke Wadding later reflected upon the events of late 1678 in a sequence of poems, scorning the allegations about an Irish Plot whilst cursing Oates's allegations and, again, affirming Catholic loyalty to the crown.

> Some news each post doth bring,
> Of Jesuits and their plots,
> Against our sacred king,
> Discovered first by Oates.
> Such plotters we may curse,
> With bell and book at mass,
> By them the time is worse,
> Then e'er we felt it was.[137]

But the opposing perception was that there was indeed a Catholic threat in Ireland. This seemed to be the view held by the authorities in London, where serious consideration was finally being devoted to the perilous condition of Ireland's defences.

The Cavalier parliament was officially dissolved by Charles II on 24 January 1679, which obviated Charles' consistent wariness of having parliaments sitting simultaneously in both England and Ireland. Soon afterwards, Ormond's advice was sought on when to hold a parliament in Ireland, specifically to deal with its security. In his reply Ormond openly suggested Ireland should receive an additional 20 companies of troops (although he never seems to have received them).[138] These would serve as a morale booster throughout the country, but the only difficulty would be how to pay for them, as in Ormond's view the possibility of an Irish parliament sitting was unrealistic (and impolitic) at this time.[139] By the end of the month the plot to murder Ormond was dealt with by the English Privy Council. No evidence of any link with plots in England was evident, but this was still suspected in the light of Dugdale's allegations. A copy of the latter's testimony ('touching a general disturbance in both kingdoms') was to be sent to Dublin, as one 'Byrne' whom he mentioned was possibly the same Byrne imprisoned in Dublin 'under so many marks of guilt', having been implicated in the assassination plot.[140]

But despite the fact that he was to have been murdered by Catholics in December, Ormond soon found himself the subject of accusation once again. In February an anonymous letter was apparently circulated throughout Ireland, claiming that Ormond, Arran, Boyle, and numerous others were involved in a plot to destroy Protestantism in Ireland and in England. The Catholic gentry supposedly indulged in lengthy late night card games with Ormond and Arran in the Dublin Castle, 'and for the rest that it is intended you may read the massacre of Paris'.[141] The latter reference was to the St Bartholomew's Day Massacre in France in 1572, another Protestant touchstone for the treatment that could be expected at the hands of Catholics. Ormond did appear to be the subject of a whispering campaign at court, based around Ranelagh and now Essex, whom he was reluctant to attack openly despite his relatively tolerant policy towards Catholics when he was viceroy; once again an indicator of his uncertainty about his standing at court.[142] On the other hand, Orrery had maintained a diplomatic silence for some time and was now told that while 'we differ more in judgement than in matter of fact', Ormond quite simply did not believe that he had 'been very candidly represented by you'.[143] Orrery, in response, assured Ormond that he never attempted to undermine him or the government, and would try to make amends.[144] Ormond's emphasis on Orrery may well have been misplaced; true, they had a long and fraught acquaintance, yet Orrery's concerns seemed consistent with a belief in an Irish plot, and he was by no means the only problem with which Ormond was faced.

More significant in political terms was that the king resolved to remove Ormond from his post as steward of the royal household, to give it instead to 'one I would gratify at the present with that place'. Charles was hardly immune to the suspicion that he and his court surreptitiously favoured Popery; this was the grounds, after all, for the sustained assault on the court that would characterize the later phases of the crisis. The suggestion that Ormond be stripped of an English rank was justified on the grounds that he was required in Ireland anyway, and Charles was not prepared to brook complaints about 'any marks of unkindness in this matter because I have given so many proofs to the contrary'.[145] Ormond eventually returned his commission, but was aware that such a loss of prestige, with its implicit hint of royal disfavour, could easily turn to his detriment. 'I have reason to expect all the attacks of the disaffected party in the parliament. The place I am in, and the principles they know I profess will whet their malice and their ingenuity to find faults with me': following on from this was the possibility that the king could be forced at some stage to dismiss him.[146] Ormond was once more obliged to defend himself from further insinuation. 'It is true, I speak with some Papists in the closet, but so have all chief governors since the Reformation, and so they still must do, til it shall please God to convert the nation.'[147]

Throughout February, in the wake of the treaties of Nijmegan that ended the Franco-Dutch war, there were further indications of French naval activity that was suspected of being directed towards Ireland. Dugdale's allegations may have coloured this assessment, though by the end of the month the threat was not perceived to be as serious as it had originally seemed.[148] But Orrery did not think so, arguing with some insight along similar lines as Ormond that the Catholic Irish would themselves encourage the French. He claimed, with considerable hyperbole and in letters to numerous correspondents, that the entire north and west of the country was disaffected, and that the impending disbandment of Louis XIV's armies would provide an incentive to employ them abroad rather than risk domestic unrest (an argument that had been used about the Irish officers who had arrived in Cork the previous year), and where better 'unless in his majesties dominions'?[149] He suggested that immediate steps should be taken to prepare for this, given that the French would almost certainly get assistance from Munster 'Papists'. He argued that most of the province's major coastal towns were vulnerable to French forces, and Ireland was, in his view, the optimum location for a French invasion. The disgruntled natives would welcome the French, and might even provide a ready pool of recruits for them.[150] However, Michael Boyle, in what seemed to be a statement of the government's position, stoutly rebutted these concerns. The French preparations were probably – though not definitely – for a purpose other than invading Ireland. While some matters, such as the banishing of Catholic clergy, might require further attention, Irish defences were as good as both resources and intelligence would permit at this time.[151]

The Irish administration continued to proceed with caution. Ormond maintained that the application to Ireland of English penal legislation against Catholics would be impractical and imprudent, for both political and material reasons.[152] However, Ormond knew that he and his government had to maintain a delicate balance, for he was aware of the political dangers arising in England on the eve of an English parliament sitting once again in March ('I think monarchy will not be struck at the root, but I fear it will be very close lopped').[153] Paradoxically, preparations for an Irish parliament had received a new impetus just before this, perhaps due to misplaced optimism regarding the imminent meeting of its English counterpart (to which Ranelagh had failed to be elected). As had previously been suggested, confirmation of the decrees of the court of claims was deemed essential, but defending Ireland was the government's main priority, which brought up the perennial question of finance once again. The ideal solution might simply be the presence of more Protestants in Ireland, as little could be done to reduce the numbers of Catholics, but plainly this was not realistic.[154] This delicate balance in Irish affairs was illustrated when Ormond suppressed a plot by Protestant apprentices and labourers in Dublin to attack places of Catholic worship, and break up masses: this was deemed to be too provocative to be permitted.[155] In the absence of a parliament to provide the necessary funds to guarantee Protestant security, Ormond was of the opinion that avoiding unrest was perhaps the best that could be done. Waiting for an improvement in the English political climate was unavoidable.[156] The emergent (if fragmented) Whig opposition had become dominant, as the simmering inclination to curb the royal prerogative and mount an attack on York found fuller expression in England.

Dubious allegations continued to emerge of French designs on Scotland and Ulster, and of the imminent arrival in Ireland of ships laden with weapons.[157] The accusations that had come to light in February against Ormond, Arran, and Boyle had continued to circulate in the southeast, and were now forwarded to Dublin.[158] Ormond stoutly defended his actions since the onset of the crisis, and was concerned at claims that he himself was a Catholic and that 'by very pregnant consequence with having knowledge and being party to the plot and though this be against all sense and Mr Oates's evidence'.[159] 'I am here in my old station, pelted on at all hands; time was I was some where believed too much an enemy to the French and papists, now I am said to be absolutely at their service, but I feel myself just as I was.'[160] While he might scorn such allegations, he could also request that Ossory suggest to the king that he mobilize support for Ormond in parliament, 'to get me fair play', for if parliament had gotten the scalp of so prominent a figure as Charles's chief minister Thomas Osborne, earl of Danby (forced from power for supposedly favouring the introduction of the twin bugbears of popery and arbitrary government), then Ormond could also fall; while Ireland seemed increasingly wearisome, 'I would not be thought unfit for it on the grounds that may be given for my removal.'[161] However, the accumulation of broadly similar allegations about an Irish plot ensured that the English parliament, newly dominated by the Whig opposition, would become increasingly preoccupied with such assertions, given that it was increasingly concerned with the Popish Plot in general (the London republication of Henry Jones' *Sermon of Antichrist* in March 1679 may have been linked to the impending parliamentary session). According to one of Ormond's informants writing on 22 March, 'both houses this day expressed great concern and zeal against Papists and Popery', which meant that some attention would invariably be devoted to Ireland: at least some members of the English political elite were of the opinion that the Irish government (and by implication Ormond) were 'too indulgent to Papists'.[162] Finally, and perhaps most significantly, at a council meeting on Ireland 'my lord Shaftesbury in his ingenuous manner shook his head and said he did not like the management of affairs there'.[163]

IX

Anthony Ashley Cooper, first earl of Shaftesbury, came from an upwardly mobile and well-connected gentry family in Dorset. He initially took the royalist side in the English civil war, but defected to parliament in 1644. He sat as MP for Wiltshire under the Protectorate, but was alienated by the increasingly autocratic tendencies of Cromwell's regime in the 1650s and became reconciled to the monarchy after it was restored in 1660. An independent minded Privy Councillor who was notably sympathetic to dissenters, Shaftesbury was increasingly distrusted by the king and fell from favour in the 1670s. He subsequently carved out a niche as a prominent opponent of the government. However, over time, he had become increasingly concerned about York's Catholicism and the question of the succession. The Whig groupings that emerged in parliament during the Exclusion Crisis were composed of a number of factions, and did not make up a single coherent political interest inside or outside parliament. But Shaftesbury emerged as the most vocal advocate of excluding a Catholic – York – from the succession.

Shaftesbury eschewed the high church Anglican royalism exemplified by Ormond, and had clashed with both Ormond and Ossory in the 1660s over attempts to prevent Irish cattle exports to England; bad blood had lingered. When Shaftesbury, in a famous speech soon afterwards, pointed to the dangers of Scotland and Ireland in the House of Lords ('that kingdom cannot long continue in English hands, if some better care be not taken of it'), he was, by implication, criticizing Ormond and his conduct. Ossory responded, pointedly asserting that his father had served the crown loyally in the 1640s, and had never advocated peace with France, war with Holland, or religious toleration: all stances that, with the possible exception of making peace with the French, Shaftesbury had adopted during his career.[164] Ossory informed Ormond of the incident, and that he intended to deflect this unwelcome attention by providing the lords with an account of the Irish government's proceedings in relation to the Popish Plot.[165] Wyche concurred, and both Coventry and

Longford suggested that Arran be dispatched to London to counter any allegations of misconduct on Ormond's part. Longford also sent Ormond a copy of Shaftesbury's speech 'that your Grace may from thence see how necessary it is to look about you'.[166]

On 31 March Ossory presented this account of the Irish government's proceedings to the Lords.[167] It offered no radical analysis or prescription, being similar (if not identical) to a report compiled by the Irish administration before Christmas, and it was subsequently published both in Dublin and London.[168] It began by reiterating the original orders issued by the Privy Council to deal with the plot in Ireland, and recounted how they had been carried out. It listed the proclamations issued and their purpose, and the measures taken against individuals such as the Talbot's, along with a number of Jesuits. It referred to the disarming of Catholics and the securing of garrisons, and the attempts to put the militia back into a state of readiness. True, many of the Irish expelled from corporate towns (as ordered) had returned. But it was argued that they were permitted back by those English Protestants who had required their services. Ormond himself had acted as a guarantor for the purchase of extra weapons, and military arrangements were as good as could be expected without extra finance from an Irish parliament (in itself a hint). Finally, it outlined the guiding principle of the Irish government over the preceding months: Ireland and England were too different to be subject to the same laws and policies. Prudence and leniency marked out a wiser course than outright repression, and for the time being, there was no overriding reason to alter this position.

The statement Ossory presented may have rebounded to his detriment: he was forced off the Privy Council soon afterwards. But arguably it also ended a distinct phase of activity, as its entire purpose was to offer a defence of the Irish government in a rapidly deteriorating English political situation. Ever since the first disclosures had come to light, Ormond had been subjected to a variety of pressures as a whispering campaign was mounted against him at court. This had its antecedents prior to the disclosure of the plot, in Ormond's plans for the government, and most especially for the revenue. The plot simply provided a pretext for those, such as Ranelagh, who were vulnerable in the face of such policies. This pressure was intensified by a number of factors. Ormond's presence in Dublin guaranteed a level of ignorance about politics in London, despite his best attempts to keep himself informed. His chosen policy suggested a leniency towards Catholics that was easily magnified into outright sympathy. There was neither a basis nor a facility for the outright repression demanded by some. But a reminder of the reasons for such demands was provided in April by the eventual publication of Titus Oates' allegations, complete with details of the forthcoming 'conquest of Ireland' and its subjugation to the 'tyranny of the Pope and French... by a general rebellion and massacre of the Protestants as formerly'.[169]

What Ormond had seemed to view as a holding position in Ireland might prove difficult to maintain, but paradoxically, as the plot hysteria intensified it would have to be maintained. The beginning of the first exclusion parliament in England ensured the centrality of Irish affairs to the question of England's own safety, which after all, was essentially the basis for the concerns about the Popish Plot.

X

In the meantime the Irish government continued to conduct its business. The day after Ossory's response to Shaftesbury in the lords, two proclamations were issued in Dublin, one offering rewards for information leading to the arrest of Catholic clergy (£10 for a bishop or Jesuit and £5 for the remainder), and the other ordering the internment of the families of Tories, and the automatic arrest and transportation of priests in areas of Tory activity; an explicit linking of the two.[170] News of both was officially printed in London, presumably for the benefit of the sceptical.[171] In the wake of Ossory's speech, and in the absence of sinister events in Ireland, there was a discernible shift in emphasis towards politics in London, in both court and parliament.

Ormond undoubtedly believed that Shaftesbury was acting against him at this time, and identified him as a threat. He had apparently done so in the past, but according to Ormond, 'then I was not Frenchman enough'. Ormond was also aware that he would become especially vulnerable if it were known that York had secured his appointment as viceroy. The fickle nature of English politics weighed heavily upon Ormond's mind, though the appointment of Essex to the treasury seemed to provide at least some respite, removing as it did one rumoured contender for his position: perhaps prudently, Ormond congratulated him on his appointment.[172] Parliamentary proceedings in London carried some weight in Ireland, as fears of a Catholic plot seemed to give a greater resonance to other issues. As another bill to prohibit the export of Irish cattle was debated in the House of Commons, the issue of Ireland's existing trade links to France was highlighted by Sir John Maynard, lawyer, MP for Plymouth, and fervent believer in the Popish Plot, who declaimed in a faintly imperialist manner that 'I would not put Ireland into a condition to make them as considerable as ourselves.'[173] On the other side of the Irish Sea, in Dublin, William Petty observed that 'the news we have of the parliaments zeal to defend Ireland against the Pope and king of France is very grateful to many, and I find there are several clubs and meetings to draw up advices to be sent for England upon that account'.[174] But while suggestive of a level of public concern about the Irish ramifications of the Popish Plot, the details of such activities remain obscure.

Despite this, Peter Talbot seemed to have been forgotten as he lay dying in Dublin Castle, his pleas for a priest in his terminal decline throwing the allegations against him into stark relief.[175] The actual paucity of subversive activity in Ireland can be seen in the attention garnered by a single incident. On 4 April Ormond and the Irish council had ordered that Catholic worship be suppressed in all Irish cities and towns.[176] One of the Mayor's officers in Dublin subsequently attempted to break up what he thought was a mass and was later assaulted for his trouble.[177] A proclamation was later issued seeking information about this, but this minor incident was magnified and reported in places as far apart as Lisburn and London, and was compared to the fate of Edmund Bury Godfrey.[178] Sheriffs in Dublin were nonetheless ordered to crack down on surreptitious Catholic worship, and by 12 April Ormond could claim that all 'mass-houses' in Dublin had been suppressed.[179] These measures were not necessarily prompted by tangible problems; nothing that could actually prove the existence of a Popish Plot had emerged. But in the absence of actual events on which to base fears, some would seek to whip up such fears. Richard Cox in Cork, for example, took the view that things were too quiet, and

> Being a sincere Protestant and a good Englishman, I could not be silent when I thought all was at stake, but took an opportunity to express my zeale *pro aris et focis* in an elaborate charge

which (being chairman) I gave at the Quarter-Sessions, held for the county of Cork, at Bandon, in April 1679, at a critical season when the Popish plot began to be ridiculed. It will not be vain to say, that I did it with that spirit and good sense that mightily animated the Protestants, and as highly provoked the Papists.[180]

Precisely what the 'elaborate charge' was remains obscure. But his claim (admittedly decades after the fact) that 'I thought all was at stake' is telling, and suggestive of genuine fear for Protestant security in Munster. Orrery was concerned that domestic unrest in England over the exclusion issue would encourage the disaffection of Irish Catholics, and remained no less concerned about the possibility of a French invasion.[181] Some might disagree as to precisely where the real threat came from: a Lieutenant John Dancer was accused of declaring Oates's allegations to be 'a damned Presbyterian Plot' whilst in a house in Kinsale in April 1679 (the fact that he was subsequently promoted suggests that little more came of this).[182] Yet the assumption that the ultimate threat was a Catholic threat continued. For example, Irish naval officers of Catholic extraction, some of whom had indeed been favoured by York in his capacity as lord high admiral, automatically and explicitly came under suspicion at this time.[183] In part this reflected the relevance of maritime affairs to the crisis; after all, the projected French invasion would be seaborne. But this also reflected an automatic assumption that the categories of Irish and Catholic were indistinguishable: Samuel Pepys, in his capacity as secretary to the admiralty, noted how one officer was 'an Irishman, which among people designed to raise doubts will make his being a Papist much more easy for belief than his being an Englishman would do'.[184] Like the officers who had arrived in Kinsale the previous autumn, their nationality marked them out.

However, the English parliament was primarily interested in Irish matters as they impinged on events in England. In March the lords had demanded that lists be drawn up by the various inns of court and other educational institutions of 'Papists', 'reputed Papists', and Irishmen, a suggestive assessment that suggested once again that while these categories were distinct, they were not considered to be too far apart.[185] Alongside demands that Ormond's government engage in repressive measures against Jesuits and priests, it was now suggested in the House of Lords that the oaths of allegiance and supremacy be imposed upon all inhabitants of Dublin, 'and other ports and forts in Ireland'. They also ordered that Ormond's Catholic brother-in-law, the prominent (if shady) Colonel John Fitzpatrick, be confined to his home, and that he be barred from within 20 miles of Dublin without Ormond's permission.[186] On 1 April the lords had sat as a committee to consider Ireland, and resolved to address the king to request that Catholics in Ireland be disarmed and that Protestants there be supplied with weapons. It was also suggested that a proviso barring Catholics from serving on juries be entered into the proposed legislation for the Irish parliament; this was agreed to.[187] The deliberations of the lords saw further efforts made to bar Catholics from practising the law, or being clerks of the peace and sheriffs without submitting to the oaths. There was also a demand for the names of guardians of children and indeed children themselves, to determine who was being educated in which religion.[188] Irish Catholics had become an issue in England once again. On 15 April the lords addressed the king to demand that Ormond seize any Catholics deemed dangerous in Ireland, and reiterated their disparate demands for anti-Catholic measures, all of which were predicated on 'the late horrid conspiracy, and the present prospect of affairs'.[189] The likely significance of the attention being paid to Ireland in the English parliament reflected the accelerating pace of events there. But this was restricted to England. Ireland was dealt with in other ways.

The Privy Council did not accede to these requests until the end of May: they instructed Ormond that weapons were to be imported for use by Protestants and that Catholics were to be comprehensively disarmed, while also assuring Ormond that his efforts were appreciated.[190] In the meantime rumblings of discontent about Ormond's conduct in Ireland, and that of others such as Michael Boyle, had continued, as John Fitzpatrick remained a source of contention.[191] Having been ordered to leave Dublin by the king (at the behest of the lords), he became the subject of a smear campaign by Essex and Shaftesbury, which was also extended to Boyle.[192] While Essex and Shaftesbury (who were distant relatives) were dominant in differing factions of the burgeoning Whig movement, they seemed to find a sense of common purpose with regards to Irish affairs. Any attack on Fitzpatrick would inevitably rebound on Ormond, yet despite this he remained 'parliament proof', as his proceedings in Ireland seemed to meet with approval in London.[193]

But this did not alleviate the hostility towards Fitzpatrick, which precluded any vigorous campaign by Ormond in his defence. The best that could be done for him was to threaten Shaftesbury with evidence of his own previous goodwill towards Fitzpatrick.[194] Yet Ossory could still report to his father that 'great whispers are against you ... I hope to God the worst they can do will be to remove you from your present station'.[195] Hostility to Ormond was also occasionally evident in Ireland: in May 1679 a James and Joanna Gurney reported how a neighbour exclaimed had that Ormond 'was a rogue and deserved to be hanged'.[196]

Despite the viceroy's perennial concerns, the new parliament sitting in England had seemed to reinvigorate English policy towards Ireland.[197] The restructuring of England's own defence arrangements seemed to be on the verge of being replicated in Ireland, though the question of parliamentary jurisdiction added yet another element of uncertainty. The strictures of Poyning's Law ensured that any legislation for an Irish parliament had to be approved in London first. Ireland may have been a separate kingdom in theory, but the reality was very different. A memorandum drawn up for Arran dealing with Ireland's constitutional position illustrated this by concluding that the English parliament was not necessarily binding on Ireland. This was not explicitly linked to any specific parliamentary legislation or resolutions, forthcoming or otherwise, but its composition could be taken as a sign that events in England could force the hand of the Irish government, in which eventuality it could offer a legal basis for resisting this. Equally, in stressing the legal primacy of the Irish parliament, it could facilitate Ormond's long-standing desire to see one in session, if only on the pretext that Ireland's security depended upon the money that only it could provide.[198] Ireland 'cannot be in disorder and danger but that it must proportionately affect England', and Ireland was supposedly quite capable of its own defence if the resources could be provided.[199] But until now, they had not been.

XI

It was probably inevitable that in such a climate the condition of Ireland would prompt further reflection. In April, amidst what was apparently a welter of similar memorandums, Sir William Petty drafted three papers on current events to send to Southwell, one of which explicitly dealt with the pertinent question of 'intestine rebellion' in Ireland, and how best to prevent it.[200] Petty emphasized the disproportionate wealth and strength of the Protestant community, but the possession of that wealth compromised them, for they were obliged to employ large numbers of Catholics. These were, he argued, easily manipulated by a clerical and intellectual elite (such as lawyers), though these could easily be 'disposed of'. He also suggested that perhaps the Catholics could be detached from their leaders, and could be converted to the established church. He went so far as to suggest that Irishwomen should be removed from the country and replaced with Englishwomen, which could only be beneficial in terms of altering the religion and culture of the Catholic Irish. But he was undoubtedly aware of reality as it stood at this juncture: he stated that the Protestant interest had to be defended against the simmering hostility of Catholics, 'whom religion and the loss of estate have made implacable against the English'.[201] Indeed, the defence of the Protestant interest was a crucial and consistent theme in Petty's analyses of Irish society: the basis for much of the 'political arithmetic' that proved to be his intellectual legacy.[202] Southwell was asked, if he was of a mind to distribute them, to show the treatises to those who 'desire to have Ireland well saved from Popery and the French' and who had 'some power to execute what is good, for all that is practicable'.[203] Petty later inquired about them, for while 'the apprehensions of men are changed since they were composed... the temper of these papers I conceive to be such as may serve in all times'.[204] It was a revealing aside.

Orrery, on the other hand, seemed relatively happy with domestic affairs.[205] But he remained an obvious if unwelcome conduit for the fears of Munster Protestants as the broader question of Protestant security in Ireland remained an issue in London.[206] Despite this, English politics shifted the limited attention it had paid to Ireland away from there at this juncture: the imminent exclusion proceedings in parliament and the eventual outbreak of rebellion in Scotland became new preoccupations. In Ireland there had been little change: it was now rumoured that Ormond's replacement by William Savile, marquess of Halifax (supported by Charles illegitimate son James Scott, duke of Monmouth, and opposed by Essex), was imminent.[207] Halifax, Henry Jones, Lady Ranelagh, and possibly even Monmouth all emerged as new detractors, while there were also the related issues of security and, of course, the unresolved question of Ranelagh's accounts.²⁰⁸ Indeed, these were intertwined, as Ranelagh was perfectly willing to exploit suspicions of Ormond that stemmed from the viceroy's association with the court, and his willingness to do so was facilitated by Essex's control of the treasury. But Ranelagh, whose unsuccessful attempt at election had been backed by the king, remained vulnerable due to the imminent conclusion of his undertaking and the examination of his accounts, and Ormond, in turn, was inclined to exploit this to his advantage.²⁰⁹

It was at this juncture that the crisis underwent a decisive and formal change when, on 15 May, the first reading of a bill to exclude York from the succession took place. Charles's response was to prorogue parliament on 27 May, thence to dissolve it on 12 July. Ironically, an Irish proclamation of 14 May had declared 28 May a fast day 'to defeat popish conspiracies and implore a blessing on parliament'.²¹⁰ Ormond and the Irish council authorized the publication of specified prayers to be used on this day, reiterating the outline of the plot and reaffirming loyalty to the king, all the while drawing upon the liturgical rites used to commemorate the gunpowder plot 'for deliverance from the Papists our enemies'.²¹¹ There was no mention made of the more obvious liturgical commemoration of 1641; it would have been a more inflammatory choice.

Either way, the possibility of danger was conceded. Oliver Plunkett, in hiding, observed that those Catholic clergy still in Ireland were being continually harassed, often at the behest of ever-increasing numbers of informers, and the Catholic laity were too afraid to help them.²¹² Yet despite the attention devoted to the Popish Plot, the issues facing the Irish government in the months after it came to light were no different to those it had faced beforehand. The fact that the crisis had not managed to alter them was a strong indication that the allegations were groundless, and that the 'plot' did not exist. It was ironic then that amidst such concerns about potentially rebellious Irish Catholics, Scottish Presbyterians would provide the reality of rebellion instead.

3
Institutions and the 'Irish Plot', May 1679–November 1680

The English parliament was prorogued on 27 May, but events in Scotland rapidly overshadowed all else. On 3 May 1679 Archbishop James Sharp had been assassinated outside St Andrews by disaffected Presbyterians. A subsequent attack by government forces on an armed conventicle at Drumclog on 1 June prompted the outbreak of a Covenanter rebellion in the west of Scotland. It ended at Bothwell Brig on 22 June when the rebels were defeated by an Anglo-Scottish force under Monmouth, whose star would rise in the aftermath.

A perennial concern about unrest in Scotland was that it might spill over into Ulster or provoke unrest amongst Scottish Presbyterians in the province. Titus Oates, in his original allegations, claimed that the Jesuits had also intended to foment a rebellion in Scotland. Ormond was no friend of dissenters. At this time he was naturally more concerned with Presbyterians than Catholics, especially as 'fanatic' preachers were absconding to Ulster in the aftermath of the rebellion.[1] Ironically, latent fears about the security of Protestant Ireland were highlighted by a Protestant rebellion, as the upheaval in Scotland illustrated that the reality of Protestant subversion within the three kingdoms was potentially of greater significance than its as yet unproven Catholic counterpart. In Ireland, the well-worn theme of military finances (or the lack therof) was inevitably highlighted at a time of potential military exertion.[2] This renewed emphasis on finance (and thereby security) was more pertinent against the backdrop of a rebellion that also had connotations in the broader crisis; after all, events 'such as these were the beginning of our troubles before 1641'.[3] Consequently, the security of Ulster remained a major concern, both on its own terms and as an adjunct to events in Scotland. Both Catholic and Presbyterian insurrection could easily be encouraged by events elsewhere, though events in Scotland were deemed unlikely to impede proceedings in the Popish Plot.[4] But the reality of Presbyterian rebellion provided a counterpoint to the ongoing, and unsubstantiated, allegations of a Catholic plot. The events in Scotland highlighted the broader question of Ireland's internal and external security, and exacerbated the impact of the Popish Plot on the establishments of the Irish administration. Alongside this, the development and promotion of an alleged 'Irish Plot' soon began to be promoted as a political tool in England during the ongoing crisis over the succession.

I

The potential repercussions of the Scottish rebellion preyed upon Ormond's mind. Given his recurring scepticism about the existence of a Catholic plot, the Scottish rebellion was bound to take precedence. Troops were to be put into readiness and deployed in Ulster, with the explicit possibility that they would be sent over to Scotland if required.[5] Rumours persisted that Presbyterians in Ulster were emboldened by events in Scotland, though at least some Presbyterian ministers were prepared to pledge their loyalty to the government.[6]

Concerns about unrest resonated across the country. In Dublin, the Lord Mayor was to be granted an allowance, having 'been at great charge in order to the raising the militia for the safety of the city in this time of danger'.[7] On 30 June a proclamation ordered the arrest of all arrivals from Scotland until their credentials could be established ('no-one is to harbour them'); the ongoing traffic between Scotland and Ireland ensured that the rebellion remained a preoccupation.[8] But the lack of money remained a running sore for the government, despite the fact that in early June the ongoing saga of Ranelagh's accounts had seemed on the brink of finally being resolved.[9] While the eventual successes against the Scottish rebels justified measures to prevent 'insurrection or invasion', the condition of the Irish revenue guaranteed 'the danger of this Kingdom to itself, and in consequence to the rest of his dominions to his Majesty'. Again, an Irish parliament was the obvious means of raising money to rectify this, and Ormond bemoaned the continual delays in calling one, despite there having been 'some intervals that to me at this distance seemed long enough for the work'.[10] Monmouth's eventual victory offered the possibility that the king might devote time to security in general and that of Ireland in particular.[11] Instead, it prompted the dissolution of the English parliament lest Monmouth's new popularity provide both him and Shaftesbury with a new ascendancy, as Charles began to flirt with the idea of aligning himself with either the Dutch or the French.[12]

Despite this interlude, the continual allegations of Catholic plots in Ireland had not abated. 'We have had most dreadful accounts of massacres in Ireland and French landing and putting all Protestants to fire and sword, but of this we have no confirmation these three weeks.'[13] But Ireland remained quiet. This may have influenced the Privy Council's decision to release Richard Talbot (who had been imprisoned for six months in Dublin Castle) on health grounds under a £10,000 surety; in early July he was even permitted to go to France to receive treatment for a badly swollen testicle ('an extraordinary swelling in one of his stones, near as big as a gooses egg, much discoloured, and as he said very hard and sore'), thereby permitting a convenient exile in France while he awaited permission to return that would not be forthcoming.[14] The council also ordered the release of Mountgarret, who was to be bailed due to his poor health.[15] Thus, two figures named and implicated in the supposed Irish Plot were released, albeit under certain conditions; hardly a suggestion of unwavering faith in the danger that they allegedly posed.

The prorogation of the English parliament seems to have offered Ormond a lucky escape from a hostile political climate in England, a pattern that would be repeated for the remainder of the year: he would not find himself in such a precarious position again.[16] This did not mean that he would not come under pressure; but it would not be critical pressure. Orrery told Essex that Ormond 'has not engaged to undertake for the safety of this kingdom'.[17] After the interlude provided by the Scottish rebellion, this was a return to more traditional preoccupations. But there were some grounds for optimism, as previously thorny issues seemed to reach resolution. The convenient removal of Talbot from the political scene coincided with what appeared to be Ranelagh's reluctant acquiescence in the production of his accounts.[18]

Ireland had continued to lurk on the fringes of the Popish Plot in England; but perhaps no more than the fringes. At the opening of the trial of the five Jesuits (Fenwick, Groves, Harcourt, Turner and White) on 13 June 1679, the prosecution opened its case with a damning indictment of Catholics, who 'kill the Protestants by thousands, without law or justice, witness their bloody doings at Mirandel, their massacre at Paris, their barbarous cruelty in Ireland, since the year 1640, and those in Piedmont, since 1650'.[19] Later in the same trial, Oates reiterated his belief in the existence of an Irish dimension to the plot, and that Ormond's murder would be an integral part of it.[20] At Sir George Wakeman's trial in July, he repeated his earlier claims that there was an Irish Plot, and that Peter Talbot was involved in it. An army was to be raised in Ireland, and once again, a crucial element was to be 'the poisoning of the duke of Ormond'.[21] Ormond was thereby cast as a potential victim of the Catholics rather than their accomplice.[22]

While the issues that preyed on his mind were no different at this point, Ormond began to seem more content in his charge. Coventry had previously urged Ormond to remain in Ireland, as his presence in London 'would but precipitate the designs of your enemies', and should anything happen in Ireland in Ormond's absence it 'would not escape odd reflection according to the humour of the present conjuncture'. Ormond had previously been inclined to resign, but Charles had not been inclined to accept it: he may have wanted to keep a traditionally reliable servant in place at an uncertain time. Moreover, such danger as the viceroy was in stemmed from within the court; in parliament (when it had sat), his support 'was so considerable that it was that which secured you'.[23] The eventual suppression of the Scottish rebellion alleviated some of his fears about the condition of Ulster, and barring either civil war or invasion there was still nothing to fear from Catholics.[24] Indeed, such attitudes were becoming more widespread, and were influenced by other factors. Protestant businessmen and merchants in Galway petitioned for the return of the Catholics who had been expelled from the city and offered to take responsibility for their loyalty, given that trade and the local economy had suffered: hardly an indication of a belief in any imminent rebellion. However, while the Irish council overwhelmingly agreed, the king refused to concede this, as the expulsion order had originally been prompted by an address of the English House of Lords.[25] To disregard this would be impolitic at best, and the decision illustrated the gulf in perception between Dublin and London, for there did not seem to have been any discernable threat. It also illustrated the gulf in terms of authority. Fears about the condition of Ireland were dictated by the exigencies of English politics as much as by Irish realities. The flux of English politics was never far away, but consequently, its currents could be manipulated. For example, Longford was convinced at this juncture that Ranelagh, given his increasingly precarious position, could be easily crushed, and that it would be prudent for Ormond to do so: the prospect of his resurgence could prove disastrous.[26]

In the meantime, rumours against Ormond began afresh. He was accused of being 'disaffected' to Protestants, deeming them the greater danger (which was indeed his opinion).[27] But he was also informed of the king's good favour, of Charles's displeasure at the persistent rumours of his dismissal, and of his stubborn refusal to replace him.[28] This could only have been reassuring.[29] Indications of pressure being exerted on Ranelagh also seemed to bode well, as a dispute amongst the farmers of the Irish revenue suggested that the details of the accounts would finally be made public, while there were rumours abroad of Ranelagh's corruption which if substantiated would prove disastrous for him and his partners.[30] However, the absence of an Irish parliament remained problematic, especially as the ongoing petitioning campaign to call a new parliament in England would soon prompt elections there. In the meantime, Ormond was conscious that there was potentially a window of opportunity in which to call one in Ireland. He had wanted to do so since his reappointment, but 'there was then no discovery of the plot that hath so employed his Majesty'.[31] Yet there had been no concrete discoveries of a plot in Ireland, or of evidence to justify the belief in one.

The pattern established over the previous year since the plot allegations first emerged remained largely unchanged. Ormond remained vulnerable as the possibility of his impeachment in a future English parliament had now arisen.[32] Ranelagh had still not come to an accounting and was fighting a rearguard action against having to provide one.[33] Nonconformists in Ulster still remained a likely source of unrest.³⁴ But while such considerations remained relevant against the backdrop of the Popish Plot, no further proof of the existence of a Catholic plot had actually emerged. While there was no shortage of conjecture and paranoia in Ireland, there was a dearth of actual testimony and evidence. True, deponents in England had amplified some of Oates' original claims by making reference to a plot involving Ireland. The original allegations about a plot to assassinate Ormond and the king claimed that while the Jesuits were behind this, the actual killers were to have been Irish: an awareness of Irish involvement in the plot allegations in England was unlikely to have been dissipated, and such innuendoes were evident in occasional scattered reports in the London press.³⁵

Ormond at this time did not unduly concern himself with issues in England that did not directly impinge on him or his government, though he continued to defend his conduct.³⁶ It was inevitable that news of such insinuations would spread. The prominent Antrim landowner and politician Edward Conway, Viscount Conway, was informed by his agent George Rawdon that 'Lord Ranelagh is long looked for in Dublin': a hint that he may have been suspected of being the source of some such rumours. Rawdon also confirmed that there was no indication of an Irish parliament being called, especially when an English parliament was in session. But for Rawdon, these events remained distant to the point of abstraction. Far removed from the centre of power, the Tories of Ulster were of more immediate relevance to him, most especially the notorious Redmond O'Hanlon, who was on the run in Leitrim.³⁷ In time, Tory activity would become particularly relevant to the allegations about an Irish Plot. And such allegations would soon receive a major lease of life. Up to this point, there had been no Irish equivalents to Oates's allegations from anybody who could provide first-hand testimony about the existence of an Irish Catholic plot. However, in September 1679 rumours and assumptions gave way to what seemed to be concrete evidence, in the form of the testimonies of David Fitzgerald and Eustace Comyn.

Fitzgerald was a Limerick Protestant who would later play a major role in the development (and eventual collapse) of allegations about a Catholic conspiracy in Ireland, though his initial allegations remain obscure.³⁸ But Comyn's allegations are not. Originally from Painstown, County Meath, he claimed that some five years previously, in Carrick-on-Suir, he had heard John Brennan, the Catholic bishop of Cashel, bemoan the fact that 'if he had more money than he had, he had not enough of it to help those of his own religion'. He had also spoken of the impending arrival of 'those of his own religion, Frenchmen, that would come in to this kingdom and England to take the kingdom for themselves'. York 'was the right king, and not he that has many bastards'. The malicious intentions of the Catholics were revealed in the fact that Brennan allegedly gave £200 to Sir William Davis to assassinate Comyn, who apparently had more to tell, though the examining justice of the peace had been sceptical of his claims.[39] In time, these allegations would assume a more immediate relevance within the burgeoning Whig campaign to exclude York from the succession.

II

In late August 1679 Charles II fell seriously ill, and the potential vulnerability of the succession prompted a brief crisis within a crisis. Whether or not this directly affected the emerging Irish allegations seems unlikely; the same is true of York's eventual removal to Scotland in September once Charles had recovered. At a more prosaic level, it was reported in September 1679 that 'Daniel MacCarte', 'a notorious Irish priest' had been captured on 25 August on the verge of giving the last rites to a woman in London, and had been identified by Oates.[40] As the author of one anonymous London broadsheet concluded, 'such circumstances as these induce us to believe, that the Papists are so far from being discouraged in their hopes of perpetuating their late horrid conspiracy, that they still proceed in it and pursue it, with fresh vigour'.[41] Soon after this a proclamation was issued offering a reward for information on the 'four ruffians appointed in the late traitorous conspiracy to go to Windsor to assassinate the King', three of whom were apparently Irish; a pardon would also be forthcoming to anyone who could provide such information by 20 October.[42] In October it was reported in the Whig press that 'letters from Ireland, give an account of a dangerous and mischievous design, which has been lately discovered there, contrived by the Popish faction, for the destruction of the Protestants'. Weapons had been discovered, and 'a considerable person' – possibly John Fitzpatrick – was thereby implicated.[43] October also saw the election of an English parliament that was broadly in favour of 'exclusion', however defined, but the possibility that it would become a forum for grievances about Ireland (or anything else) was forestalled by its prorogation until the following year.

Again, the prorogation of the English parliament makes it difficult to draw a link between it and the flurry of new Irish allegations. Ormond's administration in Dublin was effectively sidelined, as Ireland's alleged role within the Popish Plot had emerged in England. A warrant was issued in November 1679 for the arrest of two of the ostensible Irish assassins of the king (Patrick Lavallyan and Denis O'Kearney) who were believed to be in Ireland, but Ormond was simply to ensure that they were sent to England when captured.[44] The full investigation of their allegations would not take place in Dublin. This potentially awkward development can be contrasted with more promising news about the most obvious group of potentially troublesome subjects in Ireland: a declaration of loyalty to the government from Presbyterian preachers in Ulster. Aware that, yet again, aspersions of disloyalty were cast upon them, they had addressed themselves to Arthur Forbes, earl of Granard (who was notably sympathetic to Presbyterians) in September with assurances of their loyalty and their intention to discourage sedition amongst their flock, insofar as they did not contravene their own principles. The difficulty of getting a unanimous declaration was acknowledged, but should it be required, those ministers who had subscribed would undertake to get one[45] After it had been highlighted by the recent rebellion in Scotland, security in Ulster would always be more concerned with Presbyterians then Catholics.[46] Yet such security remained on a shaky foundation. The straitened finances of the Irish government were evident when, three weeks later, soldiers quartered in Lisburn were granted limited credit 'in the intervals of receiving their pay'.[47] It was also ordered that a number of those implicated by David Fitzgerald be arrested: these included Theobald Burke, Lord Brittas, and Peirce Lacy, an Irish soldier in the French service.[48] Fitzgerald had first come to official attention through Orrery, but such difficulties as Orrery had presented might not last, for it was generally accepted that his health was in terminal decline.[49] Ossory had already suggested that Orrery's elder brother Richard Boyle, earl of Burlington, be earmarked for some of his commands. Burlington was loyal to the king, but more pertinently was not deemed hostile to Ormond, and the perceived magnanimity of such a gesture could only reflect well on the beleaguered viceroy.[50]

In late September the exiled York indicated his enthusiasm to see an Irish parliament in session, preferably before Christmas.[51] But he was of the view that only the elderly Ormond could control it, and the viceroy's age made speed an imperative.[52] However, investigation of the plot allegations was intruding on the Irish government's other business. Ormond ordered the arrest of the remaining Catholic bishops in Ireland, as soon as their whereabouts could be determined.[53] He specifically ordered the arrest of Plunkett and Patrick Tyrrell, the incumbent bishop of Clogher. This would be 'an extraordinary service to the king' but also 'of great advantage to me'.[54] There were also more substantial allegations of an Irish Plot that would prove to have a greater resonance made by Hubert Boark of Waterford against Richard Power, earl of Tyrone, a former governor of Waterford (and MP for the county) who had seen considerable military service abroad. Alongside these were a number of allegations about unspecified arms shipments to Waterford and Dungarvan, weapons that were supposedly intended for Catholics as a prelude to a French invasion. The various persons implicated here had been secured (apart from Tyrone himself), though their accusers remained elusive.[55]

The essence of these allegations resembled their predecessors. The Jesuits were supposedly at the vanguard of a plot to capture Limerick. Troops were being raised for this purpose, and foreign assistance was being solicited (Patrick Lavallyan, one of the Irishmen whom Oates had claimed was to assassinate the king, was also now reported to be near Limerick).[56] By mid-October 1679, Ormond had sent an account of 'the plot David Fitzgerald undertook to discover' to London, adding that he had not completed his investigations before 'my Lord of Orrery got notice of it, writ it over, and so it is gotten into print, with such reflections and remarks as I doubt not he designed'.[57] This text was based on allegations made against Tyrone by another informer, John MacNamara, and concerned itself with a plan to capture Limerick and 'cut the poor Protestants throats'.[58] Publication seemed to render further investigation of these allegations worthless by providing advance warning to those whom he might have implicated.[59] This was a serious matter, as Ormond was willing to concede the very real possibility that the claims were actually true.

It was bound to magnify his dislike and distrust of Orrery (though Orrery's death on 16 October 1679 alleviated such concerns).

The timing of these investigations was awkward. Ormond remained quite aware that such new discoveries could cause bills for any prospective Irish parliament to be set aside.[60] Despite the proliferation of new allegations since the start of the year, the prospect of a rebellion being raised was being taken very seriously by the Irish government.[61] More active measures against such plots were to be undertaken in Ireland at the behest of the English government. In late November both king and council instructed Ormond to prepare bills for the exclusion of Catholics from parliament and state office, for the implementation of the test acts, 'and such other necessary bills for suppressing Popery'.[62] Ormond remained optimistic about future realignments at court, especially after both Monmouth's exile and Shaftesbury's dismissal from office in the aftermath of the king's illness. However, it appeared to Ormond that Shaftesbury opposed the sitting of an Irish parliament, 'at least while I am the governor', and he remained concerned that 'the ill humour now stirring in England will be transferred hither'.[63]

III

The tension between the desire to investigate the Popish Plot and the more immediate institutional concerns of the Irish administration remained unresolved. Ormond bemoaned the time now being devoted to – or wasted on – the examination of the continually emerging flow of Irish informers.[64] Yet this became a moot point as the bill for confirming Irish estates was opposed in the Committee for Irish Affairs in London, thus delaying the Irish parliament yet again.[65] Tyrone's father-in-law Arthur Annesley, earl of Anglesey, the Irish born lord privy seal who, perhaps unsurprisingly, eventually declined to support the Lords resolution in the belief in the existence of an Irish Plot, observed that the Committee for Irish Affairs 'cast out unanimously the Irish pretended bill of confirmation of estates, but really destruction to the English', a blunt statement of at least one opinion of it.[66] Paradoxically the bill that was intended to facilitate Ireland's security could be perceived as having precisely the opposite intention and effect. Such manoeuvres naturally attracted Ranelagh's attention. He disingenuously argued that it should be postponed until the following winter, as it could prove unhelpful to the king due to the alleged bad will towards Ormond and his government that might be expressed in it.[67] Yet it was Ormond's consistent belief that any disgruntlement expressed in a parliament would ultimately stem from the machinations of Ranelagh's undertaking; his accounts had been transmitted to Dublin in July, though his survival would be guaranteed by the royal goodwill his financial transactions had incurred.[68]

Problems soon arose with the proposed parliament yet again: no more draft legislation could be sent to London for examination until those already under consideration were deliberated upon, unless these were scrapped and drafted afresh. Matters were complicated by the king's order for the exclusion of Catholics from it, not to mention the 'suppression of Popery'.[69] Ranelagh observed the subsequent debate, in which it was suggested that Catholics be barred from civil and military employment. He took the view that this could be done legally anyway, and the imprisonment of Tyrone suggested that such measures were in step with the times.[70] Essex apparently remained opposed to the bills of confirmation and settlement, based supposedly on his ambition to succeed Ormond as viceroy, but surprisingly, he was deemed 'partial to the Irish and consequently prejudicial to the Protestant interest'.[71] The Protestant interest remained concerned about the future: in December 1679 a congregation at Youghal was warned to remain vigilant due to 'the troubles and disquiets that are amongst us'.[72]

However, the disorders of soldiers in Waterford seemed to indicate that such assiduousness was unmatched by the resources available to the authorities.[73] Rumblings of indiscipline amongst them had been ongoing for some time, and had culminated with the murder of the high constable of the town: he had urinated against the door of a tavern where a number of officers were quartered and been killed for his trouble. If, as was assumed, there was a plot, here was proof that the resources with which to deal with it were in a poor condition indeed, and the fact was advertised in London.[74] Both the soldiers and the officers continued to threaten the inhabitants into silence on the matter, and Ormond insisted that this be dealt with strenuously.[75] Such indiscipline was bound to draw attention to the perceived dereliction of their duties; in London, complaints were again being made about the delay in forcing the handover of Catholic weapons, with unflattering comparisons being made to the speed at which Blood's Plot had been dealt with in 1663.[76]

The address of the mayor, sheriffs, and citizens of Waterford to Ormond about the abuses of the soldiers (threats, abuse, robbery, and murder) was printed in London in January 1680.[77] This was not the only Irish issue to be publicized there, as further hints and insinuations about the presence or activities of Irishmen there were continually noted, along with further hints about the supposed existence of an Irish Plot.[78] There were also concerns voiced about Ormond's delay in providing details about a number of Irish informers, and that no adequate account of Ranelagh's financial dealings had been compiled.[79] Ranelagh had sought to prevent this, but was under pressure to do so nonetheless.[80] Throughout January attempts to transmit further bills to England continued, 'for the benefit of his Majesty the security of this his kingdom and the satisfaction of his subjects'. The focus remained on the confirmation bill, not least because its absence would probably block the provision of supplies.[81] On the financial question, Ranelagh's sojourn in England would seemingly be longer than expected; consequently his accounting would be delayed even further.[82] The reality of Protestant opposition in Ireland to the bills for the Irish parliament also became clearer, as did their occasionally malicious basis; alongside the inevitable involvement of unspecified English political figures, objections to them had previously been sent to London by Orrery.[83] Yet by the beginning of March the bill of settlement was expected to prove acceptable on the basis of the original argument in its favour: that the absence of it was likely to hinder any prospective supply.[84] Charles had told the Privy Council of his intention to have an Irish parliament in session by the end of the same month.[85] The bills were to be transmitted back after amendments by 'some who are never unmindful when Ireland is named' to guarantee that the oaths of allegiance and supremacy would be imposed on all members of the parliament.[86] Naturally, the possibility of a parliament sitting in Dublin did not appeal to Ranelagh, who, as he himself wrote, was 'meeting with nothing but malice and persecution' there.[87] The parliament was expected to sit in a matter of weeks: according to Rawdon, 'the news is everywhere', and he began to consider possible candidates for election. A militia bill for Ireland was also reportedly imminent, along with a strengthened security establishment in which Rawdon and Longford were tipped for senior positions (the latter would be appointed governor of Carrickfergus before the end of the month).[88] However, in the light of subsequent developments, such indications of progress proved a false dawn.

IV

On 6 December 1679 Oliver Plunkett had been arrested near Dublin. This was naturally reported in the *London Gazette*, presumably to demonstrate the zeal of the government, as were the accusations of high treason against Tyrone, and the existence of witnesses to prove them.[89] However, Ormond was aware that there was a lack of material evidence against Plunkett, though he could be detained simply for remaining in Ireland.[90] From captivity in Dublin Castle, Plunkett himself observed that he had been released from solitary confinement for the simple reason that there was no evidence against him; he was imprisoned for practising his pastoral duties.[91] From the outside it undoubtedly seemed that Plunkett had been imprisoned simply for remaining in Ireland, which meant that he might not necessarily receive a severe punishment. John Fitzpatrick assured the Vatican that Plunkett would probably be exiled or imprisoned, that his execution seemed unlikely, and that he would prevail upon Ormond to do something.[92] Plunkett himself remained cautious, informing the Vatican that the appointment of new bishops would automatically prompt further repression, which would in turn alienate the Catholic clergy and the laity from the hierarchy; his stance remained unchanged up to his death, and by then was shared by the other Catholic bishops.[93] However, Plunkett would soon be subjected to far more serious accusations, as the allegations of an Irish plot began to gain new momentum.

By mid-January 1680 David Fitzgerald's testimony was finally on the verge of being sent to London.[94] In February those of Hubert Boark and a number of others were presented to the Privy Council, and were passed on to the Committee for Irish affairs.[95] They resolved to prosecute those implicated by the allegations, including Tyrone, Brittas, and Pierce Lacy. The peers were to be tried first, and 'that in order thereunto, preparations be made for the speedy calling of a parliament in that kingdom'.[96] By now, Irish informers were becoming increasingly prominent. One such individual ('Egan alias Fitzgerald') was to travel to Cork with letters of introduction from Essex and the secretary of state, Robert Spencer, earl of Sunderland, to search for arms and incriminating papers related to the plot that were hidden in the wall of an abbey. Whatever was found was to be examined, copied, and the originals sent on to Sunderland.[97] However, in late March 1680 a report was published in London about the activities of a Franciscan friar, John Fitzgerald: presumably the same individual who had claimed to know of the material supposedly hidden in the wall, and possibly the same 'Mr Fitzgerald' who had made allegations about sinister Catholic activities in Sligo and attracted Orrery's attention in 1678.[98] Letters were found in his lodgings that 'proved to be in his own hand writing, and were filled with abominable treasons against his sacred majesties life, and the Protestant religion, and contained the same things that the letters he said did, that were to be found hid in the wall in Ireland' (his seizure whilst seemingly in the process of forging testimony was attributed to misplaced zeal).[99] By April Fitzgerald was en route to Ireland again, having apparently sidestepped this difficulty.[100]

By the spring of 1680 detailed allegations about the existence of a Catholic conspiracy in Ireland were coming thick and fast. In February the Privy Council had examined more papers relating to the allegations made against Tyrone and Brittas that seemingly involved plans for a French invasion and the capture of Limerick. Those implicated were now to be arrested for high treason.[101] But despite the allegations, scepticism about the existence of a plot was evident once again. Ormond noted that the cases against Tyrone and Brittas were not the same plot that David Fitzgerald had claimed to know of, and any prosecution would be forced to rely on Fitzgerald's testimony, and it was unclear at this stage whether he would produce any more.[102] It would soon be obvious that, irrespective of whether the claims of these Irish informers were true or not, the allegations that they were prepared to make would soon assume a far greater and more specific relevance.

V

The reasons for this were quite straightforward. The prospect of English involvement in an anti-French alliance in early 1680 raised the possibility that the Whigs might be robbed of the popular sentiment that had undoubtedly come to their side.[103] Possibly in order to maintain the momentum of the campaign against the court, in March 1680 Shaftesbury claimed to have obtained more information about an Irish Plot; specifically that provided by a renegade priest from Armagh, Edmund Murphy, to William Hetherington, an obscure if dubious individual whom Murphy had met in jail. Hetherington was apparently from Ganderstown in County Louth, and was imprisoned in Dundalk in 1679 for debt and dealings with Tories. He persuaded Murphy to swear to the existence of a Catholic plot in Ireland and escaped from custody in about May 1679, presenting himself to Shaftesbury in London in February 1680. He appeared before the Privy Council on 24 March 1680, and, using Murphy's allegations, sought to implicate both Ormond and Oliver Plunkett in a Catholic plot to orchestrate a French invasion.

This gave a renewed impetus to the plot allegations (even if Murphy was later described by Sir Henry Coventry as being of 'very bad character').[104] Ormond was not the primary target: this would have distracted attention from York.[105] But Plunkett was now explicitly implicated in a conspiracy that 'was to no other intent but to ruin the king and his three kingdoms and to bring in popery'.[106] Hetherington was sent back to Ireland to obtain more evidence and, in the aftermath of his revelations, it was resolved that a committee of the Privy Council should be appointed to investigate these accusations.[107] Essex, Coventry, and Shaftesbury were subsequently reported to be members of this committee, but secrecy surrounded its proceedings and virtually no information emerged from it.[108] There was an embargo placed on reports of what had transpired, though it was known to be about 'some design alleged to be of great danger to the Kingdom of Ireland'.[109] Rumours proliferated in the absence of details, but it was obvious that the revelations were being taken very seriously, as the king resolved to attend the next council meeting in order to hear them himself.[110]

As a consequence the legislation for an Irish parliament was delayed again. It was not now expected until May: the parliament would be delayed until August at least.[111] Ossory wrote to his beleaguered father that 'yours, and I may presume to say, the kings enemies, use all their artifices to blast our reputations'.[112] He also suggested that if Ireland was indeed quiet, and if the parliament could be called, Ormond should press for it 'with all imaginable vigour'. If not, he should inform the king of the reasons for his seemingly drastic change of mind. Ossory also warned him that Essex was intent on opposing such bills as Ormond presented.[113] Mails from England were stopped, but Sir William Petty came over by sea and informed Ormond of events in London. The viceroy's concern for his position was obvious when he concluded that there were deliberate efforts to keep him in the dark, and that therefore 'something is informed against me'.[114]

At this point in time, the latter fear was more reasonable than usual. Secretive proceedings around the Irish informers also tended to prompt suspicions about them, and these were often entirely justified. Those who had made allegations against Tyrone, for example, withdrew from his trial in Ireland and absconded to England when their own immunity from prosecution expired: John MacNamara was accused of horse stealing, and Hubert Bourk of other unspecified misdemeanours. Further allegations of plot discoveries in Ulster and Connacht incurred Ormond's cynicism and contempt.

> I do not so much wonder at the scandals cast upon us now as that it was not done sooner. But it was necessary to amuse the people, as with new plots so with new actors in them. The discoveries now on foot in the north and in the west of this kingdom can come to nothing by reason of the extravagant villainy and folly of the informers, who are such creatures that no schoolboy would trust them with a design for the robbing of an orchard. My Lord of Essex's tool is a silly drunken vagabond that cares not for hanging a month hence if in the meantime he may solace himself with brandy and tobacco. Murphy is all out as debauched, but a degree wiser than the other. The other fellow brought by my Lord of Shaftesbury to the council broke prison being in execution, and now the sheriff or jailor are sued for the debt. This is their true character, but perhaps not fit for you to give of them. If rogues they must be that discover roguery, these must be the best discoverers, because they are the greatest rogues.[115]

By now their importance was also obvious, irrespective of their characters. Charles instructed that they be kept apart from strangers, and that their information be kept confidential until he had seen it in full. It also seemed obvious that the imprisoned Oliver Plunkett was increasingly becoming the subject of these allegations.[116]

Scepticism was inevitable. Sir Thomas Southwell of Limerick, who was implicated by David Fitzgerald, was concerned that the accusations against him were essentially malicious. Two years previously a tenant, one 'Gerald' (possibly Fitzgerald), a 'madman', accused him of involvement in a plot when there was 'no talk of any such thing either in England or Ireland'; it apparently arose from a dispute over rent. But 'as to the Irish Plot, we believe more is spoken of there than we hear of it here'.[117] However, on 26 April 1680 a proclamation reiterated that which had previously been issued against the Catholic hierarchy on 16 October 1678, combining it with the rewards set out in that of 26 March 1679.[118] This implied an official and public belief in the existence of a plot on the part of an Irish government that remained privately sceptical about it. 'There has been great industry to make it believed all over England that Ireland is on the brink of confusion and cutting of throats.' Merchants had inquired about the condition of Ireland, as uncertainty and fear curtailed trade across the Irish Sea. Ormond blamed Sir Henry Capel (Essex's brother) for fomenting this, and resolved to furnish himself with copies of any relevant documentation that might emerge in London, for Essex was now in possession of what appeared to be incriminating material that could prove embarrassing to Ormond; namely, papers that had been found on the body of the Tory Patrick Fleming.[119]

Fleming came from an Old English family in Meath, and had become a prominent and destructive Tory on the Ulster border. He was also an associate of Redmond O'Hanlon, with whom he had been proclaimed in October 1676. Fleming subsequently sought Plunkett's assistance to obtain a pardon, and Plunkett successfully prevailed upon Essex to obtain safe passage for him out of Ireland. But in February 1678 Fleming was ambushed by soldiers while drinking in Iniskeen, County Monaghan, and after a struggle he and a number of his followers were killed and beheaded. His head was taken to Lisburn, the bodies were put on display, and while Ormond later commented that 'a good end was put to that negotiation', Fleming passed into folklore as the subject of a famed lament.[120]

A number of papers had been found on his body. One was apparently a letter written by Plunkett outlining what he had done on Fleming's behalf. Ormond had been advised to send a copy of this to England to use in the proceedings against Plunkett. The original, which had apparently been destroyed, supposedly contained a safe conduct or protection from Ormond, who caustically noted that Plunkett's activities occurred under Essex's government. It was clearly intended to discredit the viceroy.[121] It would not be the only attempt to do so. Ormond was also warned that militantly anti-Catholic bills were to be foisted upon him, as any refusal to accept them would be inevitably embarrassing. It seemed likely that he would refuse to consider them anyway. His analysis of 1678, that persecution would merely prove provocative, remained valid. It was compounded by the fact that the execution of these bills would prove disastrous to the already creaking revenue by affecting the large number of Catholic merchants in Ireland, thus damaging trade still further.[122] But in a sign that Charles still retained considerable control over English political affairs, Ossory had been reappointed to the privy council in April, and he now advised his father to disregard rumours of his involvement 'in a design of betraying Ireland to France', for 'the visible falsity of those reports has rather done us good than harm, in shewing the animosity and grounds upon which our ruin is aimed'. Perhaps less convincing was his suggestion that Ormond's good service to the king in the prospective Irish parliament would serve to 'frustrate' any attacks upon him.[123] In this regard, as in others, little had changed: Ormond remained an important servant of the crown, but such allegations as were reported – up to and including suggestions that he was plotting with York and the French – were clearly intended to discredit him, and by extension, York, with the further possibility that somehow they would serve to undermine Irish support for the king.[124]

VI

If a leading Whig such as Shaftesbury was willing to promote allegations about an Irish Plot, there were cogent reasons for doing so. In order to exclude York from the succession on the grounds that he was Catholic, it was necessary to emphasize that a Catholic monarch would have dangerous implications for the Protestants of the three kingdoms. An obvious means of doing this was to reiterate stock images of Catholic animosity and brutality towards Protestants. In English eyes, immediately relevant examples of such activity were to be found in the perceived and actual atrocities committed against Protestant settlers in Ireland during the 1641 rebellion.

There was a straightforward logic in promoting such claims. 1641 occupied a special place in the Protestant imaginations of both islands.[125] If the Popish Plot and Exclusion Crisis rested upon the assumption that a Catholic attack on Protestants in the Stuart kingdoms was imminent, then the perception of the rebellion as wholesale massacre made it an obvious example of what this might entail. The promotion of the 'Irish Plot' rested upon the intertwined assumptions that an Irish rebellion akin to that of 1641 was on the verge of recurring once more and of being transposed to England: a belief that would be shared in both islands. This was inevitably linked to the possibility of the Catholic York succeeding his brother Charles as king. The implication was clear: who better to preside over a Catholic massacre than a Catholic king? As manipulated in the service of the exclusion campaign, specific concerns about the Catholic Irish were distilled from existing perceptions, newly bolstered by information that was harnessed to a very specific political purpose: it was intended to help effect a transformation in the nature of the state by barring Catholics from ruling it. While England lacked examples of what Catholics might potentially do should they be given the chance, Ireland could provide them. For Shaftesbury and his associates, this meant raising the spectre of an Irish Plot that was to culminate in a rebellion along the lines of that of 1641, as they subsequently sought to do.

However, the specific allegations were open to question. Previous indictments against Tyrone for high treason, arising from the same allegations now being made against him, had been declared ignoramus at a sitting of the Waterford assizes.[126] The fact that these had already been thrown out by an Irish jury would naturally cast doubt on their veracity, especially when the county grand jury was also reported to have dismissed them.[127] So on at least two counts, the credibility of allegations about an ongoing Irish Plot was damaged. The plausibility of any further allegations could easily be questioned. 'At my first coming here', noted Conway, 'I heard great noise of a plot in Ireland...but since that time it has all grown cold.'[128] Ormond's own scepticism received a boost after the unsuccessful errand to find evidence in Munster. But the proliferation of similar allegations would take time to investigate, which meant the transmission of parliamentary bills from London to Dublin was now unlikely to occur before the end of May.

Despite Fitzgerald's failure to produce his evidence in Munster, yet another unnamed informer, supposedly from Dublin, had returned to Ireland and 'is gone in search of witnesses' with an escort in tow. Ormond expected their return 'by the end of this week and then they shall not stay here long'. While aware of his perennially precarious position, Ormond noted one circumstance that inadvertently suited him: the fact that Orrery was dead, which, he sarcastically observed, was 'a great misfortune to the discoverers of plots in this kingdom'.[129]

On the other hand, belief in the Irish plot was not dead either.[130] Ormond was willing to gather information to send to England, and while he continued to dismiss suggestions that he resign his post, he remained pessimistic about his chances of retaining it.[131] Murphy and Hetherington had by now left London and returned to Ireland, as had Boark and John MacNamara. Their activities in Ireland remain obscure, but Ormond was disgruntled at being sidelined when it came to dealing with both Fitzgerald and Hetherington, and the implicit suspicion this entailed (Essex was blamed for this, amongst others).[132] Ormond had been unable to understand Murphy while interviewing him, and instructed that his testimony be written down. But from what he could understand, Ormond had noticed that he did not mention any plot resembling what was written down for him, or even what Hetherington had originally claimed. Murphy had mentioned nothing of the kind until he was faced with the prospect of being returned to Dundalk, so 'it might reasonably be suspected that Murphy's pretence to the discovery of a plot was to avoid his being returned to the jail of Dundalk'.[133] Ormond's suspicions were compounded by his subsequent observation that Murphy's allegations were derived from those of another rogue friar, John MacMoyer, a Franciscan from Armagh and associate of Murphy (he had been curate of the same parish) who had made similar allegations against Plunkett in the past.[134] MacMoyer claimed to have seen a letter from Plunkett to the Vatican in 1673, claiming that 60,000 men were ready in Ireland but lacked weapons, and requesting assistance on this point.[135] The informers were casting their nets increasingly widely.

Charles instructed that these new allegations be investigated more fully: the examinations were to continue. In the meantime the informers were to be kept away from strangers, and publication of their allegations was to be delayed until a full report had been given to the king.[136] By now large numbers of Irish witnesses were arriving in London, as were personal testimonies from Ireland to be presented to the Privy Council, (many of the informer's accents were incomprehensible to English ears).[137] Despite attempts at secrecy, the allegations against Plunkett were reported in the Whig press, as was the fact that Hetherington had provided Shaftesbury with Murphy's allegations.[138] Yet, as Haley has written, 'so far as English politics were concerned the effect of the depositions was only to keep alive the general feeling that Catholics were dangerous and desperate plotters'.[139] The Irish were not the only Papists.

Such witnesses as were now in London posed questions of a different nature. Ossory, writing to his father, observed that Essex had become 'so diligent in discovering Irish Plots', and it seemed reasonable to wonder why he had not noticed them when he had been viceroy.[140] However, despite his prominent involvement in the initial investigation of the new disclosures, Essex rapidly lost faith in the credibility of these claims about an Irish Plot; one consequence of this was that it permitted Ormond to regain an input into the investigation of the allegations.[141] By now he was willing to focus upon the Catholic threat, and their alleged intention 'to design and struggle for the restitution of their religion in the kings dominions' (though this did not automatically imply belief in a plot at this particular time). Ormond soon received word that some of the informers were to be sent back to Ireland to testify against Plunkett. By this stage both John O'Moloney, the Catholic bishop of Killaloe, and Peter Creagh, the Catholic bishop of Cork and Cloyne, had also been implicated. They had come to official attention before, and were now to be arrested for complicity in the plot. It was reported that David Fitzgerald was travelling to Ireland to testify against them, as 'Popish recusants' were to be barred from the juries.[142] On the other hand, the English Privy Council were unimpressed by John Fitzgerald, and with what seemed to be outright falsehoods in what he had claimed. The abbey wall that had been central to his testimony proved a particular point of contention, and 'the king jestingly says it was my Lord of Essex's and his plot'.[143] The eventual account published by (or on behalf of) John Fitzgerald contained little to inspire confidence in his allegations.[144] Once again, proof seemed absent. In the meantime, Henry Ingoldsby (a former Cromwellian officer and a member of the Irish council deemed 'zealous' by Shaftesbury[145]) was to be dismissed from the council, 'by reason of his factious carriage in England, and traducing of the government here'.[146] The precise details remain obscure, but such a dispute may have been influenced by older enmities from the 1640s. Orrery was not the only figure to traduce Ormond and his government. There seemed to be no shortage of others.

VII

Ormond was unimpressed with the erstwhile witnesses who had arrived in Ireland to assist in Plunkett's prosecution. He was also uncertain as to how he should deal with them. They were to be kept under close guard, so as not to be 'tampered with' or given an opportunity to abscond; explicit within this was the possibility that they might yet fabricate a story, and implicitly, that they were not to be trusted. Subsequent events suggested why. If left at liberty, he suggested, they might be inclined to change their evidence against Plunkett 'who is reasonably well allied and friended in these parts'. He was especially wary of Edmund Murphy, 'who broke prison and is charged with a capital crime', but was sceptical of the Irish informers as a whole: 'nor have the rest the reputation of men of such tender consciences but that, without doing too much injury, it may be suspected they may hearken to an advantageous proposition from any hand'.[147] The links between the various witnesses remain obscure, but the differences that emerged between them are not. John MacMoyer wrote to Hetherington to express his mounting dissatisfaction with him. Despite promises to MacMoyer and his associates, Hetherington was instead 'the greatest enemy [for] our persons that ever was hitherto in nature'. Whilst professing his loyalty to king and country, MacMoyer was concerned that he and a number of others would themselves be prosecuted after Plunkett's trial. He pleaded with Hetherington to obtain a general pardon for them, for if they were to be tried, by MacMoyer's own admission there would be no shortage of witnesses against them. He stated that Hans Hamilton had aided and protected him, and had passed his testimony on to Essex.[148] But the opinion of the Catholic hierarchy, who kept themselves informed of the unfolding developments for fear that they would be the prelude to further persecution, was that this plot in which they were supposedly involved did not actually exist.[149]

It was obvious that the informers had influential and powerful friends. One was Henry Jones, to whom Murphy had been recommended by 'that honourable lord and worthy patriot the earl of Shaftesbury'. Jones recommended Murphy (whom he deemed to be in particular danger) to Colonel Roderick Mansell, an associate of Essex who had served in the army in Ulster, and who had since become aligned with the Whigs. Jones suggested that Murphy's tale should be told to the King to ensure that he would receive a pardon, 'though let not my name be used'; Essex and Shaftesbury were to be prevailed upon if further assistance was required.[150] Mansell obliged; Hetherington was scheduled to appear before the Privy Council on 16 June, as movement on their pardons was expected.[151] Jones kept himself informed of events, informing Mansell about them in turn, and providing him with a copy of a letter MacMoyer had written to Hetherington, suggesting that Dundalk was too dangerous and intimidating a venue for the witnesses against Plunkett and that his trial should be moved to Dublin instead.[152] The witnesses were apparently granted protection for the duration of Plunkett's trial, but there was no assurance of pardons thereafter, 'which I think was not intended but is so here confirmed, so as there may be in danger after to some of them...I reserve my writing to [my] lord the Earl of Shaftesbury until I may have something more for his lordship'.[153] The connections were obvious. By this time Jones had also been involved in the interrogation of David Fitzgerald, and may have been involved in the investigation of the accusations against Tyrone.[154]

However, Ossory also kept himself informed of events, and described Jones as 'not only a spiteful but a false informer' who was scheming with Mansell and Robert Ware, the son of the antiquary Sir James Ware, who was related to Jones by marriage and who had previously been responsible for publishing anti-Catholic propaganda. Boyle and Ormond suspected him of feeding allegations about a plot to unspecified figures in London. Ossory contradicted Jones' assertion that 'Murphy was prosecuted after he had accused [Henry] Baker and [Ensign] Smith', two of the soldiers who had arrested him; the opposite was true, and Jones apparently knew it.[155] The credibility of witnesses such as Murphy was to be maintained in the face of mounting evidence to the contrary.

In July Oliver Plunkett's trial finally took place in Dundalk; or more properly, there was an attempt to try him. MacMoyer had opposed the venue, but efforts to have it moved elsewhere had failed, and Plunkett was indicted on 23 July. There were 32 witnesses available to refute allegations that he had raised an army of 70,000 Catholics to massacre Protestants and had planned to assist a French invasion (the same allegations for which he would later be convicted in London). The prosecution was not so lucky. Edmund Murphy, who had previously escaped from Dundalk jail and was afraid to testify against Plunkett there lest he be hanged himself, fled to England. MacMoyer simply failed to turn up. Presumably, the protections they sought from Jones were deemed insufficient. The trial collapsed, and Plunkett was returned to Dublin. The original choice of venue had been a 'great discouragement' to the informers, given Plunkett's 'great acquaintance and interest in that part of the country', so the Privy Council finally agreed to move his eventual retrial to Dublin from Dundalk.[156] However, it would not take place there either.

VIII

Bills for a proposed Irish parliament were finally en route to England for consideration, and Ormond still wanted to call a parliament. But he had anticipated opposition to the legislation on two grounds: that of finance, given that the issue of Ranelagh's accounts had inevitably re-emerged; and factional hostility disguised as 'zeal against Popery'.[157] But

> Whoseover understands the dangerous state of the kingdom, believes there was and is still a Popish Plot, or [really] fears a French invasion or a Popish rebellion or both, cannot be of opinion that it is fit to delay or frustrate the only means of preventing or repulsing those evils.[158]

Peremptory demands based on this reality were of relevance to Whigs such as Shaftesbury, but for markedly different reasons. He had reportedly exclaimed, 'does Ireland, the snake...think to give law to England? To give money to make the king independent of his people, to raise an army if they be so powerful! It's time for England to look about them, to make it a province'.[159] It was significant in these circumstances that the Privy Council were still deliberating on the draft bills for the Irish parliament. New problems had arisen on this front, as the revenue farmers who had succeeded Ranelagh were reportedly threatening to quit should these bills be accepted as they stood. They argued that Ireland was in no position to support more taxes, and had reportedly issued a dark warning that if the current revenue farm was dissolved, 'though they all be hanged at Tyburn some great men shall pay for it, and dearly too'. The possibility of an Irish parliament being convened in the near future was now very real, but if so, the Irish farmers were prepared to state their opinion of the condition of Ireland before the English parliament, along with their reasons for opposing the legislation. Despite this, Ormond could soon report that Ranelagh, despite his best efforts 'has brought his accounts to a balance, which I am told will weigh heavy on him and his partners'.[160]

Ultimately, such concerns about finance were prompted by concerns about security, which in turn were bound to prompt further consideration of whether Ireland was in any position to defend itself. Such concerns could easily be manipulated by an Irish administration that had long bemoaned its inability to do so adequately. In July 1680 Arthur Forbes, earl of Granard, arrived in London to discuss two reports on the state of Ireland that he had provided to the king, and to offer his advice on them.[161]

Granard was a senior and experienced soldier. A presbyterian royalist of Scottish extraction, he was also a close ally of Ormond, and was well regarded and respected for his experience and knowledge of Irish affairs. His extensive experience as a senior officer made him an obvious choice for such an errand as this. The case that he put forward on behalf of the Irish government was straightforward and unsurprising: Ireland was in no condition to withstand an invasion by anyone. Irish defences were in a bad condition: fortifications in particular were decayed, and munitions remained inadequate. The army itself was dilapidated and thereby weakened, and the payment of forces in Tangiers by the Irish exchequer was another drain of money that could be put to more immediate military uses. In early July Charles had sought to add to this debt, ordering that 500 foot soldiers and 120 horse troops were to be sent from Ireland to the garrison at Tangiers.[162] It was perhaps significant in the light of Granard's statement that this deployment was subsequently cancelled, and the troops were ordered back to their former postings in Ireland. This may have been little more than a stopgap, but could also be a sign of positive things to come.[163] The need to guarantee Ireland's security had underpinned the continual demands for a parliament from the mid-1670s, but private interests (such as Ranelagh's undertaking), tardiness, and the Popish Plot had all intervened to prevent it. There was some optimism about the prospects for a parliament sitting in the near future, even if it was accepted that there would be major opposition to it in England.[164] However, on 30 July Ormond was dealt a major blow, politically and personally, when Ossory died in London after a short illness. A universally popular figure perceived by many as solidly Protestant, he had just been nominated for the position of governor of Tangiers (a post that he himself suspected was intended to get him out of the way). Despite public outpourings of sympathy and Ormond's evident grief, the looming spectre of the Irish Plot continued to overshadow other considerations, including the calling of an Irish parliament. It was ironic that continual delays in considering legislation that was ultimately intended to secure Ireland's defences was being delayed by fears of Ireland's vulnerability.

Ormond was given advance notice of an intelligence report on Ireland drawn up for the king, and based upon the memorandums previously submitted by Granard. The substance of it was not new: that the dispossessed Irish might yet join any prospective invasion force. The Irish army and defences in general were indeed in an appalling condition, but this would not be alleviated in the immediate future due to the ongoing wrangling over the parliament. Therefore, more stopgap measures were proposed. The existing army could be moved around the country (to provide a semblance of readiness), while 1000 additional foot soldiers were to be recruited in England. It was also suggested that key state salaries and pensions be stopped or suspended to free up funds.[165] Perhaps in an attempt to capitalize on what seemed to be a positive response to his original suggestions, Granard reported to the English Privy Council again on 18 August 1680. Acting for Ormond, he provided another detailed report that was substantively similar to its predecessors, and with disturbingly specific details: only 2000 men were fit for service in Ireland, and the only mounted guns in the kingdom were at the new fort at Kinsale. At least £100,000 would be required to bring the military establishment to an adequate state of readiness.[166] But Granard's report seems to have prompted imminent (if not immediate) movement on the parliamentary bills.[167] They were deemed acceptable: none, bar one on ecclesiastical livings, was laid aside, though all were questioned. The finance bill for raising a subsidy of £200,000 was the major sticking point in this instance, mainly due to the objections of Sir James Shaen, the Irish surveyor-general who had become the leading figure amongst the revenue farmers who succeeded Ranelagh in 1675. Having previously been suspected of corruption, both Ranelagh and Ormond had sought to remove him from his position, but this now seemed to have been strengthened; Shaen was well connected at court, and perhaps more significantly, had ensured that payment of the farm rents had not been disrupted. He had argued that raising revenue via a parliament was impossible, and he instead proposed an optimistic (if obscure) alternative.[168] But Ormond's personal prestige, combined with his official role, lent considerable weight to his case that the legislation for the parliament should now be proceeded with.[169] Regardless of the differing views about an Irish parliament in itself, there was consensus on the necessity to overhaul the military establishment in Ireland, and the tide of political opinion seemed to be turning in favour of a parliament in the wake of Granard's report.[170] In such circumstances, Ormond could restate his commitment to holding a parliament and his reasons for doing so.[171] It was expected that it would be called soon.[172] The Committee for Irish Affairs ordered that estimates be drawn up as to what the anticipated revenues were to be spent on, and that Ireland's potential for collecting further revenue be assessed.[173] Charles, along with Coventry, Jenkins and Sir William Temple, a senior diplomat and the son of Sir John Temple, was inclined to take Ormond's side against Shaen, despite the latter's apparent efficiency. In turn, Essex and Laurence Hyde, the first commissioner of the treasury, supported Shaen. The Irish parliamentary bills were recommended for scrutiny once again.[174]

Ormond remained unimpressed by Shaen's activities, but was also inclined to remain wary of him.[175] Admittedly, Shaen may have had other motivations than zeal for the king's service: he had been aligned with Orrery by marriage, and formerly with Ranelagh through the undertaking, though they had since fallen out. He had also been an agent for Irish lands at the restoration, and the bill to confirm Irish estates would certainly put a stop to such lucrative activities: indeed, this was one of its objectives.[176] The eventual acceptance of Shaen's proposal, the precise details of which remain obscure but which seemed to obviate the necessity to obtain funds from any Irish parliament, ensured that it would not be called. This was deeply suggestive of how little real power Ormond possessed in his station at this point: the fact that the details of Shaen's proposals were withheld even from him only confirmed this.[177]

This came amidst new claims of an imminent Catholic plot 'to be executed this month by massacre upon the Protestants',[178] which may also have dovetailed with other rumours claiming that York was now supposedly intent on going to Ireland.[179] Ormond remained sceptical of Shaen, and of his contention that Ireland was too poor to pay what was being demanded. Ormond claimed that Ireland was, at this juncture, more prosperous than at any time since the reign of Henry II; this was proven by an increase in trade, and in the value of Irish lands. After all, Ormond was (as he pointed out himself) in a good position to know this. Here was an implicit assertion that Ireland, despite its apparent vulnerability, remained stable. But as for the Irish parliament, in his view it was now no longer possible for it to sit before the English parliament sat.[180] English opposition to the proposed legislation had become far too strong to permit this within such a timeframe.[181] Indeed, no Scottish parliament would be called during this period either: Charles had enough difficulties with one parliament in England, let alone one in each capital city in the three kingdoms.

Such difficulties eroded the viceroy's morale. Ormond was disillusioned by his station as much as the continual intrigues against him, and claimed that he remained in his post through loyalty alone.[182] Others, such as Boyle, noted the detrimental effect on the authority of the government of such continual objections to legislation.[183] Ormond continued his tirades against Shaen, given that his arguments gave the perfect excuse to those who would oppose any Irish parliament. He found himself bemoaning the 'ill condition the kingdom is in when it is threatened with Popish Plots and a French invasion', but ironically, advertising this fact was not prudent, for it could prompt speculation about the Irish government's perceived laxity.[184] Equally, reports from Dublin suggested that few prominent Catholics remained there, having gone to either England or France in the previous 20 days.[185] But it was unlikely that Ormond and his colleagues would receive any credit for that.

XI

The preoccupation of the English government with institutional affairs in Ireland was an interlude, as it soon gave way to renewed concerns about the lurking possibility of an Irish Catholic conspiracy; it was even reported in England that families in the north of Ireland were now flocking to Virginia for fear of the Papists.[186] Ormond was to be accused once again of complicity in a plot, as Shaftesbury wanted him ejected from the Irish government and discredited; rumours emerged in early October about the appointment of 'a new lieutenant of Ireland'.[187] It was also reported amongst the Anglican episcopate that papal emissaries were abroad, armed with commissions permitting the conversion of the English and the Irish.[188]

Yet there was no more definite evidence than reports of this kind, which were of a piece with the allegations made by the Irish informers. Even before those had been presented to the lords, there were suggestions in Ireland that their claims may have been manipulated. Obscure allegations about a plot strongly resembling that described by David Fitzgerald had been made in Limerick by two equally obscure figures, David Nash and Donough Lyne. The resemblance was itself suspicious: John Odell, the justice of the peace who had taken their testimony, had noted that Fitzgerald's allegations 'but magnified' those of Nash, and Odell had been alarmed by suggestions that he had manipulated these witnesses.[189] Some days later, Lyne was brought before Ormond in Kilkenny to 'subscribe' to his testimony, which, Ormond reminded him, 'flatly contradicted' what he had previously sworn. Under pressure from the viceroy, the admittedly ill and incoherent Lyne admitted that 'he knew nothing of the plot but what he had from Nash'. Nash was brought in and naturally disagreed, but eventually admitted that, while certain elements of what he had claimed were indeed true, 'whatever he had said and sworn in his information taken upon oath of a plot was totally false'. For example, he had apparently accused a number of unspecified (though seemingly prominent) individuals of meeting to discuss a plot, but now stated that 'it was a meeting only of merriment, and not to lay any plot'. Sinister constructions could be placed upon innocuous events, and very often were. When asked why he had acted in this way, he 'answered that fear of his life and promise of reward had made him first accuse them, and he had been so threatened that he was induced to say anything that might save his life'.[190] But reality could be disregarded: when Arran later told a parliamentary committee headed by Shaftesbury about this recantation, Shaftesbury's response was that 'he did not wonder at it when the chancellor and Sir John Davys took the examinations'.[191] Davys was one of the clerks of the Irish Privy Council; in time he too would be implicated in this 'Irish Plot'.

In late October Longford had advised Ormond to hasten the production of another account of his administration's conduct, 'for that will be an evident vindication of the government there in their proceedings upon the discovery of the plot, and will be a conviction of the witness's falsehood'. This may have been intended to counter more potential allegations against Ormond by Ingoldsby and Tyrone's former steward Thomas Samson, who sought to implicate Michael Boyle and Ormond in the allegations against Tyrone, with Ormond to be named as 'head of the plot in Ireland'.[192] Ormond himself was aware that 'overtures of discovery of the plot in this kingdom have of late multiplied upon us', but remained sceptical of them, for reasons that made perfect sense in this climate.

> It is most rationally to be believed that there was and is a concurrence betwixt the disaffected in both kingdoms to subvert government and religion, and I would as gladly find it out and prevent it as any man; my freehold, and that a better than the king of France or the Papists would allow me if either of them were masters, being at stake.[193]

He was quite capable of damning 'the Irish Papists...having been scandalized, persecuted and betrayed by them at home and abroad'; he was hardly likely to have become fully reconciled to them even in his old age.[194] Yet he remained quietly confident at this juncture, and was dismissive of Ingoldsby's prospective allegations: 'I know not what he can say, if nobody help his invention, that can reflect on anybody here'.[195] But the centre of gravity of the Irish allegations had by now shifted to London.

X

On 16 September at least 14 Irish witnesses, including various priests, 'Burke' (presumably Hubert Boark) and 'MacNamara' (presumably John MacNamara), arrived in London to swear to the existence of an Irish Plot. They claimed to be in fear of their lives, having supposedly been denied passports and money by Ormond, though Henry Jones, who bid them to secrecy 'lest it might turn to his prejudice', had surreptitiously provided them with money. The informers were dubious characters: horse thieves and Tories were noted amongst them.[196] Yet they were greeted in London by Titus Oates himself (and provided with shoes) and were directed to Shaftesbury. He was ill and did not actually meet them, but the significance of his apparent willingness to have done so was obvious.

It was assumed to be the case that any alleged Irish Plot would be dealt with by the imminent English parliament, but pressure to do this in London would be eased if an Irish parliament met beforehand and did so. It would be assumed to be equally (if not more) zealous on the issue, and Ormond would be temporarily secure, for he could not be summoned to England in such circumstances.[197] On 22 September he was instructed to secure Tyrone.[198]

This was probably inevitable. His accuser Boark was reportedly ingratiated with Shaftesbury (who was prepared to assist the Irish informers personally if no official aid was forthcoming), whilst Robert Fitzgerald and Henry Jones were alleged by some of the informers to have been the only members of the Irish council to offer any assistance to them.[199] 'Whigs' seemed to be in a good position to exploit the Irish Plot, whilst 'Tories' were in no position to ignore this. Titus Oates himself now claimed that large numbers of Irish priests were in London. So many were supposedly in St James Park, that 'Mr Oates thought himself in another country, but durst not walk there.'[200] Certainly, the Irish witnesses seem to have been patronized – and as later events would suggest, manipulated – by elements of the Whig opposition. Such favouring of the informers was not confined to England: in Ireland, Ormond was obliged to provide guards, money, and 'all other necessary assistance' to one James Geogheghan, a defrocked

Franciscan who intended to make further discoveries in Ireland; those he implicated were to be arrested and examined, and the testimonies forwarded to London.[201] The continued presence of 'Irish papists' in London attracted unfavourable notice, given they 'are as obnoxious in their very names here as once they were in Ireland and Paris'.[202] Anti-Irish prejudice was surely a prerequisite, if fears of an Irish Plot were to be successfully promoted: occasional reminders to this effect were inevitable. More tangibly, the Privy Council finally resolved to try Oliver Plunkett in England, and he was *en route* there by 17 October.[203] The impending English parliament had ensured that the consideration of the bills for an Irish parliament was no longer a priority in London, and a visceral fear of Catholics began to assume a primacy in public discourse.[204] This even extended back to Ireland, where 'all the discourse in this country is concerning the plot and new discoveries often made', according to Orrery's son in Cork.[205] Rumours were abroad in London of 'a great resort of Papists hither for France and Ireland', which had prompted searches and arrests.[206] Indeed, on 25 October the lords ordered the mass arrests of all Irishmen residing in London, Middlesex, Westminster, and Southwark, with their names and details to be provided to the committee investigating the plot; concerns about the presence of the Irish were evident even prior to the presentation of the Irish testimonies.[207] The alleged Irish Plot could also be conjured (and scorned) in doggerel:

> Great stores of wild Irish, both civil and wise,
> Designed to join with the pilgrims of Spain,
> Many thousands being ready all in good guise,
> Had vow'd a long pilgrimage over the main,
> To arm well this host,
> When it came on our coast,
> Black bills, forty thousand, are sent by the post,
> This army lay privately on the sea-shore,
> And no man e'er heard of them since or before.[208]

A touch of scepticism seems evident in the last two lines, but on 26 October Sir Henry Capel claimed in the English House of Commons that in Ireland, the Papists are at least five to one in number to the Protestants, and may probably derive from their cradle an inclination to massacre them again: at least the Protestants have no security, but by having the militia, arms, and the commands of towns and forts in their hands.[209]

The spectre of an Irish Plot was conjured once again as new allegations emerged about a plan to kill Shaftesbury and Titus Oates. Consequently, Edmund Murphy, David Fitzgerald, and Hetherington were empowered to bring over witnesses from Ireland as they saw fit, and the Lords reiterated their demand that Plunkett be despatched to England as soon as possible, and on hearing of his arrival in London, they ordered that he be incarcerated in Newgate.[210] Likewise, after the evidence against Tyrone was examined and the lords had requested that he be brought over, it was ordered that he was to be sent to England, along with copies of the evidence against him and accounts of his original trial.[211] And from Dublin, it was now rumoured that Ormond ('the duke') was to be summoned to London 'for having not countenanced the informers'.[212]

Whether Irish matters would have come to the fore had the parliament been held the previous year is a moot point. By November it was obvious that there had been concerted efforts to foster the notion that there was indeed an Irish Plot, and that there were witnesses to prove it. Having been nurtured and patronized up to this point, the imminent opening session of the English parliament would provide these informers with the necessary forum in which to reveal what they claimed to know.

4
Irish Evidence, November 1680

Shaftesbury's promotion of obscure and dubious Irish informers eventually bore fruit in November 1680. According to Gilbert Burnet, 'some lewd Irish priests, and others of that nation, hearing that England was at that time disposed to hearken to good swearers, they thought themselves well qualified for the employment'.[1] Burnet caustically described them as 'brutal and profligate men: yet the earl of Shaftesbury cherished them much'. Allegations of an Irish Plot were given credence by their claims, and 'upon that encouragement it was reckoned that we should have witnesses come over in whole companies'.[2]

Reminders of the potential dangers of Catholic Ireland had already arisen in parliament. Speaking in the commons on 2 November, John Birch asked 'what use did the Papists make in Ireland of the favours granted them by King Charles I? Did they not make use of it to the destruction of the Protestants, by rising up in rebellion, and massacring 100,000'?[3] So when, on 4 November, the second Exclusion Bill was passed in the commons, in the lords 'the earl of Shaftesbury reported from the Committee for Examinations what their lordships thought was fit for the house to hear at the bar, concerning the conspiracy in Ireland; which his lordship divided into three parts'. These were the allegations directed at, respectively, Plunkett, Brittas, and Tyrone.[4] It soon became apparent that these elements resembled the fragments of something larger and more dangerous. The allegations are outlined below.

I

The first testimony was that of the priest Edmund Murphy.[5] He had apparently returned to Ireland in 1673 after a sojourn in Spain, and claimed that Plunkett had offered him the post of chanter of the diocese, and ordered Murphy to excommunicate a number of dissident priests as he continued to correspond with the continent. For a Catholic bishop in Ireland this was simply an unavoidable operating procedure, but it was depicted here as part of ongoing preparations for a rebellion. Plunkett had supposedly made inquiries about the manpower available to facilitate and assist a French invasion of Ireland, compiling substantial lists of those who could serve in this capacity.

Plunkett sought out Patrick Tyrell, the bishop of Clogher, who claimed that 'the king of England's authority was annexed to the Popes bull'; the insinuation of royal involvement was reminiscent of allegations that Charles I gave his imprimatur to the 1641 rebellion.[6] Both men told Murphy that 'there was a thing on foot, that would root out heresy out of the kingdom', or more specifically, 'the Protestant religion'.[7] According to Murphy, Plunkett had 7000 men ready to assist the French, in a manner that would somehow benefit York. Another priest, Ronan Maginn (one-time vicar apostolic of Dromore), told Murphy that 'the Primate would bring in the French to no other end but to murder all the Protestants in one week'.[8] But after hearing this Murphy resolved to help Maginn thwart the plot.[9] Plunkett was allegedly recruiting Tories and various other disaffected characters to his banner, from both Leinster and Ulster, and instructed those of them who had been dispossessed of their estates to go to France. One was apparently Patrick Fleming, 'the chiefest rebel in Ireland'.[10] By August 1678 Murphy and Maginn resolved to inform the authorities of this plot, but soon fell foul of a Lieutenant Henry Baker, who was also implicated. Maginn went to France soon after the proclamation for banishing Catholic clergy had been issued. Murphy went so far as to suggest that this had been intended to get himself and Maginn out of the way, and having sought to infiltrate this plot, the latter was allegedly poisoned in Flanders, and Murphy was eventually imprisoned. While incarcerated, he met William Hetherington, 'a person [imbued] with a most heroic and excellent disposition, and very zealous for the Protestant religion'.[11] Murphy also claimed, when asked, that Ormond and some unspecified others had sought to obstruct him. His allegations, like those of the informers who followed, rested upon his own assumed veracity rather than any corroborating evidence. At the time he spoke of, Plunkett had undoubtedly come into conflict with certain priests in his diocese. One of these was John MacMoyer, who had accused Plunkett of plotting a rebellion in 1676 in order to forestall an impending prosecution for supplying ammunition to Tories.[12] Murphy became further alienated from Plunkett for excessive drinking and Tory connections, amongst other things, and so was suspended from his duties.

After Murphy had finished, Plunkett was brought to the bar, replying when asked if he knew Murphy that he did 'know him too well'.[13] He admitted to corresponding with Fleming but denied any involvement in any plot. Murphy then swore that his statement was true, and that he had been delayed and obstructed in Dublin (witnesses were also supposedly shipped to Jamaica). When he attempted to testify about the existence of the plot, he had been imprisoned in Dundalk on charges up to and including murder. He also claimed that the Irish council disregarded his claims; indeed, that Sir John Davys, one of the clerks of the council, had openly dismissed them. In all, a sinister construction could be put on events that were, on their own terms, open to a number of explanations.[14]

The second testimony to be presented on 4 November was that of Hubert Boark, who claimed that in Waterford in October 1677 he heard Tyrone say that 'parlez vous Francais will be plentifully heard here ere long'.[15] Tyrone then revealed the French plans 'to subdue both England and Ireland', and offered to get Boark his estate back if he would become involved. Boark refused, and Tyrone turned on him. One John Daniell (whom Boark had previously assaulted) was co-opted to swear against him. On the one hand, Boark had claimed that Tyrone sought to silence him by framing him for this assault, while on the other, Tyrone stated that this was the reason why Boark was imprisoned in the first place.[16] By his own account Boark was imprisoned in Waterford until March 1678: he claimed that Tyrone ensured that he was denied bail, saying that he wished to see him hang. Boark attempted to petition Ormond for redress, but mysteriously, the petition never arrived.

Boark also claimed to have been intimidated from testifying against Tyrone at the next Waterford assizes. Tyrone sought to discredit his testimony by accusing him of numerous crimes, especially horse stealing, and Boark was further discouraged by the absence of witnesses who could corroborate his story.[17] He escaped and went on the run, and Tyrone prevailed on Ormond to prevent him absconding to England. Like Murphy, Boark also implicated Sir John Davys, along with John Keating, the incumbent chief justice of the Common Pleas in Ireland, who had presided over the unsuccessful assize hearings against Tyrone.[18] However, Boark somehow survived to recount his tale in London.

On 6 November more testimonies were presented to the lords. Thomas Samson, Tyrone's chief steward who had been implicated by Boark, claimed that Tyrone actually had been found guilty of high treason by a grand jury in Waterford, but that the incriminating testimony was deemed invalid.[19] He also claimed to have told Sir John Davys to search Tyrone's house for correspondence, especially with 'Doctor Fogarty' (presumably the same Fogarty who had been mentioned in Oates's original allegations), but that this was never done. John MacNamara's subsequent statement provided further material with which to damn Tyrone. He claimed to have been sworn into the conspiracy in 1677 by William Bradley, a justice of the peace in Waterford who had a commission from the French to be a colonel of horse in the county.[20] MacNamara claimed to have seen a list of names of those in Munster who would raise the rebel forces in the event of the French invasion, in which case there was a plan to capture and hold Limerick: Brittas, David Fitzgerald, John Fitzgerald, and Pierce Lacy were all implicated. Tyrone intimated to him that there may have been a personal motive for his involvement in the plot: 'tis the providence of God, to bring some downfall on that unjust king, the duke of Ormond and his children, that wronged me in so high a nature on the account of Villiers': possibly 'Edward Villiers alias Fitzgerald' of 'Dromany' (Dromana), Waterford, who in March 1680 alleged that Tyrone, who was previously his wife's guardian, had swindled him out of his estates.[21] However, the precise details remain obscure.

MacNamara also claimed to have been involved in attempts to buy Hubert Boark's silence. He seemed to corroborate Boark's allegation that Ormond had intervened at Tyrone's behest by summoning Boark to Dublin. MacNamara claimed to have attended unusually large meetings of the clergy in Waterford in 1676, being informed that a French invasion was imminent, which would result in the restoration of the Irish to their lands. 'The duke of York gives full consent, and is of our side, with the assistance of the earl of Anglesey': after all, the latter was Tyrone's father-in-law.[22]

MacNamara was followed by Eustace Comyn. He claimed to know of large sums of money provided by the French for a rebellion that had been distributed by one Keadagh Meagher, who was appointed by Plunkett and Brennan for the purpose.[23] Some of the alleged recipients had uncomfortably close links to Ormond, such as his nephew Walter Butler, who supposedly gave refuge to Oliver Plunkett in his home. There were attempts to murder Comyn but Ormond refused to protect him, and he absconded to Ulster. He was subsequently imprisoned in Carrickfergus, Trim, Dublin, and Limerick. In the meantime, Keadagh Meagher was allegedly killed for having learnt about the plot. That he was supposedly murdered for discovering something that he was involved in anyway was indicative of the garbled nature of these allegations. When questioned afterwards, Comyn confirmed that Tyrone had told him that the plan was intended 'to bring in the French'.[24]

Finally, there was David Fitzgerald.[25] He told of a plan for an uprising to be orchestrated by John Moloney, the Catholic bishop of Killaloe. This had been planned since the aftermath of the Act of Settlement of 1662. Evidently, the restoration of the Irish to their estates was an objective (a suggestion that echoed Tyrone's supposed promise to Boark). In the early 1670s 'MacNamara, Lacy, [and] O'Neale' had all come from France to Ireland, ostensibly to raise recruits for the French army. However, Fitzgerald was told that their real purpose was to enable the Irish 'to assert their liberty, and regain their rights'.[26] By 1676 troops were supposedly being raised throughout Ireland, and Peter Creagh, the bishop of Cork, claimed that the Pope had released Catholics in Ireland from their obligation to the king. Once again, James Lynch and Richard Talbot were implicated. The general purpose was to ensure that York would become king by 1678, but 'a difference between the king and parliament' was essential to the success of this plan, and would, of necessity, be carefully fostered: a suggestion that would have a considerable resonance in the midst of the Exclusion Crisis.[27] November 1678 had been the time specified for the French invasion, with Kerry deemed the ideal location. It was to be assisted by risings in key locations: Limerick would be captured and Protestants would be massacred. Given that similar claims had been published in 1679, such consistency could suggest plausibility (or equally, fabrication).[28] But nothing was to happen until the French actually landed; they were to be the catalyst. Fitzgerald also implicated his former landlord Sir Thomas Southwell, who he claimed was obstructing the discovery of the plot. And on that note, the first presentations of the Irish witnesses came to an end.

II

Collectively, these convoluted claims seemed to point to a bigger picture. The recurrent cross-referencing, the implications and innuendo, the reiterating of salient points that were either similar or the same; they strongly suggested that there was a plot, and that these informers were aware of at least some elements of it. Given that the Irish informers testified to the lords in an environment of visceral anti-Catholicism, their claims were bound to be of some relevance to an English audience. England itself lacked an appropriate model for what Catholic rebellion or invasion might actually entail, but Ireland could provide one.

The Popish Plot and Exclusion Crisis witnessed a huge upsurge in print production that mirrored that of the crisis of the early 1640s. A more specific parallel is the fact that, as in the 1640s, some of this printed material between 1678 and 1681 concerned itself with Ireland and the Irish, and usually with the inherent danger of the latter. The Popish Plot was significant in that the proliferation of printed material saw the formulation, in both style and substance, of the broad genre of the 'narrative' as 'an extended account of a series of events given by an actor or intimate witness'.[29] The various Popish Plot narratives 'represent a brilliant attempt to hijack what was at the time accepted as a news medium in order to make it a vehicle of malicious untruth'.[30] They gave a formal imprimatur to what had previously been no more than scattered rumours.

The miscellaneous jumble of Irish allegations found their way into print quite rapidly. Some of these pamphlets were official publications. Sympathetic individuals probably funded others, whether as verbatim accounts of the testimonies presented to parliament, or as more substantial versions of them (some of the printed versions expanded greatly upon the sworn depositions). Irrespective of their details, the Irish narratives remained consistent within certain limits, and at a more general level a pattern could be discerned from their broad similarities. The salient elements of this were quite straightforward: that there was a long-standing plot for an Irish rebellion, to be bolstered by a French invasion being orchestrated by the Catholic gentry and clergy. Its ultimate purpose was the destruction of Protestantism; the inducement was the restoration of the Irish to the lands lost in the 1650s and 1660s. The informers had come into contact with it, had seen enough to realize what was involved, and were compelled to attempt to thwart it. The narratives derived their authority from their presumed status as first-hand accounts. They were quite restrained, yet were detailed and intricate, if contradictory and complicated, and were often driven by the narrative of the author's own travails. Many of the informers claimed to have been threatened and persecuted, a situation exacerbated by the fact that, for some, the alleged plot seemed to penetrate to the highest levels of the Irish government, as evinced by the numerous innuendos made about Ormond's role in the 'plot'.

Consistency amongst the Irish informers was perhaps understandable, given what seemed to be the orchestrated nature of their patronage in London. Yet the similarities may also derive from the fact that the testimonies reflected long-standing perceptions, and readily fitted into the mesh of uncertain beliefs and expectations about the Irish at this time. To make sense of these Irish narratives, it is worth glancing forward in time to the points when the testimonies were actually printed, in order to assess the allegations as a whole. Derived from oral testimony, these would be compelling accounts to read or hear aloud. Yet the narrative accounts did not necessarily spell out the implications of the plot's success. Regardless of the ultimate purpose, the immediate and most fearful consequences remained unclear in many. However, one was quite blunt: 'the Popish Irish were in an expecting readiness to give the blow, and act over their butcheries of 41, but with greater barbarity'.[31]

The fear that Irish Catholics would seek to wipe out the Protestant settlers whom they vastly outnumbered did not just draw credence from the notion that Catholics were duty bound to wipe out heretics. It also drew strength from the tangible reality that the Catholic Irish might attempt to get back the lands they had so recently lost. This was the context into which the informer's claims would fit. It is worth looking at them in their totality.

III

Edmund Murphy had been the parish priest of Killeavy in Armagh, and his career was chequered: in 1674 Plunkett suspended him from his duties for drunken behaviour, and questionable dealings with Tories. Murphy's eventual allegations had been the basis for Shaftesbury's promotion of the Irish Plot, but when Murphy was examined in London in May 1680 he claimed to be unaware of any plot then in progress. He was sent back to Ireland to be maintained by the government in Dublin: since at least May 1679 Ormond's administration had been maintaining informers on the Irish revenue.[32] Murphy was later recommended to Henry Jones, who sought a pardon for him, and he subsequently accompanied Hetherington to Ulster to obtain more evidence. However, when Plunkett's first (unsuccessful) trial opened in Dundalk in July 1680, Murphy, apparently fearing arrest or retribution, refused to testify and absconded to England, where in December 1680 the lords voted to allow the publication of his testimony, which he assented to in January 1681 as *The Present State and Condition of Ireland*.[33] This was not the account presented to the lords, but was the information originally taken before the sub-committee of which Essex and Shaftesbury had been members. It was a detailed and intricate account of his activities in County Armagh in the 1670s, in circumstances that remained largely incidental to claims about an impending Irish rebellion.

Armagh had been heavily settled under the Ulster Plantation; by 1641 native Irish landowners retained only 24per cent of land in the county. The remainder was divided between the Church of Ireland, Trinity College Dublin, and a variety of Old English families and newer British settlers. The remnant retained in Irish hands was mainly in the baronies of Orier and the Fews in south Armagh. Yet while the native landowning classes had been supplanted, they remained *in situ*, and by the second half of the seventeenth century Armagh was problematic for the authorities. Economically stagnant with a low population, often impassable topography, and a fragmented society, it retained an uneasy balance between natives and newcomers, and was subject to neither's law. Such a situation would inevitably breed and facilitate lawlessness; it bred and facilitated Tories.[34]

Tories were an inevitable by-product of the disruptive events of the seventeenth century in Ireland, and were notably prevalent in Armagh.[35] Murphy's pamphlet was primarily concerned with Tory activity in Armagh and Louth and the collusion of English military personnel in those activities. It focused on the notorious Armagh Tory Redmond O'Hanlon and dealt with Plunkett indirectly. As Murphy's own testimony it was inevitably shaped by self-interest (he did not incriminate himself), but his printed testimony connected the exalted realms of alleged international plotting with the reality of life on the ground in the Armagh of the late 1670s. Murphy's was the worm's eye view. And he began with Redmond O'Hanlon.[36]

Originally from Poyntzpass, O'Hanlon came to prominence as a dangerous and elusive Tory leader in Armagh and Louth in the 1670s. Murphy claimed to be concerned that his parish was suffering from the depredations of O'Hanlon and his gang, and so he had preached against them. In response, O'Hanlon threatened to levy fines of (respectively) one cow, two cows and death upon anyone who attended Murphy's sermons. Murphy himself fled the parish after O'Hanlon murdered one of his parishioners. It was at this point that Cormucke Raver O'Murphy emerged. A thief and former herdsman to Lieutenant Henry Baker, he had joined O'Hanlon's gang and was active in September 1678 when Murphy had sought out Baker to deal with O'Hanlon. The latter proved reluctant to do this, and the reason soon became clear when Murphy's brother encountered Baker and Cormucke Raver drinking together and wrestling in a quarry. Members of the army were in league with the Tories they were supposed to be hunting. Cormucke Raver eventually split from O'Hanlon, and a feud ensued. Consequently, when a Captain William Butler sought Murphy's assistance in dealing with O'Hanlon, both settled upon the initially reluctant Cormucke Raver as the instrument. An elaborate scheme to ambush O'Hanlon was devised, but this was hampered in suspicious circumstances and Murphy was accused of becoming a Tory hunter, and being in danger he absconded to Dundalk. Further escapades ensued, until Cormucke Raver was shot by one of his own associates. Murphy continued his campaign against O'Hanlon, attempting to recruit Cormucke's disgruntled family to his cause, but he was eventually arrested for his troubles after being accused by another soldier, Ensign John Smith, of seeking to murder him (Smith was himself accused by Murphy of colluding with O'Hanlon). Eventually released from prison, Murphy became involved once again in the rapidly escalating intrigues intended to capture O'Hanlon and his band. By October 1679 he was imprisoned again, supposedly in a trumped up charge. He narrowly escaped execution to learn that he had been excommunicated by Plunkett, who intended 'to carry on the plot by means of the Tories', for 'the destruction of all the Protestants'.[37] This was Plunkett's first appearance in an account that was meant to specifically target him. As for Murphy, he was imprisoned, but managed to tell Hetherington what he knew. And from that point his account substantively petered out.

Murphy provided a deeply partisan view of Tory activity and its backdrop by one intimately involved in it. Oliver Plunkett had taken a great interest in the activities of Tories in Ulster after his appointment as Archbishop of Armagh. His background did not endear him to Armagh's clerics ('Meathmen without exception are not suitable as preachers of the word of God'),[38] but the travails of the dispossessed in his diocese who had become Tories caught both his attention and his sympathy. Acutely aware of their situation, their depredations among the peasantry, and of the retaliation against the Irish that would inevitably follow their actions, he made himself available as an intermediary between the Dublin government (particularly under Berkeley) to deal with Tories (such as Fleming) in exchange for a measure of *de facto* religious toleration. He subsequently enabled a number of Tories to leave Ireland, and continued to do so; they remained a preoccupation.[39] Indeed, just before the plot revelations came to light in London he had been concerned with the decrees of the recent Catholic synod at Ardpatrick. The first had been an instruction for Catholic priests to preach against Tories and their supporters, though this was never implemented due to the onset of the Popish Plot.[40]

Tory activity could also be depicted as an integral part of any attempt to orchestrate a rebellion: the term was synonymous with dispossession and the Catholic Irish, and allegations about supposed Irish Plots often directly linked them to Tories. Murphy almost certainly saw an opportunity to save himself as the nascent Whig opposition in England sought Irish witnesses. What he excluded from his account was equally suggestive: his own criminal past, and the awkward local rumour that he himself had killed Cormucke Raver O'Murphy.[41] Amongst those whom he implicated were Baker and Smith, the soldiers who imprisoned him in 1679, which suggests an element of revenge that may also have extended to Plunkett, though he would eventually decline to repeat his allegations at Plunkett's trial the following year.

IV

The various allegations made by Hubert Boark, John MacNamara and Eustace Comyn were linked by the fact that they were all directed at Tyrone. Both he and William Bradley had been indicted for high treason at the Waterford assizes on 11 March 1680, and Brittas, Pierce Lacy, and various other figures from both Waterford and Limerick had been implicated in this 'conspiracy' at this time.[42] Despite the prominence later accorded to these allegations in London, they were initially dismissed in Ireland.

These three remain the most obscure of the informers who testified before parliament. Boark claimed to be from Thomond, and to have been brought up a Catholic before embarking on a career as an attorney.[43] MacNamara claimed to be a Protestant from 'Cracolo' who married into a Catholic family in Waterford, and had been 'often employed in many public concerns'.[44] But Comyn was the first to come to official attention. In September 1678 he claimed that John Brennan, the Catholic archbishop of Cashel, knew of a plan for a French invasion of England and Ireland, and that he had offered to tell Ormond of a 'a Popish Plot for the destruction of the King and kingdom', and in September 1678 was kept in comparative comfort in Trim to facilitate his further disclosures. However, he did not universally impress those he came into contact with, and he made no mention of Tyrone at this stage.[45]

Tyrone's accusers had gone to England after the collapse of the original case against him. They had immunity from prosecution, to which Boark and MacNamara were both vulnerable.[46] Both were among the contingent of Irish witnesses who arrived in London in September 1680 to be greeted by Titus Oates, all of whom were reportedly hostile to Ormond and Lord Chancellor Boyle.[47] Just prior to the submission of their evidence to the lords in November, Boark and Thomas Samson were reportedly present at a meeting in Burlington's house in London that both Essex and Shaftesbury attended: a suggestive indication of the close links between these Irish witnesses and the Whig opposition.[48]

Their testimony was printed without substantive amendment, though expanded versions were also produced.[49] The published version of Boark's testimony was dedicated to the king, and contained the same allegations as had been presented to parliament, but with additional, telling details. It almost immediately deployed a swipe at English manhood that would hardly endear the Irish to prospective English readers.

> The English were good soldiers in their tongues over a cup of ale, with long pipes of tobacco in their mouths; but that they were too tender now to lie in the fields after thirty years rest, and that they were so foggy, so fat, and full of guts, that they were not able to fight any better than a company of swine.[50]

Otherwise it simply provided a broadly similar, if more detailed, version of what he had already sworn. Equally, MacNamara's published testimony (dedicated to Shaftesbury) largely reiterated his previous statements, but certain details were added: Plunkett, Brennan, and Anglesey were explicitly implicated.[51] This dovetailed with Boark's supposed tribulations whilst attempting to swear against Tyrone.[52] MacNamara also claimed that Tyrone offered sanctuary to Patrick Lavallyan 'who was to murder the King'.[53] In a nod to the British context of the crisis, details were included of 'a poor and needy Scotch-man coming in and pretending a sham-plot of the Presbyterians, and denying the Popish Plot' who was 'immediately kindly entertained and cherished, and well rewarded for his pains', though he vanished after implicating York.[54] This latter detail was almost certainly contrived: it corresponded too conveniently to the objectives of the Whigs. As well as reiterating that the Shannon estuary was to be the location for a French landing, MacNamara also claimed that the Irish army being surreptitiously raised to assist them would be equipped by massive shipments of French weapons to be landed in Waterford.[55]

A related contribution came in the form of a pamphlet credited to Thomas Samson (who had also testified before the lords) that reproduced the testimonies of Boark and MacNamara.[56] Rather suggestively, it was dedicated to Essex, and explicitly sought to vindicate the witnesses' claims, perhaps in the light of a burgeoning scepticism.[57] The introduction asserted the international nature of the Catholic plot, whilst invoking the spectre of 1641.[58] Samson claimed to be from Dorset, and had settled in Munster after his wife's death. He made his allegations out of 'the fear of God...love to the Protestant religion...my duty and allegiance to his majesty', not to mention 'self-preservation'.[59] Instead of the testimony he had sworn before the lords, Samson printed those he claimed to have provided to Ormond and the Irish council (along with that of one Edward Ivie), one of which gave an account of the trial of Tyrone and a number of others in March 1680.[60] He claimed that Tyrone was acquitted by a jury packed with Catholics, and 'kindred, tenants and friends of the earls prepared for the purpose'.[61] While replete with further detail, these added little to what had already been alleged, but cumulatively they seemed to expose other, equally sinister facets of the alleged Irish Plot.

V

The third element of the allegations provided by Shaftesbury arose from the claims of David Fitzgerald. Supposedly a Protestant, he had been a tenant on the estates of Sir Thomas Southwell of Castle Mattress, County Limerick, a substantial landowner and cousin of Sir Robert Southwell.[62] By September 1679 Fitzgerald had been questioned. Ormond viewed Fitzgerald as the most significant and reliable of the Irish informers emerging at this time, so his interrogation became an imperative.[63] Interviewed by Henry Jones, Fitzgerald expanded upon his allegations but provided no concrete evidence of interrelated plots in England and Ireland.[64] The specific nature of his claims at this time remain obscure, but the broad outline was consistent with what he later swore before the English parliament: that there were plans for a Catholic rebellion in Ireland to procure the restoration of the Catholic Irish to their lands, to be carried out in conjunction with a French invasion and a massacre of Protestant settlers.

Fitzgerald recounted his allegations to the Privy Council in London, thus prompting new indictments against those he accused, but his testimony was deemed insufficient without further corroborating evidence.[65] Doubts had already been cast upon him in Limerick, though this had no effect on the presentation of his evidence to the lords.[66] Yet much of his testimony was second-hand. Fitzgerald had not actually witnessed crucial events he mentioned that supposedly offered conclusive proof of the plot.[67] But the broadly similar nature of the accounts of the other Irish informers suggested some degree of corroboration. For example, John MacNamara implicated many of the same figures as Fitzgerald while also implicating Fitzgerald himself.[68] In the light of later events, this could be seen as evidence that the witnesses had simply been coached, but by implicating Fitzgerald in the plot MacNamara would have enhanced his credibility by suggesting that he possessed inside knowledge. Of the various informers, Fitzgerald seemingly made the greatest impression on the lords, and an expanded and embellished version of his testimony was published as *A Narrative of the Irish Popish Plot*.[69]

The two versions of Fitzgerald's allegations are worth examining as a whole. The pamphlet began with a straightforward assumption that the Catholic Irish

> suffer themselves to be led blindfold into fatal rebellions, by the pernicious counsels of their priests, [but] the world may easily believe (by their proceedings in the last rebellion) that their designs are always on foot, and tending to no less than the utter subversion of the English government in Ireland, and establishing the power in the hands of their own natives and religion.[70]

The Catholic Church was the principal actor here, and the involvement of the clergy in the ostensible plot 'to promote a rebellion in Ireland' was repeated and reiterated.[71]

Fitzgerald freely admitted that he had no direct knowledge of this. Despite this, he was quite certain that 'the conspiracy was very formidable, and had it gone on till full ripe, would have had very dire effects'.[72] He thereby set the stage before proceeding onto what he actually claimed to know, beginning with the arrival in Ireland from France of Irish officers who intended to recruit for the French service, one of whom told Fitzgerald that 'if the Dutch were once subdued, he did not question but that the French would establish the Roman Catholic religion in all the northern parts of Europe; and...that we should have the same laws established in Ireland that are in France'.[73] Fitzgerald was told by Pierce Lacy of the importance of Irish soldiers in France to such designs, and that one purpose of such a conspiracy would be the overturning of the land settlement.[74]

Fitzgerald became involved. The officers moved between Ireland and France in subsequent years, arranging meetings under the pretext of enlisting recruits, and the Catholic hierarchy continued to facilitate it. Again, Moloney, Creagh, and Lynch were all implicated as prime movers in this plot to 'be rid of that yoke of heresy which they had so long suffered under'.[75] 'The King of England had no right to Ireland, but what he had from the Pope; and that the King being an heretic, the same right returned to the Pope again' (the reference was to the twelfth century Papal Bull *Laudabiliter*). One of the plotters 'did say, that he did trust in God the natives of Ireland would not be long subjects to heretical government'; the clear implication was that Catholic government would replace it, whether under York, the French, or both.[76]

The rebellion would begin in Munster. A French landing was to take place near Tarbert on the River Shannon in November 1678, and Limerick was to be captured. The plotters had ingratiated themselves with the Limerick garrison (allegedly killing three officers in the process by excessive drinking). What that rebellion might ultimately involve was unsurprising. Irish Protestants had remained on their guard in recent years, 'having forty-one fresh in their memories'.[77] And as for how the plotters would successfully carry out the plan, 'they had no other way than to rise all in a night, and to proceed in a general massacre throughout the said kingdom, and to kill man, woman and child, and not to leave a Protestant living in the kingdom of Ireland'.[78]

However, much of Fitzgerald's account told of his troubles after learning of the plot, rather than the details of the plot itself. It was particularly concerned with the alleged attempts of his former landlord Sir Thomas Southwell to prevent him from revealing what he knew.[79] Fitzgerald rebutted suggestions that Southwell had any personal dispute with him, claiming that the dispute was meant to intimidate him into silence.[80] His account observed that the generally miserable fates of informers 'are not certainly prevailing motives to encourage any one to undertake the employment purely out of love to it'; consequently, Fitzgerald's motives might seem the purer.[81]

By way of conclusion, the final third of the pamphlet consisted of 'a seasonable address to his country-men, the natives of Ireland',[82] in which Fitzgerald (or another author) sought to dissuade them from rebellion, and to spare them 'the blood and confusions, the horrors, and desolations necessarily attending such insurrections and desperate rebellions'.[83] Reference was made to 'the blood of two hundred thousand peaceable Protestants and loyal subjects by you most barbarously butchered in the rebellion begun, 23 October 1641': a hugely exaggerated but often accepted number.[84]

There were reasons why the Irish should not embark on such a course of action (up to and including the risk of incurring the wrath of God).[85] The planned rebellion was predicated on French assistance, but could the French be trusted to provide it? The claim that the rebellion would wait until the French actually landed conveniently rendered scepticism on the ground of inactivity redundant. Would Louis XIV actually countenance a rebellion in the territory of a King who 'is the greatest and best (I had almost said) the only friend he hath in Europe'?[86] Such an insinuation about the contentious pro-Catholic leanings of Charles II was evident and telling, and may explain the assertion that loyalty was due to Charles by the Irish not only by natural right, but because of his supposed magnanimity to the Irish since his restoration.[87] Even if Louis did get involved, he would be obliged to face an English army, and an appeal to English exploits and 'gallantry' at 'Poiters, Agincourt or Cressey' offers a reminder who the audience for this pamphlet would have been.[88] In the second section the author flew a notable kite when suggesting that it was up to prospective readers to determine 'how this and a French design, and the Plot discovered against his Majesties life here in England doth agree'.[89] The third section of the pamphlet was of a very different nature and tone to the preceding segments, as Ireland in itself became peripheral. The emphasis was on the (Catholic) French, which offers the key to its meaning.[90] This view of Ireland was directed at an English audience, and like the testimonies of the other witnesses, it was harnessed to a primarily English political purpose: the barring of a Catholic from succeeding to the thrones of the three kingdoms.

5
The Decline of the Irish Plot and the Road to the 'Tory Revenge', November 1680–July 1681

At least some of the witnesses made a positive impression on the Lords. On 8 November they ordered the arrest of unspecified 'Irish ruffians' (presumably the would-be assassins of the king), and requested that Charles order some of the individuals named in the testimonies to be brought from Ireland. Irish business was to be the second item on the agenda (after the 'bill against Popery') when the house reconvened on the following Monday, and the lords requested a conference 'in the painted chamber, concerning some informations relating to the discovery of a horrid popish plot in Ireland'.[1]

On the same day Plunkett petitioned the lords for access to his servant, James McKenna (who had also implicated him), and to be incarcerated at the crowns expense: he had used up his own money while imprisoned in Dundalk, and the Catholic laity were unwilling or unable to provide money in such a repressive climate.[2] The petition naturally prompted consideration of his case, as Bourke, Hetherington, Murphy, MacNamara, and David Fitzgerald had all implicated him. On 10 November the governor of Newgate claimed that Plunkett 'believes there is some kind of plot against the English in Ireland', and that while he denied having any dealings with France, he had admitted to a correspondence with Spain. This may not have been especially sinister in itself: Catholic jurisdiction over Ireland was exercised via Brussels, which remained under Spanish control. But Plunkett's correspondence with the continent had already been painted in a sinister light by the informers.

Plunkett was summoned before the lords, where he denied and denounced the allegations against him. He claimed to be aware of

115

unspecified threats against his person by (or on behalf of) Tories: 'that his life was being aimed at, he mistrusted that there was a plot against the English'.[3] However, more allegations were provided to the lords, including one 'about bringing over a French army to Ireland to settle the Catholic religion': once again, Plunkett was alleged to be involved. The lords resolved to pardon the informer, James Crew, and to arrest the priests cited in his evidence.[4] In his testimony Hetherington had disparaged the Irish administration, and especially Ormond, whom he claimed to be 'the centre of all the conspirators'. While Murphy apparently gave a similarly critical account, David Fitzgerald gave a good account of both Ormond and his government.[5] There was certainly a degree of credence, and perhaps even gratitude, shown to the informers by parliament.[6] They made a definite impression on George Vernon, MP for Derby Town, who implored the house on 11 November to consider the exclusion bill.[7] The bill passed the commons on the same day.

I

The 'Irish Plot' came to prominence at a particular juncture. 'Exclusion', as it had emerged, became for a relatively brief period the most obvious means of tackling the vexing question of a Catholic succession.[8] The broader significance of the Exclusion Crisis arises from the fact that the dispute over the succession prompted the emergence of distinct (if inchoate) political blocs in the English parliament, with supporters of exclusion eventually labelled 'Whig' (a term for Scottish Presbyterian bandits, used to highlight their perceived subversive tendencies), while the supporters of the court and an unaltered succession were labelled 'Tory' (the term for an Irish Catholic bandit, deployed as a term of abuse at the ostensibly pro-Catholic court: it stuck).[9] These were by no means parties in a modern sense, but the English parliament of autumn 1680 witnessed the polarizing of existing attitudes towards the succession. The term 'Exclusion Crisis' is arguably 'best reserved for the brief period between the rejection of the bill in the House of Lords in November 1680 and the dissolution of the Oxford parliament in March 1681'.[10] This was also the period in which the promotion of the 'Irish Plot' was at its most prominent, for it was inextricably linked to the ongoing exclusion proceedings in parliament. To cultivate a fear of Irish

Catholics was intended to bolster the Whig campaign to prevent a Catholic accession to the throne. Since the acquittal of Sir George Wakeman in July 1679 (whom Oates had accused of plotting to poison the king) and the various executions of June–August 1679, the Popish Plot seems to have lost much of its momentum.[11] The absence of an English parliament throughout most of 1680 had also been undoubtedly problematic for the Whigs. Events such as the Meal Tub Plot of June 1680 and even the trial of Stafford in December 1680 (accused of plotting to kill the king and raising a Catholic army) can thus be seen as attempts to maintain the momentum of the Popish Plot.[12]

The same can be said about the allegations of an Irish Plot. The role of the informers was inextricably linked to the ongoing exclusion proceedings centred on parliament: it became their stage, and their testimony prompted action. Their allegations were not intended to influence opinion within parliament alone; hence their publication. The exclusion campaign had a marked popular dimension as the Whigs expanded their activities beyond parliament and into the public arena.[13] This was intended in part to compensate for the reality that parliament could be (and would be) prorogued at the king's discretion, thus robbing them of a crucial political stage.[14] Pamphlets with an Irish theme were one element of a Whig propaganda campaign that sought to keep the public aware of the dangers of Catholicism, and by implication, of a Catholic king.

Parliament's refusal to renew censorship of printing against the backdrop of the Exclusion Crisis (the licensing act lapsed on 10 June 1679) had opened the door to a proliferation of printed material. Pamphlet production in Britain doubled to *circa* 3000 titles per annum in the period 1678–1681, many of which were markedly anti-Catholic.[15] However, with one exception, most of the testimonies of the Irish witnesses were not published in Ireland.[16] The impact of the Popish Plot fractured the Irish government's previously rigorous control over printing, and numerous reprints of English tracts arising from the Popish Plot were published in Dublin.[17] There was an obvious market for such works, which would have helped to guarantee a strong awareness of the currents of the crisis in Britain. But the fact that the testimonies of most of the Irish informers were only published in London is indicative of the reality that they were, first and foremost, interventions in an English political debate.

Their publication was an engagement with the emergent 'public sphere' of early modern England.[18] Public discourse was multifaceted, incorporating and combining print, oral traditions, preconceptions, lived experience, memory, and social background, even if the printed word is the only element to have survived.[19] Tim Harris has rightly argued against a 'top-down, centre-out' approach that assumes popular politics to have been exclusively manipulated from above.[20] Such interventions in public debate overlapped with existing perceptions; in this case, the visceral mesh of beliefs and expectations about the Irish that were reflected in the testimony of the informers. The potential political utility of the Irish Plot depended upon memories and preconceptions that would, in theory, strike a chord with those who were now made aware of it. The prominence accorded to this in November 1680 stemmed from the spectre it presented to English minds of a re-run of the events of 1641 and their consequences, in a manner that would directly impinge upon them.

In a period of intense anti-Catholicism, further assertions of Catholic perfidy from an Irish angle may have seemed redundant. After all, English anti-popery could draw upon the memory of key events such as the defeat of the Spanish Armada in 1588 or the discovery of the Gunpowder Plot in 1605 to illustrate the persistent danger with which England was faced. Equally, there were more tangible contemporary fears of resurgent Catholic power on the march in Europe, most especially in the form of France. In 1681, in a treatise attributed to William Petty, Catholicism formed an obvious bond between France, Ireland, and the Papacy, and within this were certain key assumptions: that there had been an attempt to wipe out Protestants in 1641; that Plunkett and the Talbot's had been involved in a plot for a French invasion along the lines of what had been alleged; that the French would be welcomed by the Irish as their saviours from the oppression of the English; and finally that another massacre of Protestants remained a distinct possibility.[21] Reports to that effect continued to emerge. For example, the informer James Carroll, a leather worker and freeman of Dublin, claimed to have spoken to a local in Portumna, in County Galway, in April 1672 who intended to 'kill an hundred of the Protestants, Anabaptists, Independents and such like fanatic rogues'[22] He had previously claimed to have been the first discoverer of this plot, and that he had been persecuted by the Catholic William Burke, earl of Clanricarde, in order to discourage his testimony 'about the said horrid plot, which was for murdering of all the Protestants in a months time, they being twelve for one, and introducing Popery into that kingdom'. Carroll had been forced to leave Ireland, and was in dire need: Catholics had apparently already murdered his pregnant wife. Carroll's pamphlet was dedicated to Essex, and stated its intentions quite bluntly: 'the Popish Irish were in an expecting readiness to give the blow, and act over their butcheries of '41, but with greater barbarity'. Both Essex and Shaftesbury later attested to the truth of his claims.[23] And one 'inducement of his discovery, was the bloody massacre that broke forth there in the year 1641, which will never be forgotten by the Protestants, nor ever be repented of by the Papists'.[24]

The events of 1641 were inevitably (and extensively) regurgitated in print. The massacre paradigm had been evident in pamphlets printed immediately after the outbreak of the rebellion, and throughout the 1640s. The perception of the rebellion as a massacre of Protestants was nothing new, and was easily revived. Alongside such grisly depictions of its events were the printed accounts such as those of the Irish witnesses that claimed to reveal the machinations of a plot that would culminate in a rerun of 1641. The structure of the two categories dovetailed neatly. One suggested history repeating itself; the other provided the history. For the unconvinced, a pamphlet such as *An Account of the Bloody Massacre in Ireland* could end with a useful exhortation: 'see more of such cruelties in Clarke's Martyrology'.[25] Following this advice, the curious could find a virtually identical account of 1641 cast within a master narrative of the sufferings inflicted upon the professors of the true – reformed – faith.[26] The Popish Plot slotted into a chronological pattern of Catholic persecution culminating in Ireland on 23 October 1641 with the outbreak of a rebellion intended 'not to leave a drop of English blood in Ireland, and so consequently not the least spark or glimpse of gospel and pure Protestant religion'.[27] Similar examples of Protestant suffering in other times, and other place, could also be deployed. 'We may call Popery a bloody religion, if at least we may afford the name of religion to a thing made up of idolatry, usurpation, and cruelty.'[28] But for the most horrendous examples of such cruelty

We need not look any further back than the present age: in the rebellion of Ireland wherein there were more than three hundred thousand innocent Protestants destroyed, and this in a base treacherous manner, without any provocation[;] no age, sex, or quality being privileged from massacres and lingering deaths, by being robbed, stripped naked, and so exposed to perish by cold and famine, or else suddenly hanged, their throats cut, drowned in rivers, bogs and ditches, or else murdered with exquisite torture: wives ravished before their husbands faces, children forced to hang up their own parents, others compelled against their consciences to own the Romish superstitions, and swear thereunto in hopes to save their lives, and presently murthered, as if they designed to destroy souls as well as bodies: and such beastly cruelties acted as the most barbarous heathens would blush to practise. All which being acted within these 40 years, I hope is not yet, nor ever will be forgot.[29]

This author explicitly sought to remind an audience that this was precisely what Protestants could expect at the hands of the Papists, and did so because such things were supposedly at hand again.[30]

Memories of 1641 were bolstered by the records of the Protestant experiences of the rebellion that entered public discourse in the works of figures such as Jones and Temple.[31] The Popish Plot also saw the publication in London of another substantial account of 1641: Edmund Borlase's *History of the Execrable Irish Rebellion*.[32] He was the son of Sir John Borlase, one of the lord justices in Ireland at the time of the rebellion. Like his father's contemporaries Jones (who had assisted Borlase: one of his letters provided a glowing preface to his book) and Temple, Borlase devoted much space to publishing a selection of lurid witness depositions, supplementing them with whatever material he could find: he had even received a copy of the allegations made against Ormond, Arran, and Boyle in February 1679.[33] His history was apparently in print by August 1679, though its commercial sale was delayed.[34] One correspondent expressed his hope that it would be published while the English parliament was in session; a pregnant suggestion implying that it might be instructive to the members of either house.[35] The text was being circulated by September 1679, when John Tillotson, the dean of Canterbury, wrote to Borlase acknowledging the receipt of a book 'which I am now reading with great pleasure and satisfaction', and congratulated him on his 'compiling a work so seasonable at this present time, and so useful to posterity'.[36] In 1679 it was recommended from the pulpit of St Patrick's Cathedral in Dublin in front of a presumably uncomfortable Ormond during the annual 23 October sermon commemorating the rebellion.[37] But, the book was poorly received and unsuccessful.[38] Despite this, there were preparations for a second edition. The text had originally been submitted to Roger Lestrange in his capacity as licenser of the press, and he requested certain alterations 'to clear the king of the outrages in Ireland'; Lestrange claimed that he had been told some years previously not to licence any works on Irish history without the approval of Ormond, and other senior figures.[39] It seems that Borlase intended to reinsert material that Lestrange had cut, such as the alleged commission from Charles I to the Irish rebels in 1641, further assertions of the inherent cruelty of the Irish prior to the rebellion, and allegations that Charles had been willing to 'aid himself out of Ireland against the parliament'.[40] Such additions would have heightened the relevance of Borlase's work to an English audience by once again conjuring up fears of the Catholic Irish and the Stuarts supposed affinity with them.

Other works attempted to do this as well. In 1679 a collection of abstracts of the 1641 depositions (clearly inspired by Temple's work, which was republished twice in the same year) was published in London, the preface of which reassured readers that their accuracy had been checked against the originals by no less a figure than Essex when he had been viceroy.[41] They were published 'not out of any great hopes of converting Papists...but to dispose all professors of the Protestant religion to a just sense of what would have been the fruit of this instant hellish plot, had it succeeded'.[42] Generalized fears of Catholics were combined with more specific fears of an aggressive and expansionist France under Louis XIV, and potentially, by England's possible future under York.[43] For example, in David Fitzgerald's printed account, Protestantism in northern Europe seemed to be coming under pressure from a Catholic superpower, and that pressure might yet be extended to Britain. This was reminiscent of prevailing English fears of 'universal monarchy': of an overwhelming monarchical power with military, economic and territorial supremacy.[44] The Dutch had occupied this role in the 1660s, but by the later 1670s the French had taken their place. Anti-Popery in

England was bolstered by events on the continent, in the form of the sufferings of Protestants in Piedmont, Portugal, Poland, and above all, France.[45] Britain was a Protestant island hemmed in by Catholic France to its south and east and Catholic Ireland to its west: hence the 'mentality of encirclement' noted by Jonathan Scott.[46] From the late sixteenth century onwards, Ireland had become a potentially valuable asset to England's Catholic opponents on the continent. Indeed, one of the officers whom Fitzgerald alleged to be involved in the plot was supposedly the son of the Confederate general Owen Roe O'Neill: another name with which to conjure memories of the 1640s.[47] For one Whig polemicist, 'a Tory is a monster with an English face, a French heart, and an Irish conscience'.[48] That conscience had been testified to in 1641. The Protestant cause in England was potentially in danger and could be further weakened, perhaps irreparably, by the accession of a Catholic monarch. An obvious tactic to prevent this and secure an exclusively Protestant succession was to attempt to whip up fears of Catholicism to crisis point.

The Irish threat perceived during the Popish Plot derived strength and credence from a potential recurrence of 1641. There would eventually be a pamphlet debate about the veracity of the Irish witnesses, but this did not question the underlying assumptions upon which they had based their case. Those assumptions had not dissipated. The 1641 rebellion was the single most notorious episode of violence in a remarkably violent era across the three Stuart kingdoms. The memory of both the rebellion and the supposedly murderous intentions of the Catholic Irish, as hinted at in the claims of the informers, tapped into older and deeper fears: in England, of Catholicism from without; in Ireland, from within. These fears were highlighted by the allegations about the Irish Plot, and the sense that its investigation had taken on a greater urgency was evident when, on 15 November, an English proclamation was reissued in Dublin offering pardons for all disclosures of a plot made within the next two months.[49] But the promotion of the Irish Plot in London faltered on the same day, when the House of Lords rejected the exclusion bill.

II

Arran and Longford furnished Ormond with detailed and precise accounts of the proceedings of the Irish witnesses before the lords (at least up to 6 November).[50] The nature of the allegations against

Ormond had changed. Instead of being accused of masterminding or directing the plot in Ireland, he was accused by some of the informers of obstructing their testimonies and harassing them.[51] It was hardly as serious a charge, but it was perhaps inevitable as there was no evidence to justify the more dangerous allegation. Ormond gave notice that he intended to send Tyrone to London as soon as possible, along with a full account of the Irish government's proceedings with regard to the plot, perhaps along the lines of Longford's previous suggestion.[52] But the extradition of Tyrone was noted as a 'dangerous precedent'.[53] Charges against him had been thrown out in Ireland, yet he was to be tried again on the same charges in an English court, which naturally called into question the authority of the Irish government. This is essentially what would later happen to Plunkett. In early November the Irish informers repeated their allegations at the bar of the commons, who resolved to demand pardons for Boark, Comyn, Samson and MacNamara, and Murphy.[54] Charles acceded to this demand on 13 November, the same day in which bills restricting the Irish cattle trade were passed in the lords.[55]

Around this time, Charles ordered Ormond to overhaul the army in Ireland by replacing unsatisfactory officers, strengthening its discipline, and recruiting additional troops.[56] Other concerns about Irish soldiers abroad were evident when, on 27 November, an extensive address was sent from the commons to the king warning him of the myriad dangers of popery. In particular, it questioning the continued maintenance of the garrison at Tangiers, given its numerous 'Popish' governors, 'and the Irish Papists among the soldiers of that garrison have been the persons most countenanced and encouraged' (though the garrison got its supply anyway). In the two years since Oates made his original allegations, the dangerous intentions of Catholics were assumed not to have changed substantially. They supposedly remained intent on fulfilling their long-held design of introducing Popery and eradicating Protestantism, or as it was put to Charles

> To destroy your Protestant subjects in England; to execute a second massacre in Ireland; and so, with ease, to arrive at the suppression of our religion, and the subversion of the government.[57]

Implicit within the mention of a planned 'second massacre' in Ireland was the memory of what was perceived to be the first: 1641.

This had also been implied by the testimonies of the informers. Despite the defeat of the exclusion bill, on 19 November the commons committee investigating the Popish Plot had its powers extended to cover Ireland, and their interest in the Irish informers ensured that their material welfare was referred to the treasury.[58] The Irish Plot may also have been on the mind of the Whig polemicist Henry Care, whose response to the defeat of the bill was to remind Protestant readers on 19 November of the peril they faced, that their wives would be 'prostituted to the lust of every savage bog-trotter', whilst they themselves would be disembowelled, 'or else murdered with some other exquisite tortures and holy candles made of your grease (which was done within our memory in Ireland)'.[59]

Such fears seemed ironic in the light of Peter Talbot's death on 18 November.[60] Nothing had ever been proven against Talbot, and no material evidence had ever emerged against him. In a supreme irony, he was ministered to on his deathbed by his old rival Plunkett, who by now was also imprisoned in the castle and with whom Talbot had been reconciled. Officially, his death did not dissuade the Irish government from dutifully obeying its orders, and from continuing to assist the ongoing investigations in England (though equally, they had little choice).[61] Ormond's instructions were evident in proclamations issued on 29 November, threatening to punish unauthorized absences and excessive leave in the army by dismissal, and ordering Catholics with licences to hold arms to surrender both their weapons and licences; Protestants were not to hold weapons on behalf of Catholic friends or neighbours.[62] This continual prudence could easily be seen as proof that there was indeed something to fear, or at least that it was believed to be the case.

Rumours continued to thrive in such a favourable climate. It was claimed by one John Jephson – who may or may not have been the same person implicated in the plot to assassinate Ormond in December 1678 – that while travelling in France in 1676, he had overheard French officers speaking of unsuccessful attempts to land weapons and ammunition in Galway, 'about the time we expected the landing of the French and Dutch at Kinsale'.[63] At this time Hetherington was seeking more witnesses to prove something similar: he suggested that a pardon could be obtained for Patrick Tyrell if he confessed to an involvement in the plot, but 'Doctor Plunkett will surely be hanged.'[64] In early December Hetherington offered the commons the tantalizing possibility of further evidence to support the existence of an Irish Plot, claiming to know of 25 other Irish witnesses, but 'did not think it convenient that the names or circumstances of them should be known'. The commons ordered that Hetherington be granted £100 for their upkeep, and provided an additional £70 to maintain the more prominent and potentially useful witnesses: David Fitzgerald, Samson, MacNamara, Boark, and John Fitzgerald.[65]

Not surprisingly, Shaftesbury was kept well informed about events (or alleged events) in Ireland. He was told by an anonymous correspondent that Patrick Lavallyan had absconded to Cork; despite there being support for his arrest on the Irish council, the warrant was delayed, and 'the opportunity was lost, which gave great discouragement to all honest men here'. When Lavallyan's letters from France were intercepted at Youghal, they were never transmitted to England: the messenger from whom they were taken had supposedly spent time in an Irish college in France and was related to Ormond. Such insinuations could only reflect poorly upon the viceroy. Other allegations were made to Shaftesbury about the state of Protestant security in Ireland: that more troops would be required in Galway, due to both the alleged readmission of Catholics to the city and the dangerously Catholic composition of Connacht (given 'the Popish interest of the Lord Clanricard'), and that considerable quantities of weapons were still hidden in Ireland, as too much notice had been given for the disarming of Catholics, proof of which was ostensibly provided by reports that armed Catholics in Queen's County were harassing Protestants and evicting them from their homes. This correspondent dwelt on the necessity for the raising of a militia, for strengthening Protestant morale and security in Ireland. And at least some unnamed figures allegedly favoured Ormond's replacement by no less a figure than Shaftesbury.[66]

Malicious rumours against the viceroy were, yet again, giving way to more concrete allegations against him. He was accused of permitting assemblies of Catholic clergy in Dublin, of disarming Protestants with undue haste (in one day), and of permitting Catholics to retain weapons. He was accused of deliberately delaying the arrest of the late Peter Talbot, of not seizing either his or Richard Talbot's papers, and of leaving the latter at liberty (where he was supposedly favoured by Arran and Ossory); of raising a Catholic regiment; and of having being made lord lieutenant in order to facilitate the calling of a parliament, thence to raise an army to be directed at England 'to set up arbitrary government'.[67] These were reminiscent of previous accusations made against him, and as such may have been indicative of a renewed attack on the monarchy. Two weeks previously Arran had expressed the suspicion to his father that his letters were being intercepted; such allegations may have been orchestrated.[68] There were ongoing rumours that an attempt to impeach Ormond was imminent. Information had been collected to use against him, and to procure his dismissal from his post, which, according to Longford, 'is not thought secure, but in a confiding hand or with a thorough English Protestant (which is now the phrase in mode)'.[69] Presumably Ormond was seen to be neither of these things.

If this was the case, than attempts to discredit him had arisen from political purposes rather than malice: his long affinity with the Stuarts seemed to rebound to his detriment. There were continuing rumours of unrest in Ireland: Arran had heard of 'great apprehensions and new discoveries from Munster'.[70] Ormond laid this at the door of Orrery's sister, carrying on her brother's work through correspondents who were 'as zealous as he was, but not so inventive'.[71] Equally, in Connacht, the Anglican archbishop of Tuam, John Vesey, requested that Ormond send a company of soldiers to the town, due to a possible repeat of the hardships of 'the late rebellion'.[72] Such latent fears could also be kept alive by the ongoing activities of Tories, which had been a crucial element in the testimonies of informers such as Murphy. Henry Jones had become involved in efforts to procure a pardon for Murphy's adversary Redmond O'Hanlon, in exchange for his assistance in bringing other Tories to heel, after which the pardon was to be extended to his associates. O'Hanlon himself had apparently instigated the negotiations, and terms had been agreed by the beginning of November.[73] At this time the Armagh grandee Sir Hans Hamilton, an 'Old Protestant' royalist who had benefited greatly from the restoration settlement and who was involved in the search for O'Hanlon, reported to Ormond on the activities of the informer Owen Murphy, who apparently had permission from Ormond and the Irish council (prompted by an order of the English House of Lords) to apprehend and send to Dublin whoever he deemed useful 'to the discovery of the Popish Plot in Ireland'.

The mercenary nature of some of the informers was no secret, and Hamilton was wary of this, but he assisted Murphy anyway by sending suspects to Dublin as requested (though Hamilton told Ormond about this to pre-empt any complaints that might be made against him for assisting Murphy), and also provided Ormond with letters found in the possession of Redmond O'Hanlon's mother-in-law, concluding that 'if under pretence of discovering the plot such bloody murderers shall be pardoned, it will be good encouragement for others to turn Tories'.[74]

The letters in question were from Deborah Annesley (Jones' daughter) and her husband Francis. The first, dated 7 December, suggested that Ormond was prepared to support the original offer of a pardon to O'Hanlon, but 'was overruled by the council, who would not hear of him coming in'; instead, Redmond and his brother Leighlin were to be proclaimed.[75] The second letter, dated 9 December, was the more crucial of the two: O'Hanlon and his brothers would be assured of pardons if he 'will be a discoverer of the design for the French invasion here, and who in Ireland are the principal abettors'.[76] Jones was prepared to act as an intermediary to obtain them.

III

Machinations continued at a higher level of politics. In December 1680 Sir John Davys assured Ormond that any proceedings against him by his enemies in parliament would be dependent on insinuations, as the best concrete evidence that could be mustered was his alleged tardiness in issuing warrants for the arrest of Patrick Lavallyan. But 'all worthy and honest persons I meet with do speak with great honour of your Grace's person, and with great certainty of your Grace's loyalty to the King and sincerity to the Protestant religion and look upon both to be abundantly safe under your Grace's administration'.[77] On the other hand, a note of exasperation was evident when Ormond was told that he was to be accused of taking communion at the home of his sister, Lady Clancarty. He caustically recalled Oates's original allegations in 1678: he was supposed to be killed by Catholics, after all, which might strongly suggest that he was unlikely to be guilty.[78] However, such persuasive logic counted for little.

Ormond dismissed the allegations of misconduct over Lavallyan. He acknowledged the activities of Owen Murphy, who despite being authorized to find witnesses against Plunkett (presumably in Armagh), had ended up in Tipperary, and had apprehended 'about a dozen people, not like to say anything material as to Plunkett; so that I believe he takes them upon account of Eustace Comyn's mad narrative'.[79] There was a related note of desperation evident when Comyn himself asked a correspondent in Cashel for proof that he had been refused a warrant to apprehend Catholic clerics, including Brennan and Plunkett. If found, it was to be sent to Shaftesbury's address in London: a significant indication of his patronage of the witnesses.[80] But this was indicative of the paucity of actual evidence. The testimonies and indictments against Tyrone and those accused alongside him may have been ignored by grand juries in Ireland, but the allegations were easily revived in a credulous English debate, and were sent to both houses of parliament.[81] Even at Stafford's trial in November 1680 there had been hints of Irish involvement, when Stephen Dugdale claimed that the Pope 'would assist the poor distressed Irish with both men and money'.[82] At the trial, Oates claimed that in January 1678 he had seen letters from Ireland showing

> that they were as busy in Ireland as we were in England. We found that the Talbots, and other persons, were very zealous in raising of forces, and were resolved to let in the French king, provided that the parliament should urge the king to break with France.[83]

A subsequent report had provided the conspirators with 'an account how ready the Irish were to vindicate their freedom and their religion from the oppression of the English as they called it'.[84] James Lynch was implicated in a plot once again, this time by Bernard Dennis, a former Dominican who claimed that in July 1677, in Madrid, Lynch had said that Plunkett 'is resolved this year, or with the next convenience, to bring in a French power into Ireland, thereby to support the Roman Catholics in England and Ireland'.[85] This welter of Irish innuendo easily attached itself to the unfortunate Stafford, who was asked while on trial before the lords to explain 'that letter that comes from Ireland, to assure the Fathers here, that all things were in a readiness there too, as soon as the blow should be given'.[86] He would be sentenced to death on the same day, on spurious charges of attempting to have Charles II assassinated. There was no shortage of Irish allegations, and the ingredients with which to devise them seemed simple enough. If one proceeded from the assumption that Irish Catholics were intent on sending Protestants to a terrible fate, one could easily produce a credible account bolstered by whispered innuendo, sinister priests, and links to Catholic Europe. This was the framework within which the accusations against Tyrone were cast, and on 9 December (the same day on which Redmond O'Hanlon had been offered a pardon), Tyrone arrived in England to be imprisoned for treason as the lords sought more Irish witnesses.[87] The increasing attention paid to the accumulation of Irish evidence was illustrated when on the same day a motion was entered in the lords to allow Edmund Murphy to print his testimony.[88] Given that the testimony of the Irish informers had failed to influence significantly the passage of the exclusion bill in parliament, their publication may have been deliberately intended to exert an influence outside it.

However, Ireland continued to attract attention in parliament, where credence could still given to some of the informers. In the commons on 15 December Paul Foley, MP for Hereford, once again raised the spectre of a Franco-Irish plot to massacre Protestants, and according to Francis Winnington, MP for Worcester, 'by what Fitzgerald informed you at the bar, the welfare of all Ireland depends upon this session of parliament and, I believe, of England too'.[89] On 24 December Thomas Samson gave a (presumably unfavourable) account to the commons of the proceedings of Sir John Davys in Ireland 'in the prosecution of the Popish Plot there'.[90] Despite the defeat of the exclusion bill in the lords, the allegations about the Irish Plot had by no means been abandoned in the commons. Other legislative solutions to the prospect of a Catholic succession were attempted in the aftermath of its rejection, most notably in proposed bills to limit the powers of any Catholic successor, and to form an association of Protestants.[91] Proceedings on both were confined to the Lords, and, for various reasons (mainly the proroguing of parliament in January 1681), the bills were never put to a vote, but both had key clauses that amply illustrated Irelands *de facto* political subordination. The limitations bill proposed the creation of a council of 41 members to exercise control over foreign policy and the Irish government, while the association bill, drafted by Essex and possibly borrowing from a similar initiative during the reign of Elizabeth, proposed that virtually all civil and ecclesiastical office holders in Ireland and England would have to subscribe to an association of Protestants to guarantee the succession: all would have to take up arms on the king's death, for example, at least until parliament could be called. Logically, non-subscription would raise questions about the religious allegiance of those involved. Such implicit concerns about the condition of Ireland seemed to suggest that the assumed existence of an Irish Plot might have found a receptive, if limited, audience amongst the English political elite.

Further allegations of Irish plots came from Mullingar, where another informer, James Geogheghan, claimed to know of another plot to kill the king. The previous summer, in England, he had been told to expect 'a Romish King, and that this heretical king Charles II should be brought down'. There was supposedly an ongoing plan to guarantee this outcome, for 'God almighty swallowed the heretics of England, for abusing the Catholics.'[92] But there had been consistent complaints about Geogheghan's abuse of the permission he had been granted by the authorities to obtain evidence. 'It was not fit to let him go on to plunder, beat, and imprison who he pleased, English and Irish, Papist and Protestant, as his fancy, supported by strong ale and wine, should direct him.'[93] While a number of individuals whom he accused were to be arrested, Geogheghan himself was in custody, and on 20 January, after considering a request by Ormond, the Privy Council ordered that he be prosecuted for 'violences, excesses, debaucheries, and in effect plain robberies committed on Irish and English Protestants and Papists'.[94] But irrespective of the truth of such rumours, or the calibre of the informers who recounted them, the various allegations of an Irish Catholic plot tallied with certain Irish Protestant expectations. Orrery's son Roger Boyle, for example, who had succeeded to his father's title, emulated him by writing of his own belief in, and fear of, the imminent execution of an Irish Catholic plot.[95]

In January 1681 yet more rumours of such a plot were printed in London.[96] Essex subsequently presented the testimonies of Maurice Fitzgerald, Murtagh Downey and James Nash to the lords, and in turn William Bradley, Sir John Fitzgerald, and Pierce Lacy, all of whom were implicated, denied the allegations against them.[97] The presentation of these testimonies had been prompted by the initiation of proceedings against Tyrone.[98] And significantly, on 6 January the commons resolved that there was indeed an Irish Plot.[99] 'There is something in the evidence of the Irish Plot that agrees with forty-one. Then there was a great massacre in Ireland, as now intended.'[100] The next day the lords ordered that Murtagh Downey and David Fitzgerald be summoned from Ireland, came to a conclusion that would be publicly printed with the testimony of MacNamara, Fitzgerald and Nash, and demanded the concurrence of the commons in their subsequent resolution that

> There now is, and for divers years last past there hath been, a horrid and treasonable plot and conspiracy, contrived and carried on by those of the Popish religion in Ireland, for massacring the English, and subverting the Protestant religion, and the ancient established government of that kingdom.[101]

But the forum in which the informers had stated their case was stripped away by the proroguing of the English parliament on 10 January 1681.

IV

This did not, however, prevent assertions about the existence of the Irish Plot from appearing in the Whig press. 'The plot in Ireland is every day more and more discovered to be a damnable design to massacre the Protestants there, and betray that kingdom into the hands of the French.'[102] It was explicitly stated that Tyrone and other Catholic nobles (both Irish and English) were involved in the Franco-Irish plot 'to shake off, as they pretended, the English yoke, [and] make a general massacre of Protestants'.[103] Some days earlier

> a great light in the heavens, bigger than the moon, appeared directly over the city of Dublin, which in one nights time moved over several parts of the city and at length, in sight of multitudes of people, fell through the air into the sea, as they judge, and was seen no more, and that the Protestants there have dreadful apprehensions of approaching danger.[104]

Presumably this was the great comet of 1680, as seen across northern Europe. The assumption that this inevitably presaged impending danger for Protestants was automatic. A 'blazing star in the west' had been seen from Kinsale on 17 December, and was visible for a number of nights (though the official gazette declined to interpret it for good or ill).[105] It could still be asserted in the Whig press that the Irish Plot existed, and that 'the Papists have not some considerable hopes to reduce that kingdom to the see of Rome'.[106]

But the cause in which such allegations were utilized seems to have been losing momentum, and this was reflected in a manner that had a direct bearing on Irish affairs, as Ormond's difficulties began to ease at this time. Arran informed him that he probably would not have been impeached by parliament, as 'none of the sober men will allow of any article of your being either a Papist or in the plot', though it was possible that he may have been censured for a perceived lack of vigour in dealing with Catholics. Renewed preparations for an Irish parliament might once again be set in train, given the anticipated dissolution of the English one.[107] Ormond duly informed John Davys that he was probably in the clear, while being aware that new (if obscure) allegations of plots were emerging from Limerick and Galway.[108] In a manner that resembled Oates's original allegations, Presbyterians in Ulster, 'who are very numerous and greedy for land', were now rumoured to have plans for a rebellion in conjunction with some of the Irish. But while the correspondent who alleged this queried the retaining of former Cromwellians in the army, he discerned no trace of any Catholic plot.[109] This could easily be contrasted with more tangible concerns about Presbyterians in Ulster, especially in Donegal, where a 'general fast and abstinence from labour' had been declared to induce repentance for forgetting the Solemn League and Covenant, 'which cannot imply anything but the renewal thereof'.[110]

In mid-January, Charles had repeated his order to Ormond to recruit replacements for the troops that had been sent to Tangiers, but did not authorize the calling of any parliament in Ireland.[111] There were ongoing rumours that the Irish army was riddled with Catholics, as further aspersions were cast upon Sir John Davys (who, according to Arran, was 'persecuted chiefly upon your [Ormond's] account'), but Ormond downplayed these allegations, gently reminding local grandees such as Sir John Skeffington, Viscount Massareene, that they had their own responsibilities 'to govern and command', in order to 'keep the government in safety and the kingdom in peace notwithstanding suggestion and general rumours'.[112] Ormond himself was to proceed with improvements to fortifications and defences in Ireland, and to advise on what more might be required.[113] However, such control as he had over his government was being progressively weakened. In February 1681 the English treasury had decisively reasserted its control over Irish finances (a development that may have been related to the new found political strength of the court).[114] But there was no avoiding the problem of Ireland's ramshackle defences. For example, Dublin Corporation had stated that the increase in the size of the city beyond the walls since 1660

> renders it of no strength nor security to the inhabitants, and which was not only a discouragement to Protestants for settling here, but might be also an invitation to the enemies of his Majesty to invade or raise rebellion in that kingdom...the growth and strength of this city would be the security of the whole kingdom.[115]

Ormond was expected to rectify this, at a time when danger still seemed to be abroad. After all, in February a report from Bristol had made mention of 'an alarm at Youghal, as if the French had been on the coast of Ireland', though like so much else during the Popish Plot this seems to have been groundless.[116] But even the most tenuous allegations could still be deemed worthy of investigation: reports from Derry about sinister military activity, and conversations with a 'rebellious dark meaning' derived from little more than loose drunken talk overheard in a tavern, yet were still deemed worthy of being reported to the authorities, who ordered an investigation.[117] It illustrates the extent to which fears could be based on the most slender of suggestions.

Yet despite these promising signs, it appears that little had changed since Granard had delivered his report to the English Privy Council the previous summer. Men and material were still to be obtained for Ireland's defence, and were to be paid for out of the Irish government's pocket.[118] Nor had the continuing rumours in Ireland abated, that Ormond was obliged to dismiss. 'The hottest and most groundless alarms go out of Munster and I have reason to believe they are sent for out of England to fill sheets of printed papers and the peoples heads with fearful apprehensions.'[119] Forces were deployed in Munster during February 1681 due to 'frequent alarms', and arms, ammunitions, and salaries were to be provided to the militia there (this was to be extended throughout the kingdom for as long as was practicable).[120] There were continual fears in the vicinity of Dunmanway, in County Cork, about the possibility of an Irish rebellion, though the presence and strength of the militia meant that this was unlikely without some foreign assistance.[121] But equally, if it did not happen, this could be attributed to the presence of the militia, and would not automatically alleviate local fears. It was a no-win situation for the sceptical. Ormond's own scepticism was fanned by the ongoing incrimination of Oliver Plunkett; if the original grand jury had possessed the allegations now made against Plunkett, they would not have delivered a verdict of ignoramus, thus posing the obvious question of why they were not produced in the original case.[122] The obvious answer was that they had not existed.

It was at this juncture that Ormond became aware of an impending 'paper war' between Anglesey and James Touchet, earl of Castlehaven, in which he would become embroiled. Castlehaven had fought with distinction for the Confederate Catholics in the 1640s, whilst simultaneously providing a useful link between the Confederates and Ormond, to whom he was related by marriage. He published his memoirs in 1680, presumably (at least in part) with the purpose of rebutting allegations about his conduct in the 1640s made in works by writers such as Borlase. In writing his own history, Borlase had received at least some assistance from Anglesey, who in April 1680 informed the author of his happiness with the text. He observed how a potential recurrence of the 1641 rebellion remained a real concern, given the 'wolvish' nature of the Irish. 'Nothing can contribute more effectually then by the truth of history to undeceive that ignorant and unhappy people, and to let them see how they have been seduced to their ruin', even if they were 'the most barbarous though the most entirely subdued nation in Christendom'.[123]

Before this, Anglesey himself had sought to join the ranks of authors recounting the events of 1641. In July 1679 he sought material for a prospective history of Ireland (with a particular emphasis on the 1640s) that he planned to write.[124] On 22 January 1680 he 'spent all day at home in the history of Ireland which I resolve now to go on with and first to dispatch that part of it since the rebellion'.[125] He intended to fulfil this ambition by assembling materials for a history of Ireland that he embarked upon in early 1681. It was never published, and such sections as were completed were lost, but he placed a great emphasis on the 1640s: the section dealing with this was to be published before the remainder, and, in a testament to a tradition of which it was intended to be a part, the main sources from which it would draw were Jones' *Remonstrance*, and the histories of the rebellion by Temple and Borlase.[126]

Anglesey had criticized early drafts of Castlehaven's memoirs, but subsequently adopted a hostile stance to the work and its contents in public. Castlehaven certainly believed that this was to emphasize his public zeal during the Popish Plot: Anglesey had been implicated by John MacNamara, and may have feared being tainted by association with Tyrone. Borlase weighed in behind Anglesey, stoutly rebutting many of Castlehaven's assertions, and emphasizing that 'the conspiracy was so general and there had been such unheard of villainies (not in any age before) committed by the Irish ere his Majesties forces could be embodied to [assert] his power that the infection seems to have polluted the whole kingdom'.[127] He continued in the same vein, reiterating the old argument that the atrocities committed by British and settler forces in the 1640s were ultimately to be laid at the door of the Irish rebels who had made the first move.[128]

However, the dispute opened out to include Ormond. The treaties he had signed with the Confederates (such as that of 1649) were attacked for favouring Catholics. Ormond had no desire to respond in public, though he would draft a broader defence of his past conduct, on the grounds that it was inextricable from criticism of his conduct in the present. Anglesey's memoirs had surprised him more than the usual slanders to which he was accustomed. He was especially unhappy at the claims of crypto-Popery that were still being levelled at him based on his supposed conduct since the onset of the plot. 'The matter is so false and despicable, that it deserves nothing but contempt.'[129] The proroguing of the Oxford parliament obviated the necessity for drafting an account of this kind and it was never published, though the dispute flared up again in November 1681.[130] It was of a part with previous disputations over the 1640s that had recurred since the Restoration, and which rested upon the same assumptions that underpinned the belief in the existence of an Irish Plot.

V

However, it was inevitable that the lack of anything other than unsubstantiated allegations to prove the existence of an Irish Plot would prompt reflection about whether it actually existed. On 21 January 1681 the Privy Council ordered that the examinations of Irish informers be taken and forwarded to the council: the vast majority of these would play no further role in the proceedings relating to the Irish Plot, so presumably their allegations were deemed to be of little or no value.[131] The Privy Council acceded to their request for a pardon before providing any testimony, but this was to be restricted to charges of treason and misprision of treason: less significant crimes were to be excluded.[132]

The nexus of Irish informers and English politicians remained potent, and highlighted concerns that the English government could not afford to ignore, even if it had been inclined to do so. But by the beginning of January cracks had begun to emerge amongst the Irish witnesses. It was reported that Oates and David Fitzgerald were arguing over unspecified allegations made against Sir John Davys (presumably based on previous allegations that he had sought to obstruct witnesses); Fitzgerald was backing Davys, and was becoming the subject of smears himself.[133] Despite this, public assertions about the existence of an Irish Plot continued. It was reported that meetings in Cork were addressed by a sinister figure exhorting the people to rebellion: 'who this great man is, is not certainly known (perhaps another nuncio from the Pope, like that in '41, who managed that horrid massacre and rebellion)'. Rumours were abroad of French activity, and of gunpowder seized in Limerick.[134] In Dublin, it was reported that 'the Papists here are much elevated at the news of the prorogation of the parliament, insomuch that they hector about the streets with swords and other arms', thus justifying Protestant fears of their intentions.[135]

Yet by the end of January, Hetherington and David Fitzgerald, two of the key figures in the promotion of the Irish Plot, were levelling accusations against one another that would ultimately serve to discredit it.[136] Fitzgerald had by now suggested that Irish witnesses had been suborned, a claim that had already been ridiculed in the Whig press, but on 2 February he was granted a full pardon by the Privy Council.[137] A number of Irish witnesses who had previously been examined were summoned before the council. They apparently knew nothing about any Irish Plot, having been suborned by Eustace Comyn to bolster his own testimony.[138] The dispute between Fitzgerald and Hetherington was heard before the King and council on 11 February, and an account of it was published that was unashamedly hostile to Hetherington.[139] Printed anonymously in London, it exhibited a level of detail that suggested it may have had some kind of official sanction or assistance. It was obvious that some of the Irish informers (whose allegations were still unsubstantiated) had dubious pasts and had found favour with elements of the Whig opposition. As the political tide in England began to turn against the exclusionist case and its proponents, an account of a dispute between two of these ostensible witnesses may have had a certain propaganda value.

Hetherington ('the principal manager of the Irish evidence, as he styles himself'[140]) was accused of accepting and dispensing bribes to guarantee the production of false testimony, and questions were raised about his shady past and his relationship with Edmund Murphy. In turn, the charges levelled at Fitzgerald by Hetherington were also reproduced: he was accused of attempting to force witnesses to withdraw their allegations with the support of Ormond and the king, who had supposedly given him money and other inducements to 'break Shaftesbury's knot'.[141] The allegations against Fitzgerald were rebutted at considerable length, in a manner inevitably hostile to Hetherington and, implicitly, those who may have supported or assisted him. Fitzgerald was the more plausible of the two. The Privy Council ordered that Hetherington be prosecuted for tampering with witnesses and procuring allegations against Ormond, York, the queen, and Michael Boyle, and also for misleading the council.[142] Fitzgerald petitioned the council on 16 February to prosecute Hetherington and Bernard Dennis on the grounds that they were likely to abscond.[143]

Fitzgerald was not alone in his turnaround. Other informers did the same. John MacMoyer, Edmund Murphy, James Callaghan, Daniel Finan, Hugh Duffy, and George Murphy all petitioned the council for maintenance in mid-February, and on 23 February complained that they had been 'most scandalously and maliciously vilified and abused' by Hetherington, Dennis, and another obscure figure, Jerome Battye.[144] Despite what could be seen as the undermining of the Irish witnesses and their evidence (on 25 February, a further nine were discharged as unnecessary[145]), attempts to revive fears of the Irish had not necessarily abated. It was reported that Thomas Samson captured Tyrone's butler in London with bullets and a sword that could only be put to a nefarious purpose.[146] But if this kind of allegation was linked to fears of an Irish Plot along the lines of what had been suggested, it was becoming increasingly obvious that the Irish informers might not have been telling the truth. In late January it had already been suggested publicly that there was a plan 'to scandalize and subvert the Irish evidence of the Popish Plot, and to blame it instead upon Protestants', which was one of the allegations Hetherington subsequently levelled against Fitzgerald.[147] Indeed, the Middlesex grand jury had reportedly brought a bill against Fitzgerald for suborning witnesses.[148] But MacMoyer, Duffy, and Paul Gormley also accused Hetherington of attempting to induce them (and others) to swear against the Queen and York.[149] On 2 March the Privy Council heard the attorney-general's opinion that the allegations against Hetherington and the others were true, and ordered their prosecution.[150] On 11 March Fitzgerald was pardoned.[151]

However, he was not necessarily discredited. On 22 March Sir Thomas Southwell was permitted to receive a copy of Fitzgerald's testimony against him. Southwell, who was 73, denied the allegations that he (along with Brittas, Lacy, and Sir John Fitzgerald) was 'conspiring against his Majesty, and abetting a French invasion and a general massacre of all Protestants in Ireland'. Southwell was 'a true English Protestant, and the information against him arose from private revenge'; he had prosecuted Fitzgerald for non-payment of rent, and he reiterated the fact that the same charges had previously been dismissed by a grand jury in Limerick. Besides, Southwell made the fair point that as a Protestant and a substantial landowner he was unlikely to benefit from this plot.[152] Just prior to this Sir John Fitzgerald, who had been imprisoned on charges based on the allegations of Boark, MacNamara, and David Fitzgerald, had also petitioned the Privy Council for release from prison.[153] His arrest prompted a panegyric from the poet Dáibhidh Ó Bruadair (Fitzgerald was apparently his patron) stating that were Charles only to look at Fitzgerald's face, he would realize that he could do no wrong, and which damned the informers against him.[154]

Ó Bruadair may have had a point: Fitzgerald was almost certainly innocent. It was resolved that petitions for the release of Fitzgerald and Lacy were to be considered, but despite the lack of evidence against them, both they and Southwell remained in jail.[155] Belief did not require evidence: according to John Maynard in the commons, 'this damnable Popish Plot is still on foot in England, and I am sure in Ireland too'.[156]

And there was another Irish informer whom posterity did not consign to obscurity: the Catholic Edmund Fitzharris, who had written a tract with Edmund Everard (*The True Englishman Speaking Plain English*) that went beyond advocating exclusion to suggest that Charles II was just as dangerous as his brother, if not more so, and should therefore be deposed.[157] This seems to have been part of an attempt to discredit the Whigs, but it backfired: Fitzharris was betrayed by Everard, and was imprisoned on a charge of high treason: the Catholic Church was concerned that his arrest might serve to inflame feelings even further against Irish Catholics.[158] Fitzharris was alleged to have links to a plot whereby 'the king of France had a design on Ireland'.[159] As for his allegations, 'the design being of so horrid a nature in all its branches, we cannot give you the particulars'.[160] However, if such reports were intended to maintain the pressure on parliament to alter the succession, it was in vain: Charles dissolved the brief Oxford parliament on 28 March after it reintroduced an exclusion bill.

Ultimately, the careers of these informers were driven by events in England. Their significance was linked to proceedings in parliament, but after the January resolution affirming the existence of an Irish Plot their roles may have become redundant. It remains unclear to what extent Irish Protestants supported the Whig cause as it was formulated in England. There were obvious alliances and alignments (as seen by the activities of Henry Jones), but there are only glimpses of orchestrated political activity on the part of the Protestant interest. One of these, and one which reveals hints of the links between political interests in both islands, is the petition of the Clare grand jury drawn up in late February 1681, which had argued that the dissolution of the English parliament 'has encouraged the Papists in Ireland to as great insolence as the sitting of that parliament gave them terror'. It claimed that while no parliament sat, no plot could be discovered, and as Catholics supposedly felt that the proclamations against them would not be enforced, magistrates were reluctant to enforce them. Ormond was called on to press for an Irish parliament that could take the appropriate measures against this to 'secure us and our posterity from the apparent danger we are now in'.[161]

Such petitioning was a distinctive feature of English politics in 1679–1681, and the driving force behind this Irish example of it was the Catholic Daniel O'Brien, Viscount Clare, who had lost command of a regiment in 1675 after being accused of spying for the French. Some Protestants in the county opposed the petition, and Clare, in a revealing aside, informed Essex that 'it were fit some check were given to such Protestants as in these times oppose the sitting of the parliament in England, on which depends wholly our safety'.[162] Clare had also been willing to provide Shaftesbury with information on alleged Catholic activity at court in the 1670s; there was at least one tenuous link to the English opposition. Ormond disliked Clare anyway, and now seized upon him as a concrete and tangible enemy. In an ironic reversal of the accusations made against him, Ormond sneeringly castigated Clare as a 'Papist', suggesting that he had links to Spain, France, and Titus Oates, and who 'came over hither...just when the design was to be put into execution'. He also observed that his lands, near the mouth of the Shannon and close to Limerick, were a perfect spot for an invasion (as indeed some of the informers had suggested): Clare was thereby an obvious suspect, whose claims of zeal for the Protestant religion 'when the plot is discovered and frustrated' were further grounds on which to suspect him.[163]

Clare was not just concerned about Catholic designs in Ireland. In a prescient judgement that foreshadowed the events of 1688–1689, 'in my opinion it concerns the Protestant interest in England to suppress Popery without delay here, as you will have a numerous party against you, when any Popish prince falls out with the crown'.[164] But instead of achieving its stated purpose, Charles's displeasure at the activities of Clare and the grand jury in promoting such a petition, and the aspersions it implicitly cast upon him, ensured Clare's removal from the official posts he held in Ireland.[165] The petition was subsequently published in the Whig press in London.[166] But Charles's willingness to punish Clare was suggestive of the increasing confidence of the monarchy and its adherents as they weathered the storm. The waning of the crisis was also reflected in an anonymous tract that seemed to be intended as a vindication of Irish Catholic in the light of the sweeping allegations that had been made by Oates and others. The anonymous author did concede the possibility that Catholics 'have wrongfully suffered the loss of... their goods, [and] their fortunes'.[167] The tract also disputed the Protestant belief that Catholics had been absolved of their loyalty to the crown by the Pope, and were thus 'duty bound to murder Protestants, and destroy [this] nation by fire and sword, for [the] propagation of the Catholic faith'.[168] It concluded with a scathing reference to 'a sort of people who under a colourable zeal against Popery (as they term it) strike at monarchy'.[169]

The latter sentiment amply reflected Ormond's opinion of Clare. The viceroy was still concerned about the condition of the Irish army. He also remained intent on reforming it, and planned major musters of the available forces in the country. However, the fear of being posted to Tangiers seemed to be a discouragement to prospective recruits.[170] The tension between the main internal dangers in Ireland remained evident, as it had for decades. As usual, Presbyterians seemed to pose a more real danger than any Catholic plot: on 9 March the Privy Council ordered the suppression of 'unlawful meetings' in Donegal, but the possibility of Catholic subversion was also deemed worthy of attention: from Queen's County came further allegations of 'the design that is now in hand which is to subvert the Protestant religion and to advance the Roman Catholic religion'.[171] Soon after came further reports from Youghal about the discovery of correspondence, again, between Patrick Lavallyan in France ('one of the suspected ruffians who were employed to murder the king') to his family in Cork.[172] But equally, there were parallel reports suggesting that accounts such as this were illusory.

> Swearing treason against men is now grown so common that many say they dare hardly ask for their debts or distrain for their rents for fear of being sworn into the plot, and it is generally so all the kingdom over to the great disturbances of the subject, Papist and Protestant, to the filling of prisons with inconsiderable wretches and to his Majesty's considerable charge to keep the accusers and the accused from starving, for they are for the most part equally poor, and, which is hardest of all, we dare not deliver

the prisons by the trial of those accused without directions from his Majesty for fear of the scandal, which men are so apt to cast on the government and the justice of the kingdom.[173]

There were echoes in this of Sir Thomas Southwell's fears. Ormond was still scathing of the informers in the light of what seemed to be their discrediting in London. Writing to Arran from Ireland, he noted that 'Hetherington is known here to be an arch rogue, and Comyn, whilst he was here was esteemed to be something betwixt a fool and a madman'; hence, he concluded that Comyn was unlikely to have composed the narrative that he had previously dismissed as 'mad'. Hetherington was the more likely culprit.[174] But official prudence was maintained, as all judges 'in commission' were to sit on circuit for the crown during any Popish Plot trials in Ireland, and the juries were to be composed of Protestant freeholders, insofar as this was practicable.[175]

It now seemed that the Irish elements to the Popish Plot were waning, as perennial concerns came to the fore once again. 'If there follow but a tolerable calm, I suppose the condition this kingdom is in, and that it may be brought into, may be taken into consideration, for most certainly it must be of advantage or prejudice to affairs in the other two.' The final closure of Ranelagh's accounts was the next Irish business in hand, and an Irish parliament was the logical next step, though in Ormond's view the work to facilitate this had already been done: all that was required would be the decision to summon it.[176] Arran subsequently confirmed to his father that Hetherington had indeed composed Comyn's narrative, but this may well have been an incidental detail when viewed alongside the more substantive matters that finally appeared to be in train once again.[177]

VI

In political terms the tide had by now turned against the Whigs who had promoted the Irish Plot. Thus, lingering uncertainties about the Irish informers and their allegations could (and would) become more public over time. Ormond had held the informers in contempt from an early stage, and Charles was told that they were motivated by private malice, and were 'envious, malicious, viperous informers, who durst not show their face, in any place of justice'.[178] Equally, a tongue-in-cheek pamphlet (complete with brogue) ascribed to the informer Maurice Fitzgerald of Limerick sought to exonerate Pierce Lacy and Sir John Fitzgerald, whilst damning Hetherington once again for suborning evidence. It also sought the measure of those Irish witnesses who had intended to provide it.

> De parliaments did vote an Irish plot too upon my narraty, and dey did vote it upon a lye, for I never saw my narraty till I came here; but peoples makes narratyes and plots in London; and put it upon me fait.

And as for the reasons why:

> By my shoul, if you vill be giving your pardons and your moneys, you will have a tousand Kings evidences; don't you tink when cow-stealers, horse-stealers and murderers are to be hang'd, but to shave demselves from de gallows, dey will come to London and be your Kings evidence.[179]

In this light, self-interest was the basis for their claims. David Fitzgerald reportedly suggested that those Irish witnesses who chose to stand over their allegations should be hanged.[180] But informing was not automatically profitable: one 'Hurley', another Irish witness, apparently died destitute, 'for want of necessaries'.[181] Another, 'Geoghegan' (possibly James Geogheghan) was reportedly executed in Ireland as a cattle thief in the spring of 1681.[182] English official concern about the quality of these witnesses would be evident when the Privy Council sought to determine which allegations against Oliver Plunkett would be of relevance to his forthcoming trial.[183] Arran had concluded by late April 1681 that if tried in London, Plunkett 'is not like ever to see Ireland again'; there were too many witnesses against him who would be readily believed by an English jury.[184] But this would not be a matter to be dealt with in Ireland.

Plunkett was not the only loose end that remained: Redmond O'Hanlon was also unfinished business. It was later alleged that Shaftesbury intended to procure a pardon for him in exchange for his swearing against Ormond and other senior figures in Ireland. If true, this may have contributed to Ormond's resolve to deal with him for once and for all. On 4 March 1681 he had authorized William Lucas of Down 'to do his Majesty good service in the apprehending, killing, and destroying of proclaimed rebels and Tories'.[185] Lucas contacted O'Hanlon's foster brother Art, and in early April offered him a protection in exchange for his assistance.[186] Art O'Hanlon took full advantage of this and shot Redmond on 25 April 1681 near Eight Mile Bridge in County Down. O'Hanlon's body was decapitated by the time Lucas arrived, presumably by one of his followers to prevent the head being put on display.[187] But it was found and mounted on a spike above Downpatrick jail while the remainder of his body was displayed in Newry, County Down.

> For neither Redmond's limbs nor pate,
> Shall under sordid rubbish lie
> Forgot, but shall be placed on high.[188]

As with Patrick Fleming beforehand, an end had been put to the negotiation.

As for the various Irish witnesses, they did not seem to be receiving much in the way of official support: their standing had declined. There was a dispute amongst them in April over the money for their maintenance that was to have been distributed by Hetherington, which they had not yet received. A private collection, in which Shaftesbury was involved, was organized to tide them over until something more official could be arranged.[189] But continual suggestions about the falsehood of their testimony could not be disregarded. Edmund Warcup, the zealous justice of the peace for Middlesex and Westminster who was tasked with examining the various informers, assessed the information of Florence Weyer and concluded that it should be sent to Dublin so that Ormond could investigate it.[190] 'If false, the untruth of Weyer's information may detect other untruths, this being the most material information I have yet met in relation to the Irish plot.'[191] The council subsequently ordered that the utility of the various Irish witnesses be assessed, to get rid of those who were continually demanding maintenance, and to determine who would be retained for the impending trials of Plunkett and Hetherington. The decision was made by 27 April, when 16 were dispensed with.[192]

Other matters remained. Clare had sought to apologize to Ormond for any suggestion of having cast aspersions on his government, while hoping that 'neither the petition nor the presenters of it may receive any discountenance from your Grace'.[193] The grand jury subsequently retracted the petition, so Clare was 'wholly disowned and abandoned by those he drew into that snare'; an attempt at a similar petition in Limerick had failed, as the county grand jury there had declined to get involved. Ormond observed these events, along with the imminent (and unprecedented) decision of the 'loyal and well affected citizens' of Dublin to send an address to the king thanking him for his declaration of April 1681 that had condemned the actions of the Whigs and committed Charles to upholding the law and the established church.[194]

Ormond himself was still the subject of rumour and insinuation. In May 1681 a tract entitled *Ireland's Sad Lamentation* (printed in London and presumably imported into Ireland) came to official attention in Dublin.[195] It was written after the dissolution of the English parliament, ostensibly from a 'person of honour' in Dublin to 'his friend in London', and was reminiscent of the accusations against Ormond that had been circulated in Ireland in early 1679. The dissolution of parliament had ensured that 'we have little hopes, if at all any, of being secured from that Popish cruelty which most of us have felt in this age'. The particular reason for this was Ormond, who, it was alleged, had embarked on 'a progress over the whole kingdom, to see in what posture the same lay, (for what design I know not) in which journey he was much attended by Popish gentry'.[196] Despite the ostensible discovery of an 'Irish Plot', Ormond and Arran had supposedly done little to deal with it: instead, he was once more accused of protecting Richard Talbot, numerous Catholic priests, and Tyrone, along with intimidating Protestants into silence about the existence of the Irish Plot. Ormond was not openly accused of involvement in a plot to massacre Protestants, but the insinuation was obvious. 'We want an Essex, a Shaftesbury, that is to say, a good and zealous Protestant that will stand up for us in this time of eminent and scarcely to be avoided danger.' Ormond, by implication, was of a different ilk. Such insinuations were extended to Arran, Boyle, and John Fitzpatrick, whose recent conversion to the established church was dismissed, and whose pedigree was reiterated for the sake of readers: 'his father a heinous rebel, and his mother hanged for making candles of Englishmen's grease in the time of the late rebellion'.[197] But *Ireland's Sad Lamentation* was condemned by Dublin Corporation as a libel 'most unchristian, false and scandalous', being 'stuffed with most notorious falsities', and having thus declared their faith in Ormond, Arran and Boyle by condemning it, the corporation decided to issue a proclamation to the same effect.[198]

By May Ormond seemed increasingly confident in his dealings with London. He openly stated his disbelief in the accusations against Sir John Davys, and his disregard for the petition that Clare had tried to present to him; by this stage, Clare was its only advocate.[199] This seemed to mirror the turning of the political tide in England. Writing to York soon after, Ormond expressed his belief that the 'Tory' interest was indeed in the ascendant, but that the danger was not completely past.

> The wrack of the crown in the King your father's time is fresh in the memory of many of us; and the rocks and shoals he was lost upon (though they were hid to him) are so very visible to us, that if we avoid them not, we shall perish rather derided than pitied.[200]

Further suggestions of the renewed strength of the crown came in the form of reports in London suggesting that parliaments would be called in Ireland and Scotland by the beginning of August.[201]

Despite such grounds for optimism, in May Ormond and the council ordered enforcement of a proclamation of 20 November 1678 against unusually large masses in Cork.[202] Rumours of Irish Plots continued to emerge, from Roscommon and Mayo.[203] But these had been, and would remain, common currency in Restoration Ireland: the Popish Plot had merely given such suggestions a greater sense of urgency. In May, Owen O'Callaghan claimed that 'last March' he had heard Hetherington and others discuss the possibility of killing, amongst others, the Queen, Ormond, York, Arran, Michael Boyle, Sir William Davies, and Sir John Davys. He supposedly offered O'Callaghan an allowance from parliament if he would testify against them, and especially against the Queen.[204] David Fitzgerald apparently persuaded six of the Irish witnesses to testify that Hetherington bribed them to make allegations against Ormond 'and others', though it was suggested in the Whig press that this may have arisen from private malice on the part of a witness whom Hetherington declined to lend money to.[205] In June Eustace Comyn claimed to have been bribed to make further allegations, and had been told that the offer of a pardon was the reason why so many allegations of this nature had been made. Comyn also claimed to have been told by Hetherington that 'those witnesses' were worthless, and by George Coddan that there was no material evidence against Oliver Plunkett, or indeed anyone else.[206] After all, a pardon had been promised by proclamation to those who could provide any information on a plot. But these recantations made no difference to Plunkett's predicament.

VII

Plunkett's imprisonment was of inevitable concern to the Catholic Church. As far back as December 1680, the Pope had been personally concerned about his plight, as the church took the view that the English Parliament was intent on wiping out Catholicism across the three kingdoms.[207] The Spanish ambassador had unsuccessfully attempted to intercede on Plunkett's behalf, and it was hoped that York could be prevailed upon instead.[208] But such efforts came to nothing.

On 9 June 1681 Fitzharris was tried for high treason. Everard alleged that Fitzharris sought to induce him into serving 'the French and the Popish interest', most especially by writing the offending pamphlet.[209] Despite the fact that figures such as Arran testified in his favour, Fitzharris was found guilty and sentenced to death.

Plunkett's trial was also in June. According to Gilbert Burnet, it was known that Plunkett had previously censured some of the clerics who testified against him. They had already appeared before a grand jury, but the foreman, 'who was a zealous Protestant', told Burnet that they had contradicted each other so much that 'they would not find the bill. But now they laid their story better together, and swore against him'.[210] The evidence was opened by the attorney general to consist of two parts, first 'to prove a general plot in Ireland to bring in the French, to raise an army, and to extirpate and destroy all Protestants and the Protestant religion, and secondly to prove Dr. Plunkett concerned, and that as a principal agent and contriver in that design'.[211]

Plunkett was accused of involvement in such a plot by most of the witnesses against him: Florence Weyer, Henry O'Neill, 'Neile O'Neale' (*sic*), Hugh Duffy, John 'MacLegh' (*sic*), and John MacMoyer.[212] Despite his protestations about the circumstances of the trial, together they provided enough testimony to convince the court of the truth of the charges on which Plunkett had been arraigned. However, Edmund Murphy was apparently repentant and proved to be an unhelpful witness. He attempted again to implicate Ormond and York, stating that Plunkett had intended to raise 60,000–70,000 men, but only to support York against Monmouth should the need arise: this was very different to claiming that they were intent on killing Protestants *en masse*. Whilst claiming that the French were involved in this, he did not directly implicate Plunkett and stated that the other witnesses were motivated by malice. However, his performance was seen as proof that he had been tampered with.[213] As for the other witnesses, 'their testimony throughout the whole was very conformable and agreeing in all the parts'.[214] The jury took only 15 minutes to convict Plunkett, and consequently, on 15 June 1681 both he and Edward Fitzharris were sentenced to death in London for high treason.[215] The following day the various witnesses against Plunkett (with the notable exception of Murphy) petitioned the Privy Council for the pardons that were due in exchange for their testimony.[216]

There was unresolved business relating to other aspects of the outstanding prosecutions arising from the Irish Plot. On 16 June Sir John Davys petitioned the Privy Council, complaining about the delay in his trial due to the absence of key witnesses – Boark, Fitzgerald, and Samson – in England.[217] On 23 June James Carroll – now 'of Dublin' – sought compensation from the council for discovering the plot in 1672.[218] By this time Plunkett's execution was imminent. He petitioned for his defence to be adequately provided for in London, requesting passes for witnesses to travel to England, primarily to testify to the dubious and criminal character of many of the witnesses against him, such as MacMoyer, Murphy, and Hetherington, but he was denied permission to obtain copies of the various indictments made in Ireland against them.[219] Plunkett was able to provide an affidavit that contained damaging allegations against the witnesses for the prosecution; namely, that the allegations were fabrications intended to secure pardons and profit.[220] Ironically, the Privy Council ordered that the witnesses against Plunkett be pardoned for treason and misprision of treason; essentially the same charges on which they had helped to convict Plunkett.[221] David and Maurice Fitzgerald were to be retained for the eventual trials of Hetherington, Dennis, and MacNamara.[222]

Plunkett was probably beyond help at this point. Some sort of public reckoning for the Irish Plot was required. At the same time, with the Stuart monarchy having weathered the crisis of the previous three years, preparations were also being made to punish figures such as Hetherington who had orchestrated the allegations. Plunkett was apparently offered a pardon by the Whigs in exchange for a confession that would have been priceless in propaganda terms, but he refused. Essex subsequently asked Charles to pardon Plunkett on the grounds that the evidence of the witnesses against him had been worthless, but this was also refused: Charles blamed Essex for permitting Plunkett's condemnation by remaining silent at the trial, and 'I dare pardon nobody.'[223] Essex, who, like Henry Coventry, apparently never believed in the Irish Plot (despite his willingness to exploit it), may have been prompted by his conscience. He later told Gilbert Burnet of Plunkett's unwillingness to get involved in politics or intrigues, in stark contrast to the 'meddling and factious' Talbot brothers.[224] But Plunkett was the one who paid the ultimate price.

Overtures to York to intervene on Plunkett's behalf were presumably unsuccessful, as even as late as 28 June his mother-in-law, the duchess of Modena, was requested to intercede with York to have Plunkett's sentence commuted.[225] This too was unsuccessful, and on 1 July Fitzharris and Plunkett were 'drawn upon sledges to Tyburn, and there hanged and quartered according to the sentence that had been passed upon them'.[226] Both protested their innocence (Plunkett via a 'long harangue').[227] A curious footnote to the event is that Plunkett's severed head was recovered, and decades after the event, the informer Hugh Duffy would repent of his actions when confronted with it.

There was a cynical political motive for the execution: Charles had previously issued orders against executing clerics, except on his specific orders. But he admitted to the French ambassador that the execution of Plunkett was necessary to maintain the credibility of the witnesses who had testified against him, and who were to be used at Shaftesbury's planned trial.[228] The condemnation of Fitzharris can perhaps be attributed to the same consideration. Either way, with these two executions, the Popish Plot and Exclusion Crisis had reached their zenith. The arrest of Shaftesbury some days later illustrated the extent to which the monarchy and its supporters had weathered the storm. The crisis, and Ireland's role in it, was over.

Conclusion

On 2 July Arran wrote to Ormond to tell him about the executions of Plunkett and Fitzharris. 'I shall not need to send you Plunkett's speech, for it is verbatim in the newsbooks, and also sold by itself in print. He died as all people say with great resolution and Fitzharris very pitifully.' Arran also told his father about Shaftesbury's arrest on suspicion of high treason: the latter had 'cursed very much the Irish witnesses... for he guesses those are the persons that swore against him, but I am told there are as many English'.[1]

The Irish informers had been willing to testify about a variety of allegations, but as it became obvious that circumstances had turned against them they may well have chosen to swear to the truth. Shaftesbury's arrest can be seen to symbolize the end of both the Popish Plot and the Exclusion Crisis. The Stuart monarchy had survived intact. Alongside that, the death of Plunkett also had a symbolic value. His trial and execution were the most high-profile Irish elements of the Popish Plot, and were undoubtedly motivated by cynical political necessities. Even before this, the claims about the existence of an Irish Plot, and of the impact this had had upon Ireland itself, had gradually been undermined and rendered irrelevant. In this way, Plunkett's execution was an anomaly. But it also signified the end of the Irish dimension to the Popish Plot. Indeed, with these events, the crisis as it had manifested itself in England and Ireland had come to its end. What remained in the aftermath would be little more than loose ends.

When Titus Oates' allegations first came to light in 1678, Ormond's government in Dublin had assiduously sought to deal with the possibility that Ireland may have had a significant role to play in this alleged conspiracy, and did so promptly. The potential existence of a Catholic plot would be of great significance in a country that was effectively a colony, administered and governed by a Protestant minority who had gained their privileged position at the expense of the Catholics who made up the bulk of the population of the island. How secure was this nascent ascendancy, and how real was the possibility that the Catholic Irish would seek to reverse their dispossession? After all, less than a decade later, when presented with the opportunity, Catholic Ireland attempted to do precisely that. It seems reasonable to suggest that the inclination to do so would also have existed during the Popish Plot. There is a grain of truth in Ormond's suggestion of 1678 that the Catholic Irish would be cowed by the possibility of retaliation. But the original allegations had explicitly stated that the Catholic Irish would be assisted and supported by the French, a prospect that would render them a far more formidable enemy. Underpinning these possibilities was the memory of 1641: it was both benchmark and precedent. Irish Protestants undoubtedly remained concerned that they might be in danger from such a plot. Many held this perception, and the stark realities of the Ireland in which they dwelt ensured that such perceptions reflected distinct possibilities.

The impact of the Popish Plot also came against the backdrop of the institutional preoccupations of the government in the late 1670s, and naturally became intertwined with them. If there was going to be a Catholic rebellion in Ireland, then the kingdom would have to be defended, which would require money, which would require a parliament, which in turn required an investigation of Ranelagh's undertaking, which was ultimately rendered irrelevant by the facts that Ranelagh was pardoned and no Irish parliament met before Charles' death in 1685. But the hidden importance of the undertaking cannot be underestimated, for Ranelagh had sought to deflect the unwelcome attention it had garnered by attempting to smear Ormond as a closet-Catholic. Such factional rumour mongering, as directed at the viceroy and other senior figures in Ireland, was a constant feature of the crisis. But its origins and usefulness were firmly rooted in English politics. Alongside the impact of the crisis upon Ireland was the related fact that Ireland became an adjunct to the crisis in England.

The ongoing attempts to procure evidence in Ireland to prove the existence of an Irish Plot were driven by the requirements of the Whig opposition in the Exclusion Crisis. But just as the original testimonies of the Irish informers did not sway the House of Lords into voting for exclusion, the publication of the various pamphlet accounts did not seem to impact on public or parliamentary opinion. Certainly, by the spring of 1681 the loyalist response was evident in the propaganda battle.[2] Despite the best efforts of those who promoted it, the Irish Plot did not revive the anti-Catholic hysteria of the Popish Plot. There is also a curious tension between the fact that the notion of an Irish Plot was deemed plausible enough to promote, and the tardiness of the English government in actually making provision for Ireland's defences. Ormond had rued how legislation ultimately intended to secure Ireland from invasion and rebellion was of secondary importance in London, and thus was continually delayed. This had been especially obvious when the allegations about the Irish Plot were presented to the English Privy Council: the Irish parliament was effectively shelved. It seems obvious, given the priorities accorded here, that while the possibility of an Irish rebellion was considered, its significance was perceived purely in terms of how it would impact upon England. The fate of both Ireland and the Protestants who would be on the front line of any rebellion there were little more than afterthoughts.

In April 1679, during a debate about the Irish cattle trade in the English House of Commons, Sir Edward Harley observed that 'it is strange that out of our kindness to Ireland, we should be unkind to the imperial territory...Ireland is but a colony of England; now can any story give an account that colonies have been so indulged, as to prejudice the territory from whence they came?'[3] One could readily debate the contentious argument about whether early modern Ireland can be categorized as a kingdom or a colony. This is a pointless distinction, for Ireland was both. Its legal status as a separate kingdom was declared in 1541. Its status as a colony is best suggested by the reality that the Restoration settlement ensured that the bulk of its available land would remain in the hands of Protestant settlers. Ireland's colonial status is also suggested by its constitutional subordination to England, a subordination that, during the crisis, became more evident in practice as well as theory. The fact that Plunkett was tried in England on the charges for which he was previously acquitted in Ireland suggests that decisions made in Ireland were easily disregarded. Even Ormond and his administration had been increasingly sidelined, being relegated to the level of factotums obliged to facilitate the supply of such evidence as was sought; they had little control over what was demanded of them. The same was true in institutional terms, as the ongoing attempts to call an Irish parliament were stymied by events in London, and, crucially, control of Ireland's revenue was increasingly reserved to London: a parliament may have been rendered redundant anyway. Shaftesbury's call to make Ireland a province, and thus subordinate it to English interests, seems inadvertently prescient in hindsight.

But one crucial fact remains: no evidence of any Catholic plot emerged in Ireland during the crisis. The Protestant interest retained fears and uncertainties about the intentions of the dispossessed Catholics amongst whom they dwelt, while those same Catholics retained hopes about the reversal of the settlement that had confirmed their dispossession. But such fears had been evident throughout the Restoration: while they may have been highlighted and accentuated during the Popish Plot, they were nothing new. Figures such as Orrery or Henry Jones, who had connections to the English political scene and who actively sought to promote suggestions that an Irish Plot existed, were essentially making bricks without straw. They had little material with which to work other than perennial fears and concerns. The Catholic Irish remained quiescent, and Ormond himself remained sceptical about the existence of any Catholic plot, not to mention the motivations of those such as Orrery who maintained that such a plot existed. There were indeed internal security problems in Ireland, from Presbyterians on the one hand, and Tories on the other. But Catholic Ireland did not seem inclined to rise, and from the early stages of the plot Ormond had perceived the dangers of acting in a manner that could provoke it, even if this ensured that aspersions would be cast upon him. After all, the treatment meted out to the Cameronian's in Scotland illustrates that the servants of the Stuarts were quite capable of acting in a brutal and repressive manner. But the Cameronian's in Scotland were a relatively minor sect: unlike Irish Catholics, they did not make up most of the population. It is worth considering a brief counterfactual: how would a different viceroy have acted? How would a figure such as Orrery have dealt with the crisis? Or a British appointee who lacked the particular attributes that Ormond possessed? Ormond was essentially the right man in the right place at the right time. This was the essence of Southwell's judgement in May 1682. He appears to have been right. Even prior to this, in mid-July 1681, Ormond himself had been confident that Ireland was in no danger of invasion, especially now that Plunkett was dead (despite his scepticism, Ormond had retained some lingering suspicions about the activities of the deceased primate).[4] By the end of the month he could report to Charles in terms reflecting the reality that the Stuart monarchy had survived:

> It is true there is no faction in any of your other kingdoms, but hath some abettors and well wishers in this... I presume not to look beyond seas or so far into foreign designs and actions as to prognosticate what dangers they may in time produce to England, my foresight being bounded by a nearer prospect, and that methinks plainly enough shews that you are put to defend and vindicate your royal authority at home which must be effected before you can employ it abroad with any probability of success. This is a position so manifestly true that I hope God will let your people see it and dispose them to that obedience, which only can preserve them from the slavery they seem to fear and from the confusion their leaders seem to affect. From both God protect your Majesty and your kingdoms.[5]

Aftermath, 1681–1691

Memories remained. At least one tract was later written to reassert Plunkett's guilt and validate the witnesses against him.[1] While Plunkett was dead, his accusers were not, and the pamphlet could be seen as a defence of their own position in what was likely to prove a vulnerable time for some of them. There would also be attempts to suggest an Irish link with the so-called 'sham-plot': the circuitous allegations that claimed that part of the Catholic plan in the Popish Plot was to mask it as a form of Presbyterian unrest.[2] Indeed, in 1682 William Hetherington published a tract refuting the claims that he had manipulated witnesses, and reproducing once again the testimonies of some of the informers with whom he had been involved; he also sought to link these to allegations of a 'sham-plot'.[3] Hetherington remained loyal to Shaftesbury, but his fortunes eventually declined with those of his patron: in November 1681 he was arrested on a charge of *scandalum magnatum* brought by Ormond and was ordered to pay £10,000 damages. His inability to pay saw him imprisoned again, and in March 1682 he was accused of involvement in a plot to assassinate the king. His personal circumstances had changed for the worse, and the pamphlet may have been an attempt to salvage something from his previous activities.

As for Shaftesbury, who had been accused of high treason, the case against him was politically motivated and flimsy, and was eventually dropped. Ironically, he later became embroiled in a plan to orchestrate a rising and assassinate both Charles and York before absconding to Amsterdam where he died in January 1683. Essex would follow Shaftesbury's lead and also became involved in this new Whig conspiracy – the so-called 'Rye House Plot' – but he was arrested and imprisoned in the Tower of London, where he was found with his throat cut in July 1683. It remains unclear whether this was suicide or murder, but the latter seems the more likely. Ironically Titus Oates outlived virtually everybody else involved in the Popish Plot, dying in 1705 after a life best described as shady.

I

But Ireland's role in the crisis ended with Plunkett's death. The Irish witnesses and their allegations were of little further value in England, and slowly began to trickle back to Ireland. In July 1681 Owen Murphy was reimbursed for his expenses and was permitted to return to Ireland, whilst Eustace Comyn was granted a full pardon on the same day.[4] Not all were so lucky: in October 1681 Ormond was authorized by the English Privy Council to prosecute anyone who had sought to suborn witnesses to testify against himself, Boyle, and Davys.[5]

In October 1681 the Privy Council ordered the release of Marcus Forristal, the Catholic bishop of Kildare, who was to have his possessions and money restored to him (if practicable). He was not to be charged with involvement in any plot: only with remaining in Ireland beyond the period specified for Catholic clerics.[6] There were, of course, lingering suspicions: in June 1681 Massareene expressed his conviction that 'I really believe the Popish Plot goes still on with the Romish clergy, who, you see, are still amongst us, yet will neither be taken nor appear.'[7] But Forristal's release hardly suggested that such suspicions applied to him. Some witnesses remained active. In October the Privy Council considered the petitions of eight persons incriminated by the informers Murtagh Downey, Maurice Fitzgerald, and Owen O'Callaghan. In November 1681 the council ordered that these three were to be sent back to Ireland to give evidence 'upon the petition of divers gentlemen in prison in Ireland', for 'their evidence would be of no use here'.[8] John and Dennis MacNamara, Edward Ivie, and Bernard Dennis testified against Shaftesbury at his trial in November 1681.[9] Tyrone himself was released in December 1681 on condition that he give himself up if required, and his accusers were to be prosecuted in Ireland.[10] Soon afterwards, John Fitzgerald readily undermined his own allegations by stating that

Israel Tonge had arranged to plant the letters he had been supposed to discover in 1680.[11]

In February 1682 the Privy Council ordered that information on the Popish Plot in Ireland, provided by one James Fitzpatrick of Quin, Clare, was to be given to the magistrate Edmund Warcup, who was to ensure that certain named individuals be sought in London.[12] Some days later Warcup reported back. Nobody had been found.[13] Given the collapse of the allegations about the Irish Plot, this was unsurprising. In May 1682 three of Plunkett's (unnamed) accusers were condemned to death in Ireland, though one retracted his accusations against the Primate.[14] After the acquittal of a number of those accused in Munster, the informers and the plot even earned the scorn and contempt of Ó Bruadair, with Charles II and the judge who acquitted them earning his praise.[15] In *Suim purgadora bfear nEireann* ('The purgatory of the men of Ireland') Ó Bruadair offered a rare Catholic Irish perspective on the Popish Plot, assessing it in much darker terms by viewing both it and the activities of the Irish informers as part of the slow crushing of Catholic Ireland in the years since the 1640s.[16]

By August 1682 Edmund Murphy was reportedly working on a farm in Kent, and he vanished from the record soon afterwards. And by October 1682 Peter Creagh, the bishop of Cork, was declared innocent after one of his two accusers recanted.[17] The Catholic bishops who were supposedly instrumental in the organization of the Irish Plot were thereby released. Perhaps the most eloquent (if ultimately ironic) statement about the continued existence of any Irish Plot was the decision by the Privy Council, in February 1683 and on foot of his own petition, to permit Richard Talbot to return to Ireland.[18]

II

The travails of the informers were incidental. There were more important considerations. In April 1682 Dublin Corporation offered a petition of loyalty to both Ormond and the king.[19] Throughout 1682–1683 similar petitions were drawn up throughout Ireland, and Tim Harris has suggested that these corresponded to the English petitions issued during the so-called 'Tory revenge', as the king and court sought to consolidate their position across the three kingdoms whilst avenging themselves upon their opponents.[20] The majority of such Irish petitions assured Charles of the support of his Protestant subjects. It remains virtually impossible to gauge whether the English political divisions of 1679–1681 were replicated in Ireland: the absence of an Irish parliament ensured that there was no institutional forum in which such beliefs could find expression. But, as in England and Scotland, by the final years of Charles II's reign the danger to the Stuart dynasty in Ireland was seen to have passed, and the succession had been secured.

Ormond's tenure as viceroy ended in February 1685 with the death of Charles II. He was subsequently lauded in an anonymous broadside for his steady and composed service during the crisis, in terms reminiscent of Southwell's previous assessment.

> Into your hands, then, which before it graced,
> The noble instrument again was placed;
> On which, a long, soft tune, again you played,
> When jarring discord did all else invade.[21]

The Popish Plot carried an occasional resonance in subsequent years, though the fortunes of those accused in it were mixed. Brittas was earmarked for a command in January 1686, 'having been perfectly ruined by Mr Oates's plot', and Pierce Lacy had also been impoverished by two years imprisonment: he petitioned the incumbent viceroy Henry Hyde, earl of Clarendon, for assistance in January 1686, and his petition was recommended for consideration given 'how much he suffered in the time of Oates's villainy'.[22]

However, there was a greater resonance accorded to the specific concerns that the Popish Plot had highlighted in Ireland, for they had not yet been satisfactorily resolved. In the early 1680s William Petty again turned his attention to the condition of Ireland in general, and its defences in particular.

> Suppose the ports and garrisons of Dublin, Wexford, Waterford, Youghal, Cork, Kinsale, Dingle, Tralee, Limerick, Galway, Sligo, Derry, Carrickfergus, and Drogheda to be in the hands of Catholic officers, under one Catholic general, who commands perhaps 15 garrisons and 15 regiments; it is manifest that the said general and 30 officers can if they agree let in the French.

It followed, then, that the Catholic Irish

> would triumph in full splendour of religion, the protection of the mightiest prince, the exercise of all offices, the merit of extirpating heresy, and revenge even by massacre upon the British and Protestant interest, and to be delivered from the fear of a Protestant successor.[23]

The invocation of a Catholic Irish 'massacre' by way of revenge was deeply suggestive. The passing of the Popish Plot did not alter the reality that Ireland was seen to be vulnerable to foreign attack. And such concerns as were expressed by Petty, of internal subversion assisting a Catholic – French – invasion, were reminiscent of the allegations previously made by informers such as David Fitzgerald.

Fears of French assistance to the Catholic Irish did not fade way after 1681: far from it. In 1688, in the wake of the 'Glorious Revolution', an assessment of the condition of Ireland was provided to William of Orange. The Irish were now seen to be a far more formidable enemy than they had been in 1641, given that they possessed advantages that they had lacked in the 1640s: numerical, strategic, and geographical supremacy, military strength, major support from a continental power, and royal authority, for James was still king of Ireland. Despite lacking these advantages in the 1640s, they had still managed to form a government and hold out for 12 years. But now

> they have the king's authority added to the fury of their priests. They have interests and councils of France to abet them, and the kings authority will be now so much at the mercy of France, that in effect the king of France will be now king of Ireland. Nor will a Popes Nuncio be long wanting thence, to unite the minds of the clergy in this war of religion.[24]

To any observer in 1641–1653, or 1678–1681, such an assessment could only have sounded familiar. Familiar too was the rhetoric of the Williamite war, and of the ghosts it sought to conjure. The 1680s had retained an undercurrent of unease facilitated by uncertainty about the present, and certainty about the past. When Nicholas French's *Narrative of the Earl of Clarendon's Settlement and Sale of Ireland*, was reprinted in 1685, an 'English Protestant' offered a riposte; after all, the legitimacy of the Restoration settlement was at stake.[25] Indeed, one chief secretary had noted how 'the Irish talk of nothing now but recovering their lands and bringing the English under their subjection, which they who have been the masters for above 400 years know not how well to bear'.[26] Unsurprisingly, given the Catholic revival of the 1680s (especially the danger to the land settlement posed by the 1689 Jacobite parliament), along with the stark fact that French forces were in Ireland supporting a Catholic monarch, the Williamite war triggered an outburst of printed material similar in tone to that employed in previous generations.

III

York succeeded his brother Charles as James II in 1685. Irish support for him inevitably meant Catholic support, and within this the long-promised Catholic plot, of which 1641 had been one episode, could now be discerned.[27] Catholic confidence under the Jacobite regime was illustrated in 1686 by events in Galway. During the Popish Plot Catholics had been expelled from the city, and were barred from participation in its governance, but in June 1686, on Clarendon's orders, Catholic merchants in Galway (and other towns) were to be admitted as freemen without taking the oath of supremacy. If elected to office, their names were to be forwarded to Clarendon to facilitate their formal dispensation from the oath, if appropriate. The reasoning behind this echoed issues that had arisen during the Popish Plot itself: Catholics were useful to the local economy, and there was no legal basis for their exclusion from the freedom of corporate towns.[28] This was a world apart from the fearful reluctance of Charles to readmit Catholics to the city during the Popish Plot. In July 1686 Clarendon, on foot of a petition from Galway's Catholics blaming the incumbent mayor for misusing funds, ordered him not to stand for the post again, and not to delay the admission of Catholics to the common council: indeed, he was expressly ordered to admit them promptly.[29] On the other hand, William King later claimed that Catholics had not forgotten other aspects of the Popish Plot, and that they sought to take advantage of the fact that James had apparently never issued a general pardon on his accession. 'No sooner had they got judges and juries that would believe them, but they began a trade of swearing, and ripping up what they had pretended their neighbours had said of his late majesty whilst duke of York some years before, especially in time of the Popish Plot', and malicious prosecutions supposedly proliferated.[30]

The intertwining ethnic, social, and religious divisions of Ireland in the reign of Charles II inevitably became more pronounced under his brother as they seemed to become open to alteration. During the Popish Plot, demands for a parliament had hinged upon the issue of Protestant security but none was ever called. The previous parliament of 1661–1666 had implemented the land settlement and laid the foundations for a nascent Protestant ascendancy. The next Irish parliament of 1689 would be tasked with its destruction.

Even prior to the outbreak of war in 1689, the outrage of Irish Protestants at their potential fate was noted, as was their willingness to defend themselves: the deaths of Essex and Edmund Bury Godfrey were invoked as reminders of the perfidy of the Papists.[31] Ireland had long overcome 'that great devastation caused by that tedious and bloody rebellion begun in the year "41"' to attain a level of prosperity and happiness, 'for all affairs were managed with the same equality and indifference towards all manner of persons; so that the very Papists could not complain of an unequal distribution of justice'.[32] Sir John Temple had argued something similar: the depoliticized nature of such an idyllic scene ensured that when 'malicious and prying Popish neighbours', who had been encouraged by policies favouring Catholics, began 'without doubt, to think of some such bloody practices as were put in execution in the year forty-one', and seek to emulate them, it could readily be ascribed to their nature.[33]

James was continually vilified: "tis certain, that the Irish never had power to hurt the English and Protestants of that kingdom, but for the advantage they had of a Popish king who divested the Protestants of all power, civil and military' and placing it instead 'into the hands of Irish papists'.[34] The events of 1641 and the involvement of the French illustrated 'what favour Protestants are to expect under a Popish king, and in a kingdom where Popery is predominant'.[35] Another account of James' alleged conduct assured readers that the author would not 'enter into a tedious discourse of all the measures taken since 1660 to subvert the Protestant religion'; to the right audience that would be unnecessary.[36] The complaints about the methods used to undermine Protestant power – purges of the civil and military establishments, and the consequent transfer of control to Catholic hands – were fundamentally similar to the claims of some of the informers during the Popish Plot; continuity once again. And James had opened the centre of power to Catholic influence, most especially in the form of his viceroy Richard Talbot, now earl of Tyrconnell, who was markedly more enthusiastic for redressing Irish Catholic grievances than his king. But the implications of Tyrconnell's policies – especially the possibility of a reversal of the land settlement – proved decisive in ensuring their gravitation towards William.[37] Some pamphleteers attempted to draw a distinction between James and his viceroy, 'as the late King coming for Ireland...gave us some hopes, it would abate the cruelty of the enraged Tyrconnell'.[38] But in rhetorical terms the distinction between the two was irrelevant.

As depicted, the purpose of Tyrconnell's actions sounded familiar: the attempted destruction of the Protestant community in Ireland.[39] The involvement of Catholic clergy and the French was discerned once more.[40] Indeed, in a virtual recap of what David Fitzgerald had claimed, the Irish were being manipulated by the Jesuits and expected assistance from the French, who were to land in Munster, most likely Kerry.[41] And again, the spectre of 1641 remained near to hand: 'a day never to be forgot'.[42] The assault upon Protestants by Tyrconnell and his forces 'so nearly resemble their beginnings in their last so horrid rebellion in forty one'.[43] For the more imaginative pamphleteers putting words into Tyrconnell's mouth, the point could be emphasized with hopefully greater veracity, and in doing so collapsed any distinctions between himself and his royal masters, most especially his Catholic queen: 'It was but in the year 1641 200,000 heretics fell victims to the holy cause, in this island; and were I master of as many islands, they should all be offered up a tribute to your majesties shrine.'[44] Recurring themes were present; unprovoked slaughter, the connivance of Catholic priests, foreign invasion, and perhaps most dangerously, subversion at the heart of power. It was from such perennial fears that Irish Protestants sought to secure themselves. The soliciting of English support, as in the 1640s, was an obvious way out of the dilemma. But to do so after the event would be too late, and the precedent that came to hand was the obvious solution: the events of 1689–1691, as discerned in the chaos of war (the presence of Catholic forces, a Catholic revival, and a possible reversal of the land settlement) suggested confirmation of what had been feared since 1641. This was by no means far-fetched. According to William King, writing with the benefit of hindsight,

> If they hated us so much in 1641, that without provocation, and whilst in possession of their estates, they rose as one man, and attempted to destroy us; if they were so set on it, that they ventured to do it without arms, discipline, or authority on their side, and where the hazard was so great, that it was ten to one if they succeeded; what could we expect they would do now, when provoked to the height by the loss of their estates, when armed, disciplined, and entrusted with the places of strength, power and profit in the kingdom?[45]

The Williamite invasion had in itself little to do with the plight of Irish Protestants, but as the Jacobite cause was defeated in Ireland, the island's Protestant community sought to transfer its allegiance to a new king, and thereby preserve themselves. Even if, as has been suggested, the Catholic threat perceived in the latter stages of the seventeenth century in Ireland has been overstated (and the relative quiescence of Ireland during the Popish Plot can be depicted as the proof of this), 'Irish Protestants emerged from the crisis of 1688–1689 convinced that they had narrowly escaped the destruction of everything they had gained over the preceding century.'[46] Even those contemporary observers who discounted the reality of another Irish Catholic rebellion remained aware of the potential for one, especially if a foreign power were to be involved. It was the memory of that deliverance from destruction by William of Orange that proved the most enduring marker on the Irish Protestant calendar.

But the older date of 1641 remained potent. A sermon preached in London on 23 October 1690 struck an ominous note when it stated that vigilance would be required by Protestants in Ireland, for the Irish Catholic had been proven to be irredeemable.[47] The deep hostility of Irish Protestants towards the Catholics whom they lived alongside and amongst may have been mutual, but perhaps uniquely in Western Europe, it was the social and religious group who made up the minority of the population who would emerge as the winners, as the colonists of the seventeenth century became the ascendancy of the eighteenth. The legislative victory extracted by the Protestant community in the 1690s to secure itself proved a durable one, but the memory from which it drew purpose never passed out of history. It could and would rationalize as the aggressor, and thus the justifiably punished, those who became the forgotten Catholic underclass of eighteenth-century Ireland.[48]

IV

This lay in the future. But Protestant memories were not the only memories, and after the Jacobite defeat in 1691 Catholic Irish minds also devoted time to their version of the past. York had succeeded to the throne as James II, and the Irish, who had suffered in spite of their loyalty, expected his accession to usher in the restoration of their religion and estates.[49] It was no surprise then that 1678, the year in which the Popish Plot had first come to light, was perceived by the Old English author of 'A light to the blind' (almost certainly Nicholas Plunkett) as 'the famous year, wherein the monumental troubles of his Royal Highness began'.[50] The opposition to the succession in 1678 was seen to stem from a fear of Catholics, and from this had stemmed the numerous plots, in which Titus Oates and his 'contradictory, and improbable' tale had been but one actor, and which had been intended to destroy Catholicism in the three kingdoms and to disinherit the rightful king, for 'it made the nations tremble, and struck a terror into the King himself'.[51] The disloyalty of Protestants was therefore proof that they needed to be ruled with a strong hand. And that disloyalty had become evident during the exclusion campaign, depicted as the first rebellion in the sequence of rebellions (including that of Monmouth in 1685) that had its final success in the Glorious Revolution. For the anonymous author, the continuity between 1678 and 1688 was obvious.[52] The Popish Plot had been the prelude.

Abbreviations

BL: British Library.
BL Add.: British Library, Additional Manuscripts.
Bodl.: Bodleian Library, Oxford.
Commons jn.: *Journals of the House of Commons, 1547–* (London, 1742–).
CSPD: *Calendar of State Papers Domestic. Charles II* (28 vols, London, 1860–1947).
CSPI: R. P. Mahaffy (ed.), *Calendar of the State Papers Relating to Ireland [in the Reign of Charles II] Preserved in the Public Record Office. 1660–(70), with Addenda, 1625–70* (4 vols, London, 1905–10).
CSPV: Allen B. Hinds(ed.), *Calendar of State Papers and Manuscripts Relating to English Affairs Existing in the Archives and Collections of Venice* (38 vols, London, 1867–1947).
Essex papers, i: Osmond Airy (ed.), *Essex papers, vol. 1: 1672–1679* (London, 1890).
Essex papers, ii: C.E. Pike (ed.), *Selections from the Correspondence of Arthur Capel, Earl of Essex, 1675–1677* (London, 1913).
Folger: Folger Shakespeare Library, Washington DC.
Gilbert MS: Dublin Public Libraries, Gilbert Collection.
Grey, *Debates*: Anchitell Grey (ed.), *Debates of the House of Commons: From the Year 1667 to the Year 1694* (10 vols, London, 1763–69).
HMC Rep.: Historical Manuscripts Commission, *Reports 1–* (London, 1870–).
HMC Egmont: *Report on the Manuscripts of the Earl of Egmont* (2 vols, London, 1905–09).
HMC Hastings: *Report on the Manuscripts of the Late Reginald Rawdon Hastings* (4 vols, London, 1928–47).
HMC Leyborne-Popham: *Report on the Manuscripts of F.W. Leyborne-Popham, esq.* (London, 1899).
HMC Montagu: *Report on the Manuscripts of Lord Montagu* (London, 1900).
HMC Ormonde, os: *Calendar of the Manuscripts of the Marquess of Ormonde*, old series (2 vols, London, 1895–99).
HMC Ormonde, ns: *Calendar of the Manuscripts of the Marquess of Ormonde*, new series (8 vols, London, 1902–20).
Kings Inns: Library of the Honourable Society of Kings Inns, Dublin.
Lords jn.: *The Journals of the House of Lords, 1509–* (London, 1767–).
NAI: National Archives of Ireland.
NLI: National Library of Ireland.
Nunziatura di Fiandri: Cathaldus Giblin (ed.), 'Catalogue of material of Irish interest in the collection *Nunziatura di Fiandra*, Vatican archives', part 2, in *Collectanea Hibernica*, 3 (1960), pp. 7–144; part 8, *Collectanea Hibernica*, 12 (1969), pp. 62–101.

Parliamentary debates: *A Collection of the Parliamentary Debates in England* (24 vols, Dublin, 1739–49).
Parl. Hist.: William Cobbett (ed.), *Cobbett's Parliamentary History of England* (36 vols, London, 1806–20).
Plunkett letters: John Hanly (ed.), *The Letters of St. Oliver Plunkett, 1625–1681* (Dublin, 1979).
NAUK: National Archives of the United Kingdom.
RIA: Royal Irish Academy.
State trials: William Cobbett (ed.), *Cobbett's Complete Collection of State Trials and Proceedings for High Treason, and Other Crimes and Misdemeanours from the Earliest Period to the Present Time* (33 vols, London, 1809–28).
Steele, *Proclamations*: Richard Steele, (ed.), *A Bibliography of Royal Proclamations of the Tudor and Stuart Sovereigns, 1485–1714* (2 vols, Oxford, 1910).
TCD: Trinity College, Dublin.
V & A: Victoria & Albert Museum.

Notes

Introduction

1. Existing accounts include Thomas Carte, *History of the Life of James, First Duke of Ormond* (6 vols, Oxford, 1851), iv, pp. 542–638; Richard Bagwell, *Ireland under the Stuarts* (3 vols, Dublin, 1909–1916), iii, pp. 127–40; J.R. Jones, *The First Whigs: The Politics of the Exclusion Crisis, 1678–83* (London, 1961), p. 124; Alice Curtayne, *The Trial of Oliver Plunkett* (London, 1953); James Ernest Aydelotte, 'The Duke of Ormond and the English Government of Ireland, 1677–85' (Ph.D, University of Iowa, 2 vols, 1975), i, pp. 24–9; T.W. Moody, F.X. Martin and F.J. Byrne (eds), *A New History of Ireland, vol. III: Early Modern Ireland, 1534–1691* (Oxford, 1976), pp. 432–3; John Kenyon, *The Popish Plot* (London, 1972), pp. 224–5, 233–4; J.C. Beckett, *The Cavalier Duke: A Life of James Butler First Duke of Ormond, 1610–88* (Belfast, 1990), pp. 115–22; S.J. Connolly, *Religion Law and Power: The Making of Protestant Ireland, 1660–1760* (Oxford, 1992), pp. 24–32; Mark Knights, *Politics and Opinion in Crisis, 1678–81* (Cambridge, 1994), pp. 265, 307; David Dickson, *New Foundations: Ireland 1660–1800* (2nd ed., Dublin, 2000), pp. 19–21; Anne Creighton, 'The Catholic Interest in Irish Politics in the Reign of Charles II' (Ph.D, Queens University Belfast, 2000), pp. 253–75; Thomas J. Doyle, 'The Duke of Ormond, the Popish Plot, and the Exclusion Crisis, 1677–82' (M.Litt, National University of Ireland, 2004). The most comprehensive account of the Popish Plot in relation to Ireland currently in print is Tim Harris, *Restoration: Charles II and His Kingdoms, 1660–1685* (London, 2005), pp. 377–406. For Oliver Plunkett, see Tomás Ó Fiaich, 'The fall and return of John MacMoyer', *Seanchas Ard Mhacha*, 3 (1958), pp. 51–86; John Brady, 'Why was Oliver Plunkett arrested?', *Irish Ecclesiastical Record*, 5th ser., 83 (1955), pp. 41–7; idem, 'Oliver Plunkett and the Popish Plot', i–iii, *Irish Ecclesiastical Record*, 5th ser., 89 (1958), pp. 1–13, 340–54; 5th ser., v, 90 (1958), pp. 12–27; Breifne Walker, 'Blessed Oliver Plunkett and the Popish Plot in Ireland', *Irish Ecclesiastical Record*, 5th ser., 109 (1968), pp. 313–30; Tomás Ó Fiaich, *Oliver Plunkett: Ireland's New Saint* (Dublin, 1975); John Hanly, 'Saint Oliver Plunkett' in A.J. Hughes and William Nolan (eds), *Armagh: History and Society* (Dublin, 2001), pp. 413–55.
2. Aydelotte, 'The Duke of Ormond and the English Government of Ireland', i, p. 25.
3. R.F. Foster, *Modern Ireland, 1600–1972* (London, 1988), p. 117.
4. J.C. Beckett, 'The Irish Armed Forces, 1660–1685' in John Bossy and Peter Jupp (eds), *Essays Presented to Michael Roberts* (Belfast, 1976), p. 41. A similar interpretive model was previously formulated for England in Jonathan Scott, *Algernon Sidney and the Restoration Crisis, 1677–1683* (Cambridge,

1991), pp. 1–49, and idem, *England's Troubles: Seventeenth-Century English Political Instability in European Context* (Cambridge, 2000).
5. Tim Harris, 'The British dimension, religion, and the shaping of political identities during the reign of Charles II' in Tony Claydon and Ian McBride (eds) *Protestantism and National Identity: Britain and Ireland, c.1650–c.1850*, (Cambridge, 1998), pp. 131–56; Grant Tapsell, *The Personal Rule of Charles II, 1681–85* (Woodbridge, 2007), pp. 159–90; Harris, *Restoration*, pp. 171–4, 377–406.
6. Sir Robert Southwell to Sir John Perceval, 16 May 1682 (cited in Aydelotte, 'The Duke of Ormond and the English Government of Ireland', i, pp. 28–9).

1 Restoration Ireland

1. *Lords jn.*, xiii, pp. 313–30.
2. The following discussion draws freely upon: John Miller, *Popery and Politics in England, 1660–1688* (Cambridge, 1973); K.H.D. Haley, ' "No Popery" in the reign of Charles II' in J.S. Bromley and E.H. Kossman (eds), *Britain and the Netherlands, v: Some Political Mythologies* (The Hague, 1975), pp. 102–119; Michael G. Finlayson, *Historians, Puritanism, and the English Revolution: The Religious Factor in English Politics Before and After the Interregnum* (Toronto, 1983); Peter Lake, 'Anti-Popery: the structure of a prejudice' in Richard Cust and Ann Hughes (eds), *Conflict in Early Stuart England: Studies in Religion and Politics, 1603–1642* (London, 1989), pp. 72–106; David Cressy, *Bonfires and Bells: National Memory and the Protestant Calendar in Elizabethan and Stuart England* (London, 1990); Anthony Milton, 'A qualified intolerance: the limits and ambiguities of early Stuart anti-Catholicism' in Arthur F. Marotti (ed.), *Catholicism and Anti-Catholicism in Early Modern English Texts* (Basingstoke, 1999), pp. 85–115; Brenda Buchanan (ed.), *Gunpowder Plots* (London, 2005); Arthur F. Marotti, *Religious Ideology & Cultural Fantasy: Catholic and Anti-Catholic Discourses in Early Modern England* (Notre Dame, 2005).
3. John Foxe, *Acts and Monuments [...]. The Variorum Edition* (hriOnline, Sheffield 2004). Available at: http://www.hrionline.ac.uk/foxe/ (Accessed: 10.01.2008).
4. Lake, 'Anti-Popery', pp. 73–4, 80.
5. Brian Mac Cuarta, 'Religious violence against settlers in south Ulster, 1641–2', in David Edwards, Padraig Lenihan and Clodagh Tait (eds), *Age of Atrocity: Violent Death and Political Conflict in Early Modern Ireland* (Dublin, 2007), pp. 154–75.
6. Cathy Carruth, *Unclaimed Experience: Trauma, Narrative and History* (Baltimore, 1996); Jeffrey C. Alexander, 'Towards a theory of cultural trauma' in idem, et al. (eds), *Cultural Trauma and Collective Identity* (Berkeley, 2004), pp. 1–30.
7. Nicholas Canny, *Making Ireland British, 1580–1650* (Oxford, 2001), pp. 461–550.
8. TCD Love MS 7, 236–8, ff. 400–9.

9. [Henry Jones], *A Remonstrance of Divers Remarkeable Passages Concerning the Church and Kingdom of Ireland* (London, 1642) p. 1.
10. [Jones], *Remonstrance*, p. 8.
11. A recent exception is Raymond Gillespie, 'Temple's fate: reading *The Irish Rebellion* in late seventeenth-century Ireland' in Ciaran Brady and Jane Ohlmeyer (eds), *British Interventions in Early Modern Ireland* (Cambridge, 2005), pp. 315–33.
12. T.C. Barnard, 'The uses of the 23rd of October 1641 and Irish Protestant celebrations', *English Historical Review*, 106 (Oct. 1991), p. 891.
13. Temple, *Irish Rebellion*, preface, A2v.
14. Ibid., A3v.
15. Ibid.
16. Gillespie, 'Temple's fate', p. 333.
17. Temple, *Irish Rebellion*, preface, A3r.
18. Ibid., A4r.
19. Ibid.
20. Ibid., B1r.
21. Ibid., p. 5.
22. Ibid., p. 6.
23. Ibid., p. 7.
24. Gillespie, 'Temple's fate', pp. 325–6.
25. *The Last News from Ireland* (London, 1641), np.
26. *Still Worse News from Ireland* (London, 1641), np.
27. *The Irish Petition to the Parliament in England* (London, 1641), np.
28. Cromwell to General Council at Whitehall, 23 March 1649, W.C. Abbott (ed.), *The Writings and Speeches of Oliver Cromwell* (4 vols, Cambridge, Mass., 1937–1947), ii, p. 38.
29. Toby Barnard, 'The Protestant interest, 1641–1660', in Jane Ohlmeyer (ed.), *Ireland from Independence to Occupation, 1641–1660* (Cambridge, 1995), pp. 218–40.
30. *CSPI., 1660–1662*, pp. 167–8, 173–6.
31. Creighton, 'The Catholic interest in Irish politics', pp. 126–40.
32. John Lynch,*Cambrensis Eversus*, Matthew Kelly (ed.) (2 vols, Dublin, 1848), i, pp. 35, 59.
33. John Dillingham to Lord Montagu, 26 May 1664 (*HMC Montagu*, p. 166).
34. Sir John Perceval to Sir Robert Southwell, 28 Jan. 1665 (*HMC Egmont*, ii, p. 12).
35. 'An act for keeping and celebrating the twenty-third of October, as an anniversary for thanksgiving in this kingdom' (14 & 15 Cha. II, ch. 23); Barnard, 'The uses of the 23rd of October 1641', pp. 892–93.
36. Nicholas French, 'The Bleeding Iphigenia' in S.H. Bindon (ed.), *The Historical Works of the Right Rev. Nicholas French, D.D.* (2 vols, Dublin, 1846), i, p. 19.
37. French, 'Bleeding Iphigenia', p. 141.
38. Ibid., pp. 164, 167.
39. Ibid., pp. 201–3.

40. [Henry Jones], *A Sermon of Antichrist, Preached at Christ-Church, Dublin, Nov. 12, 1676* (2nd ed., London, 1679), A2.
41. Jones, *A Sermon of Antichrist*, p. 23.
42. Coventry to Ormond, 13 Aug 1678 (*HMC Ormonde*, ns., iv, p. 183).
43. Anne Creighton, 'The Catholic interest in Irish politics', passim.
44. Sir William Temple, 'An essay on the present state and condition of Ireland' in idem, *Select Letters to the Prince of Orange... Vol. III* (London, 1701), pp. 197–216.
45. Temple, 'An essay on the present state and condition of Ireland', p. 213.
46. William Petty, 'The political anatomy of Ireland' in C.H. Hull (ed.), *The Economic Writings of Sir William Petty* (2 vols, London, 1899), ii, pp. 155–7.
47. Petty, 'Political Anatomy', pp. 164, 167, 201–3.
48. Jim Smyth, 'The communities of Ireland and the British state, 1660–1707' in Brendan Bradshaw and John Morrill (eds), *The British Problem, c.1534–1707: State Formation in the Atlantic Archipelago* (Basingstoke and London, 1996), pp. 246–49.
49. Phil Kilroy, *Protestant Dissent and Controversy in Ireland, 1660–1714* (Cork, 1994), pp. 225–43; Richard L. Greaves, 'That's no good religion that disturbs government': The Church of Ireland and the nonconformist challenge, 1660–88' in Alan Ford, Kenneth Milne and James McGuire (eds), *As by Law Established: The Church of Ireland since the Reformation* (Dublin, 1995), pp. 120–35.
50. Éamon Ó Ciosáin, 'The Irish in France, 1660–90: the point of no return' in Thomas O'Connor and Mary Ann Lyons (eds), *Irish Communities in Early Modern Europe* (Dublin, 2006), pp. 85–102.
51. Sir Robert Southwell to Sir Philip Perceval, 24 Jan. 1678 (*HMC Egmont*, ii, pp. 69–70).
52. J.C. Beckett, 'The Irish viceroyalty in the Restoration period' in idem, *Confrontations: Studies in Irish History* (Plymouth, 1972), pp. 67–86; Aydelotte, 'The Duke of Ormond and the English Government of Ireland', passim.
53. Private instructions for Essex, 12 July 1672 (BL, Add MS 21, 505, f. 29).
54. Godolphin to Essex, 12 Apr. 1673 (BL, Stowe MS 201, f. 349).
55. Essex to Arlington, 20 Aug. 1672 (*Essex papers*, i, pp. 14–16).
56. Ibid., 8 Oct. 1672 (*Essex papers*, i, p. 34).
57. *Commons jn.*, p. 270.
58. Ibid., pp. 276–7.
59. Essex to Arlington, 18 Jan. 1673 (*Essex papers*, i, p. 49–50).
60. Ibid., 20 Jan. 1673 (*Essex papers*, i, p. 50).
61. Ibid., 25 Jan. 1673 (*Essex papers*, i, p. 52).
62. Essex to Coventry, 18 June 1676 (*Essex papers*, ii, pp. 56–8).
63. Ibid., 24 July 1676 (*Essex papers*, ii, pp. 66–7).
64. Bishop of Killala to Essex, 22 Jan. 1677 (*Essex papers*, ii, pp. 94–5).
65. [Nicholas French], 'The Unkinde Desertor of Loyall Men and True Frinds', (Louvain, c.1676) in Bindon (ed.), *The Historical Works of the Right Rev. Nicholas French*, ii, p. 15; Éamonn Ó Ciardha, ' "The Unkinde Deserter" and "The Bright Duke": Contrasting views of the dukes of Ormonde in the Irish royalist tradition' in Toby Barnard and Jane Fenlon (eds), *The Dukes of Ormonde, 1610–1745* (Woodbridge, 2000), pp. 177–85.
66. Gilbert, MS 109, p. 1.
67. Ormond to Coventry, 4 Sept. 1677 (*HMC Ormonde, ns*, iv, pp. 35–8).

2 The Popish Plot in Ireland, September 1678–May 1679

1. *Lords jn.*, xiii, p. 313.
2. Ibid., p. 314.
3. Ibid., p. 315.
4. Ibid., p. 317.
5. Ibid., pp. 320, 323.
6. Ibid., p. 327.
7. Miller, *Popery and Politics in England*, p. 158.
8. Kenyon, *Popish Plot*, p. 86.
9. Quoted in Alan Marshall, *The Strange Death of Edmund Godfrey: Plots and Politics in Restoration London* (Stroud, 1999), p. xi.
10. Harris, Restoration, p. 137.
11. Toby Barnard, 'Conclusion. Settling and unsettling Ireland: the Cromwellian and Williamite revolutions' Ohlmeyer (ed.), *Ireland from Independence to Occupation*, pp. 268, 277–83; *CSPV, 1671–72*, p. 24.
12. Robert Armstrong, *Protestant War: The 'British' of Ireland and the Wars of the Three Kingdoms* (Manchester, 2005), pp. 230–4.
13. Deposition of John O'Daly, 27 Mar. 1674 (*HMC Egmont*, ii, pp. 32–3).
14. Steven C.A. Pincus, 'From butterboxes to wooden shoes: the shift in English popular sentiment from anti-Dutch to anti-French in the 1670s', *Historical Journal*, 38 (1995), pp. 351–7.
15. Sir Robert Southwell to Sir Philip Perceval, 24 Jan. 1678 (*HMC Egmont*, ii, pp. 69–70).
16. Aidan Clarke, *Prelude to Restoration in Ireland: The End of the Commonwealth, 1659–1660* (Cambridge, 1999), p. 320.
17. Creighton, 'The Catholic interest in Irish politics', p. 146.
18. D.W. Hayton, *Ruling Ireland, 1685–1742: Politics, Politicians and Parties* (Woodbridge, 2004), p. 15.
19. Anne Creighton, 'The remonstrance of December 1661 and Catholic politics in restoration Ireland', *Irish Historical Studies*, 34 (2004), pp. 16–41.
20. W.P. Burke, *The Irish priests in the penal times, 1660–1760* (Waterford, 1914), p. 52; Charles to Ormond, 30 Sept. 1678 (Bodl., Carte MS 38, f. 718).
21. Ormond to Southwell, 5 Oct. 1678 (*HMC Ormonde*, os, ii, p. 277).
22. Ormond to Boyle, 7 Oct. 1678 (*HMC Ormonde*, ns, iv, p. 211).
23. Aydelotte, 'The Duke of Ormond and the English Government of Ireland', i, pp. 30–98.
24. Joseph Williamson to Ormond, 28 Sept. 1678 (*CSPD 1678*, pp. 428–9).
25. Longford to Ormond, 8 Oct. 1678 (*HMC Ormonde*, ns, iv, pp. 214–15).
26. Ormond to Coventry, 8 Oct. 1678 (Kings Inns, Prendergast papers, xi, pp. 455–6); Warrant for arrest of Peter Talbot, 8 Oct. 1678 (Kings Inns, Prendergast papers, xii, pp. 583–4).
27. Ormond to Boyle, 8 Oct. 1678 (*HMC Ormonde*, ns, iv, p. 212).
28. Creighton, 'The Catholic interest in Irish Politics', pp. 255–6; Ormond to Coventry, 14 Oct. 1678 (Kings Inns, Prendergast papers, xi, pp. 456–8).

29. Ormond to Boyle, 8 Oct. 1678 (*HMC Ormonde*, ns, iv, p. 212).
30. Ormond to Southwell, 10 Oct. 1678 (*HMC Ormonde*, os, ii, p. 277).
31. Ormond to Southwell, 13 Oct. 1678 (*HMC Ormonde*, os, ii, p. 278).
32. Ormond to Longford, 15 Oct. 1678 (NLI MS 11,971, ff. 49–51).
33. Gilbert MS 207, f. 13.
34. Ormond to Southwell, 15 Oct. 1678 (*HMC Ormonde*, os, ii, p. 278).
35. Papers read before Lord's committee, 24, 30 Oct. 1678 (*HMC Rep. 11, app 2*, p. 17); *Lords jn. xiii*, pp. 303–4.
36. NLI MS 1,793, ff. 23–4.
37. [Luke Wadding] *A Small Garland of Pious and Godly Songs, Composed by a Devout Man* (Ghent, 1684), pp. 50–1.
38. Examination of Walter Harris, 17 Oct. 1678 (Carte, MS 38 f. 703).
39. Michael Boyle to Orrery, 28 Oct. 1678 (Edward MacLysaght, *Calendar of the Orrery Papers* (Dublin, 1941) p. 206).
40. Unknown to Sir John Ellis, 29 Oct. 1678 (BL Add MS 28, 930, ff. 129–30).
41. Anonymous deposition, 23 Oct. 1678 (Bodl., Carte MS 38, f. 715); Jeremiah Jones to Ormond, 12 Nov. 1678 (Bodl., Carte MS 38, f. 709); William Addis to Henry Benn, Lt. Richard Locke to Henry Benn, 30 Nov. 1678 (*HMC Ormonde*, ns, iv, p. 256).
42. John Shadwell to Ormond, 30 Nov. 1678 (*HMC Ormonde*, ns, iv, pp. 254–5).
43. Captain Robert Fitzgerald to Ormond, 7 Nov. 1678 (Bodl., Carte MS 214, f. 328).
44. Edward MacLysaght, *Irish Life in the Seventeenth Century* (Cork, 1950), pp. 273–4, 258–63.
45. Oral culture and the dissemination of news in Ireland have not been systematically studied. A useful model is Adam Fox, *Oral and Literate Culture in England, 1500–1700* (Oxford, 2000), pp. 335–405, while a classic and instructive account of the spread of rumour in a different context is Georges Lefebvre, *The Great Fear of 1789: Rural Panic in Revolutionary France* (London, 1973). For print culture in early modern Ireland, see Raymond Gillespie, *Reading Ireland: Print, Reading and Social Change in Early Modern Ireland* (Manchester, 2005).
46. NLI MS 1793, ff. 23–4, 26–7, 29–31; Steele, *Proclamations*, ii, pp. 114–16.
47. This discussion draws freely upon Hans-Joachim Neubauer, *The Rumour: A Cultural History* (London, 1999), and Nicholas DiFonzo and Prashant Bordia, *Rumor Psychology: Social and Organizational Approaches* (Washington DC, 2007).
48. Annabel Patterson *et al.* (eds), *The Prose Works of Andrew Marvell* (2 vols, New Haven, 2003), ii, pp. 179–377.
49. Carl F. Graumann and Serge Moscovici (eds), *Changing Conceptions of Conspiracy* (New York, 1987), p. 3. For specific historical case studies, see Barry Coward and Julian Swann (eds), *Conspiracies and Conspiracy Theory in Early Modern Europe: From the Waldensians to the French Revolution* (Aldershot, 2004).
50. Steele, *Proclamations*, i, p. 443; NLI MS 1,793, f. 26.
51. Burke, *Irish Priests in the Penal Times*, p. 52.

52. NLI MS 1,793, f. 27.
53. Ormond to Coventry, 5 Nov. 1678 (Kings Inns, Prendergast papers, xi, pp. 257–60).
54. Miller, *Popery and Politics in England*, pp. 162–9.
55. Williamson to Mayor of Chester, 9 Nov. 1678 (*HMC Rep. 8, app. 1, sec. 2*, 390b).
56. Depositions regarding Irish officers, 21 Nov. 1678 (*HMC Rep. 8, app. 1 sec. 2*, 391a).
57. Kenyon, *Popish Plot*, pp. 102–3; Grey, *Debates*, vi, p. 220.
58. NAUK PC 6/14, 17 (12 Nov. 1679).
59. David Dickson, *Old World Colony: Cork and South Munster, 1630–1830* (Cork: Cork University Press, 2006), pp. 46–52; Paul M. Kerrigan, 'Charles Fort, Kinsale', *The Irish Sword*, 13 (1979), pp. 323–9.
60. Orrery to Southwell, 1 Nov. 1678 (V & A, F.47.A.46, f. 35).
61. Ormond to Coventry, 10 Nov. 1678 (Kings Inns, Prendergast papers, xi, pp. 261–3).
62. Capt. Francis Hamond to Orrery, 11 Nov. 1678 (*HMC Ormonde*, ns, iv, p. 230); Josias Percival to Orrery, 11 Nov. 1678 (*HMC Ormonde*, ns, iv, pp. 230–1); Orrery to Percival and Hamond, 12 Nov. 1678 (*HMC Ormonde*, ns, iv, p. 232); Orrery to Southwell, 15 Nov. 1678 (V & A, F.47.A.46, f. 41); Orrery to Ormond, 16 Nov. 1678 (Kings Inns, Prendergast papers, xi, pp. 491–2).
63. Coventry to Ormond, 26 Nov. 1678 (*HMC Ormonde*, ns, iv, p. 245).
64. Orrery to Lt. Col. Meade, 28 Nov. 1678 (*HMC Ormonde*, ns, iv, pp. 245–6).
65. Ormond to Orrery, 26 Nov. 1678 (NLI MS 11,971, ff. 73–5).
66. Steele, *Proclamations*, i, p. 444; NLI MS 1793, f. 30.
67. Ossory to Ormond, 23 Oct. 1678 (*HMC Ormonde*, ns, iv, pp. 219–20).
68. Ormond to Southwell, 6 Nov. 1678 (*HMC Ormonde*, os, ii, p. 279).
69. Ormond to Capt. Mathew, 12 Nov. 1678 (*HMC Ormonde*, ns, iv, pp. 232–3).
70. Ormond to Southwell, 19 Nov. 1678 (*HMC Ormonde*, os, ii, p. 279).
71. Ormond to Wyche, 20 Nov. 1678 (*HMC Leybourne-Popham*, pp. 242–3).
72. Anglesey to Ormond, 23 Nov. 1678 (*HMC Ormonde*, ns, iv, pp. 242–3); Ormond to Anglesey, 29 Nov. 1678 (*HMC Ormonde*, ns, iv, pp. 251–3).
73. Kenyon, *The Popish Plot*, p. 105.
74. Wyche to Ormond, 26 Nov. 1678 (*HMC Ormonde*, ns, iv, pp. 244–5).
75. Ossory to Ormond, 26 Nov. 1678 (*HMC Ormonde*, ns, iv, pp. 243–4).
76. Orrery to Ormond, 22 Nov. 1678 (NAI Wyche papers, 1/1/25); 29 Nov. 1678 (*HMC Rep. 6, app*, p. 733–4); 3 Dec. 1678 (*HMC Ormonde*, ns, iv, pp. 260–2); 10 Dec. 1678 (*HMC Ormonde*, ns, iv, pp. 270–4); Orrery to Lord Lieutenant and Council, 6 Dec. 1678 (*HMC Ormonde*, ns, iv, pp. 262–4).
77. Orrery to Ormond, 29 Nov. 1678 (*HMC Rep. 6, app*, pp. 733–4).
78. Ormond to Southwell, 2 Dec. 1678 (*HMC Ormonde*, os, ii, p. 281); also Ormond to Southwell, 30 Nov. 1678 (*HMC Ormonde*, os, ii, pp. 279–81); Ormond to Ossory, 30 Nov. 1678 (*HMC Ormonde*, ns, iv, p. 254).
79. Ormond to Orrery, 23 Nov. 1678 (NLI MS 11,971, f. 69)

80. Ormond to Orrery, 26 Nov. 1678 (NLI MS 11,971, ff. 73–5)
81. Kenyon, *The Popish Plot*, p. 102.
82. J.T. Gilbert (ed.), *Calendar of the Ancient Records of Dublin in the Possession of the Municipal Corporation* (16 vols, Dublin, 1889–1913), v, p. 167); NLI MS 1793, f. 29; Arran to Wyche, 30 Nov. 1678 (NAI Wyche papers, 1/1/26).
83. Ormond to Ossory, 30 Nov. 1678 (*HMC Ormonde*, ns, iv, p. 254); Ormond to Ossory, 10 Dec. 1678 (Ibid., pp. 269–70).
84. Orrery to Malet, 10 Dec. 1678 (BL Add MS 32,095, f. 139).
85. Ormond to Wyche, 1 Dec. 1678 (NLI MS 4,846, f. 19).
86. Ormond to Southwell, 30 Nov. 1678 (*HMC Ormonde*, os, ii, pp. 279–81).
87. Ormond to Coventry, 4 Dec. 1678 (*HMC Ormonde*, ns, iv, p. 261); Ormond to Southwell, 7 Dec. 1678 (*HMC Ormonde*, os, ii, pp. 281–2).
88. Burke, *Irish Priests in the Penal Times*, pp. 52–65, 73–4.
89. Orrery to Ormond, 10 Dec. 1678 (*HMC Ormonde*, ns, iv, pp. 270–4).
90. Orrery to Malet, 3 Dec. 1678 (*HMC Rep. 5, app.*, p. 318).
91. *London Gazette*, 5–9 Dec. 1678.
92. Anthony Spilman to George Robens, 1 Nov. 1678 (*CSPD, 1678*, p. 500); same to same, 8 Nov. 1678 (*CSPD, 1678*, p. 509).
93. Ormond to Orrery, 7 Dec. 1678 (*HMC Ormonde*, ns, iv, pp. 265–8); Coventry to Ormond, 14 Jan. 1679 (*HMC Ormonde*, ns, iv, p. 303).
94. Ormond to Orrery, 17 Dec. 1678 (Bodl., Carte MS 70, ff. 525–6).
95. Ormond to Southwell, 18 Dec. 1678 (Bodl., Carte MS 39, f. 676).
96. Orrery to Malet, 14 Dec. 1678 (BL Add MS 32,095, ff. 146–7).
97. Wyche to Ormond, 10 Dec. 1678 (*HMC Ormonde*, ns, iv, p. 270); Ormond to Coventry, 18 Dec. 1678 (Bodl., Carte MS 146, p. 148); Ormond to Burlington, 21 Dec. 1678 (Bodl., Carte MS 70, ff. 529–30).
98. Orrery to Ormond, 17 Dec. 1678 (*HMC Ormonde*, ns, iv, p. 277).
99. NLI MS 1,793, f. 32.
100. Orrery to Malet, 27 Dec. 1678 (BL Add MS 32,095, ff. 143–5).
101. *London Gazette*, 26–30 Dec. 1678.
102. *A True and Perfect Account of the Discovery of a Barbarous & Bloody Plot Lately Carried on by the Jesuites in Ireland for the Destroying of the Duke of Ormond* (London, 1679), pp. 2–4.
103. *London Gazette*, 2–6 Jan. 1679.
104. Ormond to Orrery, 28 Dec. 1678 (NLI MS 11,971, f. 109).
105. Ormond to Orrery, 11 Jan. 1679 (*HMC Ormonde*, ns, iv, pp. 300–1).
106. Wyche to Ormond, 30 Nov. 1678 (*HMC Ormonde*, ns, iv, pp. 256–8); Testimony of Thomas Shadwell, 5 Dec. 1678 (*HMC Rep. 11, app. 2*, pp. 21–2); Resolution of Lords to King (Bodl., Carte MS 72, f. 422); *Lords jn.* xiii, p. 402.
107. Plunkett to John Brenan, 14 May 1670 (*Plunket letters*, pp. 84–7).
108. Kenyon, *The Popish Plot*, p. 120.
109. Information of Edmund Everard, 21 Dec. 1678 (*HMC Rep. 13, app. 6*, pp. 141–5). A slightly amended version of his testimony would be published c.April–May 1679, having been presented to the English House

of Commons: *The Depositions and Examinations of Mr Edmund Everard* (London, 1679).
110. Liam Chambers, *Michael Moore, c.1639–1725: Provost of Trinity, Rector of Paris* (Dublin, 2005), p. 37.
111. Grey, *Debates*, vi, p. 391.
112. Information of Miles Prance, 27 Dec. 1678 (*HMC Rep. 11, app. 2*, p. 52).
113. *Domestic Intelligence, or News Both from City and Country* 14 July 1679.
114. Kenyon, *The Popish Plot*, p. 111.
115. *Lords jn.*, xiii, pp. 437–9.
116. Ibid., p. 441. These allegations against 'Dominick Kelly' would also be reiterated in print: *A True Narrative of the Late Design of the Papists to Charge their Horrid Plot upon the Protestants* (London, 1679), pp. 6–7, 12.
117. *Lords jn*, xiii, pp. 500–1.
118. Information of Stephen Dugdale, 11 Jan. 1679 (Bodl., Carte MS 81, f. 488).
119. Deposition of Stephen Dugdale, 11 Jan. 1679 (*HMC Rep. 13 app. 6*, pp. 122–5).
120. Coventry to Ormond, 14 Jan. 1679 (*HMC Ormonde*, ns, iv, p. 303).
121. Information of William Brooke, 19 Jan. 1679 (*CSPD, 1679*, pp. 39–40)
122. Deposition of Stephen Dugdale, 31 Jan. 1679 (*HMC Rep. 13 app. 6*, p. 130).
123. Information of Stephen Dugdale, 11 Jan. 1679 (Bodl., Carte MS 81, ff. 488–91).
124. Information of Stephen Dugdale, 31 Jan. 1679 (*HMC Rep. 13, app. 6*, p. 130); Osmond Airy (ed.), *Burnet's History of My Own Time* (2 vols, Oxford, 1897–1900), ii, p. 195.
125. Jones, *First Whigs*, pp. 22–3.
126. *An Account of the Bloody Massacre in Ireland: Acted by the Instigation of the Jesuits, Priests, and Friars* (London, 1679). This was a reprint of the relevant sections of another tract: *A Looking Glass for England* (London, 1667). The pamphlet of 1678 was also reprinted in 1689, in an edition with depictions of torture and a brief account of the Spanish inquisition: *A Relation of the Bloody Massacre in Ireland, Acted by the Instigation of the Jesuits, Priests and Friars* (London, 1689).
127. *An Account of the Bloody Massacre in Ireland*, p. 4.
128. Ibid., p. 8.
129. Ibid., p. 5.
130. Ibid., p. 6.
131. Ibid., pp. 5–6.
132. Ibid., p. 5.
133. Ibid.
134. Ibid. This passage copies and paraphrases Temple, *The Irish Rebellion*, p. 104.
135. David Hayton, 'From barbarian to burlesque: English images of the Irish, c. 1660–1750.' *Irish Economic and Social History*, 15 (1988), pp. 5–31.
136. Harris, *Restoration*, pp. 146–52.

137. Andrew Carpenter (ed.), *Verse in English from Tudor and Stuart Ireland* (Cork, 2003), pp. 474–5.
138. Danby to Ormond, 30 Dec. 1678 (Bodl., Carte MS 118, f. 176); Ormond to Danby, 13 Jan. 1679 (Bodl., Carte MS 118, f. 178).
139. Ormond to unknown, 13 Jan. 1679 (NLI MS 11,971, f. 5); Ormond to Coventry, 16 Jan. 1679 (Bodl., Carte MS 146, p. 153).
140. NAUK PC 2/67, 69 (31 Jan. 1679).
141. Unknown to unknown, 5 Feb. 1679 (*CSPD 1679-80*, pp. 71–3); NLI MS 13,014.
142. Strafford to Ormond, 4 Feb. 1679 (*HMC Ormonde*, ns, iv, p. 318); Ormond to Southwell, 6 Nov. 1678 (*HMC Ormonde*, ns, iv, pp. 278–9).
143. Ormond to Orrery, 25 Jan. 1679 (*HMC Ormonde*, ns, iv, pp. 309–10).
144. Orrery to Ormond, 28 Jan. 1679 (*HMC Ormonde*, ns, iv, pp. 312–13).
145. Charles II to Ormond, 15 Jan. 1679 (*HMC Ormonde*, ns, iv, p. 401).
146. Ormond to Ossory, 14 Feb. 1679 (*HMC Ormonde*, ns, iv, pp. 323–4); Southwell to Ormond, 22 Feb. 1679 (*HMC Ormonde*, ns, iv, pp. 329–30).
147. Ormond to Longford, 3 Feb. 1679 (Bodl., Carte MS 81, f. 180).
148. Coventry to Ormond, 4 Feb. 1679 (*HMC Ormonde*, ns, iv, pp. 317–18), same to same, 11 Feb. 1679 (*HMC Ormonde*, ns, iv, p. 322); same to same, 28 Feb. 1679 (*HMC Ormonde*, ns, iv, p. 335); Brisbane to Coventry, 25 Feb. 1679 (*HMC Rep. 4, app*, p. 243).
149. Orrery to Boyle, 28 Feb. 1679 (*HMC Ormonde*, ns, iv, pp. 336–8).
150. Orrery to Primate Parker, 28 Feb. 1679 (BL Add MS 21,135, ff. 62–3).
151. Boyle to Orrery, 8 Mar. 1679 (*HMC Ormonde*, ns, iv, pp. 350–3).
152. Ormond to Coventry, 17 Feb. 1679 (Kings Inns, Prendergast papers, xi, pp. 267–9); Richard Aldworth to Ormond, 3 Mar. 1679 (*HMC Ormonde*, ns, iv, pp. 340–1).
153. Ormond to George Mathew, 1 Mar. 1679 (*HMC Ormonde*, ns, iv, p. 340).
154. Coventry to Ormond, 1 Mar. 1679 (*HMC Rep. 6, app*, p. 729); Ormond to Coventry, 17 Mar. 1679 (*HMC Rep. 6, app*, pp. 729–30); Ormond to Wyche, 7 Mar. 1679 (Bodl., Carte MS 70, f. 537).
155. Folger, Newdigate Newsletters: MS L.C. 755 (6 Mar. 1679).
156. Ormond to Lord Treasurer, 7 Mar. 1679 (NLI MS 11,971, ff. 5–6).
157. J. Brisbane to Danby, 19 Mar. 1679 (*HMC Rep. 14, app. 9*, pp. 403–4); Information of Matthew Fox, 19 Mar. 1679 (NAI Wyche papers, 1/1/31).
158. 'Anonymous accusations against Ormond', 20 Mar. 1679 (*HMC Ormonde*, ns, iv, pp. 361–4).
159. Ormond to Southwell, 20 Mar. 1679 (Carte, *Ormond*, v, p. 137); Ormond to Southwell, 20 Mar. 1679 (BL Add MS 21,484, ff. 29–30).
160. Ormond to Col. Edward Cooke, 20 Mar. 1679 (*HMC Rep. 6, app.*, p. 740).
161. Ormond to Ossory, 20 Mar. 1679 (*HMC Ormonde*, ns, iv, pp. 364–5).
162. Col Edward Cooke to Ormond, 22 Mar. 1679 (*HMC Ormonde*, ns, iv, pp. 368–71).
163. Ossory to Ormond, 22 Mar. 1679 (*HMC Ormonde*, ns, iv, pp. 366–7).
164. *Parliamentary Debates*, i, pp. 273–6; *Parl. Hist.*, iv, col. 1115–18; for Ossory's response, see Marshes Library, MS Z 3.1.1 f.116.
165. Ossory to Ormond, 25 Mar. 1679 (*HMC Ormonde*, ns, v, pp. 1–2).

166. Longford to Ormond, 29 Mar. 1679 (*HMC Ormonde*, ns, v, pp. 4–5); Wyche to Ormond, 29 Mar. 1679 (*HMC Ormonde*, ns, v, p. 5).
167. *Lords jn.*, xiii, pp. 488–91.
168. 'A narrative of the proceedings of the Lord Lieutenant and Council in Ireland since the intimation to them...of the plot in England', 31 Mar. 1679 (NLI Ormond MS 2,385, ff. 7–20) (printed in *HMC Ormonde*, ns, v, pp. 15–20); 'A narration of the proceedings', 5 Apr. 1679 (*HMC Ormonde*, os, ii, pp. 254–8); Ormond to Southwell, 18 Dec. 1678 (*HMC Ormonde*, os, ii, pp. 282–3); *An Account of the Publick Affairs in Ireland since the Discovery of the Late Plot* (London, 1679).
169. Titus Oates, *A True Narrative of the Horrid Plot and Conspiracy of the Popish Party Against the Life of His Sacred Majesty, the Government and the Protestant Religion* (London, 1679), p. 65.
170. NLI MS 1,793, f. 35; Steele, *Proclamations*, ii, p. 144.
171. *London Gazette*, 7–10 Apr. 1679; 10–14 Apr. 1679.
172. Ormond to Ossory, 31 Mar. 1679 (*HMC Ormonde*, ns, v, pp. 13–15); Ossory to Ormond, 5 Apr. 1679 (*HMC Ormonde*, ns, v, pp. 29–30); Ormond to Essex, 7 Apr. 1679 (*HMC Ormonde*, ns, v, pp. 33–4).
173. Grey, *Debates*, vii, p. 91.
174. Petty to Southwell, 8 Apr. 1679 (*Petty-Southwell Correspondence*, p. 73).
175. Peter Talbot to Ormond, 11 Apr. 1679 (Bodl., Carte MS 38, f. 693).
176. Burke, *Irish Priests in the Penal times*, p. 67.
177. Ibid.
178. George Rawdon to Conway, 8 Apr. 1679 (NAUK SP 63/339/9); Steele, *Proclamations*, ii, p. 114; *London Gazette*, 21–24 Apr. 1679.
179. Burke, *Irish Priests in the Penal times*, p. 68; Rawdon to Conway, 8 Apr. 1679 (NAUK SP 63/339/9); Order of Lord Lieutenant and Council, 11 April 1679 (Bodl., Carte MS 70, f. 541).
180. Richard Caulfield (ed.), *Autobiography of the Rt. Hon. Sir Richard Cox, Bart.* (London, 1860), p. 11.
181. Orrery to Southwell, 8 Apr. 1679 (BL Add MS 34,274, f. 140); Orrery to Malet, 8 Apr. 1679 (BL Add MS 32,095, f. 174).
182. J.D. Davies, 'More light on Irishmen in the Stuart Navy, 1660–90', *The Irish Sword*, xvi (1986), p. 326.
183. Ibid., 'The navy, parliament and political crisis in the reign of Charles II', *Historical Journal*, 36 (1993), pp. 275, 278, 280.
184. Cited in Davies, 'The navy, parliament and political crisis', p. 275.
185. Returns of Papists in the Inns of Court, Doctor's Commons, and Herald's College, 29 Mar. 1679 (*HMC Rep. 11 app. 2*, pp. 103–4).
186. *Lords jn.*, xiii, p. 491.
187. Ibid., p. 493.
188. Ibid., p. 499.
189. Ibid., pp. 518, 527–8.
190. NAUK PC 2/68, 59 (28 May 1679)
191. Primate Boyle to Lady Ranelagh, 14 Apr. 1679 (*HMC Rep 6., app.*, pp. 735–6)
192. Ossory to Ormond, 15 Apr. 1679 (*HMC Ormonde*, ns, v, pp. 45–9).

193. Longford to George Mathew, 15 Apr. 1679 (*HMC Ormonde*, ns, v, pp. 50–1); Ossory to Ormond, 15 Apr. 1679 (*HMC Ormonde*, ns, v, pp. 45–9).
194. Ossory to Lady Ormond, 19 Apr. 1679 (*HMC Ormonde*, ns, v, pp. 53–4).
195. Ossory to Ormond, 22 Apr. 1679 (*HMC Ormonde*, ns, v, pp. 54–5).
196. Information of Joanna Gourney, 8 May 1679 (Bodl., Carte MS 39, f. 57); information of James Gourney (Bodl., Carte MS 39, ff. 51–3).
197. Wyche to Ormond, 22 Apr. 1679 (*HMC Ormonde*, ns, v, pp. 58–9).
198. Col. Edward Cooke to Ormond, 15 Apr. 1679 (*HMC Ormonde*, ns, v, pp. 48–50); Memo to Arran, 17 Apr. 1679 (Bodl., Carte MS 39, ff. 89–91).
199. Ormond to Massareene, 26 Apr. 1679 (*HMC Ormonde*, ns, v, pp. 64–5).
200. Southwell to Ormond, 19 Apr. 1679 (*HMC Ormonde*, ns, iv, p. 504).
201. 'Considerations how the Protestants or non-Papists of Ireland may disable the Papists there both for intestine rebellion and also for assisting a French invasion... in the present year 1679', c. *CSPD 1679–80*, pp. 353–7; BL Add MS 72,852, ff. 170–1. This latter was sent to Southwell, and is dated 5 Aug. 1679.
202. Ted McCormick, 'Transmutation, inclusion and exclusion: political arithmetic from Charles II to William III', *Journal of Historical Sociology*, 20 (2007), pp. 62–4.
203. Petty to Southwell, 3 May 1679 (*Petty-Southwell Correspondence*, pp. 76–8).
204. Petty to Southwell, 10 June 1679 (*Petty-Southwell Correspondence*, pp. 78–9).
205. Orrery to Ormond, 2 May 1679 (*HMC Ormonde*, ns, v, pp. 77–8).
206. Rev. Christopher Vowell to Orrery, 5 May 1678 (*HMC Ormonde*, ns, v, pp. 81–2); Coventry to Ormond, 5 May 1679 (*HMC Ormonde*, ns, v, pp. 82–3); Col. Edward Cooke to Ormond, 10 May 1679 (*HMC Ormonde*, ns, v, pp. 88–91).
207. Conway to Sir George Rawdon, 3 May 1679 (*HMC Hastings*, ii, pp. 387–8).
208. Conway to Rawdon, 3 May 1679 (*HMC Hastings*, ii, pp. 387–8); 'A.B' to Ormond, 13 May 1679 (*HMC Ormonde*, ns, v, pp. 95–7); Coventry to Ormond, 17 May 1679 (*HMC Ormonde*, ns, v, pp. 105–6); Massareene to Ormond, 13 May 1679 (*HMC Ormonde*, ns, v, pp. 99–100); Privy Council to Lord Lieutenant, 21 May 1679 (*HMC Ormonde*, ns, v, pp. 112–13); Sir Robert Howard to Ormond, 15 May 1679 (*HMC Ormonde*, ns, v, p. 104); Ormond to Sir Robert Howard, 24 May 1679 (*HMC Ormonde*, ns, v, p. 113); Ormond to Shaftesbury, 25 May 1679 (*HMC Leybourne-Popham*, pp. 244–5).
209. Sean Egan, 'Finance and the government of Ireland, 1660–85' (Ph.D, Trinity College, Dublin, 2 vols, 1983), ii, pp. 99–103; Jones, *The First Whigs*, p. 38.
210. Steele, *Proclamations*, ii, p. 114.
211. *A form of prayer to be used on Wednesday the 28th of May* (Dublin, 1679), A 3r.
212. Plunkett to Cerri, 15 May 1679 (Hanly, *Plunkett letters*, pp. 529–31).

3 Institutions and the 'Irish Plot', May 1679–November 1680

1. NAUK PC/2/68, 53 (23 May 1679).
2. Ormond to Sunderland, 3 June 1679 (*HMC Ormonde*, ns, v, pp. 120–1); NAUKPC2/68, 110 (7 June 1679).
3. Boyle to Ormond, 14 June 1679 (*HMC Ormonde*, ns, v, p. 131).
4. Ormond to unknown, 17 June 1679 (Bodl., Carte MS 146, p. 188); Michael Boyle to Orrery, 14 June 1679 (*Orrery papers*, p. 211).
5. 18 June 1679, BL Add MS 28,930, f. 139; Michael Boyle to Orrery, 24 June 1679 (*Orrery papers*, p. 212).
6. 'Letter to a friend', 25 June 1679 (Bodl., Carte MS 45, ff. 431–4); Petition to Ormond, 25 June 1679 (Bodl., Carte MS 45, f. 529).
7. *c.*24 June 1679 (*Calendar of Ancient Records of Dublin*, v, p. 177).
8. Sir Philip Percival to Southwell, 27 June 1679 (*HMC Egmont*, ii, p. 82); Steele, *Proclamations*, ii, p. 115; R.M. Young, 'News from Ireland: being the examination and confession of William Kelso, *c.*1679', *Ulster Journal of Archaeology*, ser. 2, vol. 2 (July 1896), pp. 274–9; Ormond to Rawdon, 26 June 1679 (*Rawdon Papers*, pp. 262–3).
9. NAUK PC2/68, 110 (7 June 1679).
10. Ormond to Essex, 1 July 1679 (NLI MS 802, f. 11).
11. Ormond to Southwell, 2 July 1679 (V & A, F.47.A.40, f. 55).
12. Knights, *Politics and Opinion in Crisis*, pp. 56–8.
13. Sir Nicholas L'Estrange to John Perceval, 7 June 1679 (*HMC Egmont*, ii, p. 82).
14. NAUK PC 2/68, 141 (23 June 1679); NAUK PC 2/68, 174 (11 July 1679); 'Testimony of Mr Gurner', 10 Nov. 1679 (Bodl., Carte MS 243, f. 343).
15. NAUK PC 2/68, 183 (24 July 1679).
16. Doyle, 'Ormond', pp. 86–106.
17. Orrery to Essex, 24 June 1679 (BL Stowe MS 212, f. 356). Orrery to Essex, 7 July 1679 (BL Stowe MS 212, ff. 361, 363–8); Ossory to Ormond, 8 July 1679 (*HMC Ormonde*, ns, v, p. 152).
18. Privy Council to Ormond, 11 July 1679 (Bodl., Carte MS 39, f. 738; *CSPD 1679–80*, pp. 196–7).
19. *State trials*, vii, col. 321.
20. Ibid., col. 327–8.
21. Ibid., col. 631.
22. Ibid., viii, cols. 327–8, 631.
23. Coventry to Ormond, 17 May 1679 (BL Add MS 25,125, ff. 65–8).
24. Ormond to Burlington, 15 July 1679 (*HMC Ormonde*, ns, v, p. 155).
25. Ormond to Coventry, 17 July 1679 (Kings Inns, Prendergast papers, xi, pp. 452–4); Coventry to Ormond, 25 July 1679 (*HMC Ormonde*, ns, v, p. 163).
26. Longford to Arran, 22 July 1679 (*HMC Ormonde*, ns, v, pp. 159–60).
27. Longford to Ormond, 5 Aug. 1679 (*HMC Ormonde*, ns, v, pp. 167–9); Coventry to Ormond, 30 Aug. 1679 (*HMC Ormonde*, ns, v, p. 196); NAUK PC2/68, 182 (24 July 1679).

28. Nicholas Armourer to Arran, 8 Aug. 1679 (Bodl., Carte MS 39, ff. 64–5); Arlington to Ormond, 8 Aug. 1679 (*HMC Ormonde*, ns, v, p. 175); Coventry to Ormond, 9 Aug. 1679 (*HMC Ormonde*, ns, v, pp. 177–8).
29. Ormond to Arran, 12 Aug. 1679 (*HMC Ormonde*, ns, v, p. 178).
30. Boyle to Ormond, 12 Aug. 1679 (*HMC Ormonde*, ns, v, pp. 178–81); Rawdon to Conway, 13 Aug. 1679 (*CSPD 1679–80*, pp. 218–19).
31. Ormond to unknown, 26 Aug. 1679 (NLI MS 802 ff. 3–4).
32. Unknown to Arran, 24 Sept. 1679 (Bodl., Carte MS 39, f. 68); Ossory to Ormond, 23 Sept. 1679 (*HMC Ormonde*, ns, v, pp. 212–13).
33. Longford to Ormond, 2 Sept. 1679 (*HMC Ormonde*, ns, v, pp. 196–7).
34. Coventry to Ormond, 18 Sept. 1679 (*HMC Ormonde*, ns, v, pp. 208–10).
35. *Domestic Intelligence*, 14 July 1679; Ibid., 23 Sept. 1679.
36. NAUK PC2/68, 206 (19 Sept. 1679).
37. Rawdon to Conway, 14 Sept. 1679 (*CSPD 1679–80*, pp. 241–2; NAUK SP 63/339/35).
38. Ormond to Bishop of Limerick, 7 Sept. 1679 (*HMC Ormonde*, ns, v, pp. 199–200); Ormond to Michael Boyle, 21 Sept. 1679 (*HMC Ormond*, ns, v, p. 212).
39. 'The examination of Eustace Comyn', 28 Sept. 1679 (*CSPD 1679–80*, p. 254).
40. 'Domestick intelligence', 2 Sept. 1679 (*CSPD, 1679–80*, pp. 234–5).
41. *A True and Perfect Narrative of the Manner and Circumstance of Apprehending that Notorious Irish Priest, Daniel Mac-Carte* (London, nd), p. 2.
42. Proclamation, 8 Sept. 1679 (*CSPD, 1679–80*, p. 238); *London Gazette*, 8–11 Sept. 1679.
43. *Domestic Intelligence*, 3 Oct. 1679.
44. 'Warrant to Captain Thomas Fitzgerald', 12 Nov. 1679 (*HMC Ormonde*, ns, v, p. 236).
45. Granard to Conway, 30 Sept. 1679 (*CSPD 1679–80*, pp. 254–5).
46. Capt. Henry Ball to Conway, 2 Oct. 1679 (*CSPD 1679–80*, p. 256).
47. Ormond to chief magistrate of Lisburn, 25 Oct. 1679 (*Rawdon Papers*, p. 264).
48. Order for arrest, 17 Oct. 1679 (Bodl., Carte MS 38, f. 522); Ormond to Ossory, 18 Oct. 1679 (*HMC Ormonde*, ns, v, pp. 223–4).
49. *Domestic Intelligence*, 14 Oct. 1679.
50. Ossory to Ormond, 18 Oct. 1679 (*HMC Ormonde*, ns, v, pp. 224–5).
51. Coventry to Ormond, 28 Oct. 1679 (*HMC Ormonde*, ns, v, p. 231).
52. York to Hyde, 25 Sept. 1679 (BL Add MS 15,892, ff. 83–4).
53. Ormond to Coventry, 30 Oct. 1679 (*HMC Ormonde*, ns, v, pp. 231–2).
54. Ormond to Hamilton, 28 Oct. 1679 (*HMC Ormonde*, ns, v, p. 231).
55. Ormond to Southwell, 8 Nov. 1679 (V & A, F.47.A.40, ff. 65–6).
56. *Domestic Intelligence*, 12 Dec. 1679.
57. Ormond to Ossory, 18 Oct. 1679 (*HMC Ormonde*, ns, v, pp. 223–4).
58. *Domestic Intelligence*, 16 Dec. 1679.
59. *A Full and True Relation of a New Hellish Popish Plot in Ireland, Carried on by the Papists in the Province of Munster* (London, 1679).
60. Ormond to Southwell, 9 Nov. 1679 (V & A, F.47.A.40, f. 67).

61. Ormond to Southwell, 11 Nov. 1679 (V & A, F.47.A.40, f. 69).
62. NAUK PC 2/68, 291 (28 Nov. 1679).
63. Ormond to unknown, 30 Nov. 1679 (NLI MS 802, f.6r).
64. Ormond to Southwell, 1 Dec. 1679 (V & A, F.47.A.40, f . 75).
65. Coventry to Ormond, 7 Dec. 1679 (*HMC Ormonde*, ns, v, p. 249).
66. Anglesey Diary, 6 Dec. 1679 (BL Add MS 18,730, f. 63).
67. Ranelagh to Conway, 5 Dec. 1679 (*CSPD 1679–80*, pp. 299–300).
68. Egan, 'Finance and the government of Ireland', ii, pp. 104–5, 107–9.
69. Ormond to unknown, 10 Dec. 1679 (NLI MS 802, f. 7).
70. Ranelagh to Conway, 13 Dec. 1679 (*CSPD 1679–80*, p. 311).
71. Ossory to Ormond, 13 Dec. 1679 (*HMC Ormonde*, ns, v, p. 253).
72. Cited in Harris, *Restoration*, p. 383.
73. Ormond to Southwell, 14 Dec. (V & A, F.47.A.40, f . 79).
74. *Domestic Intelligence*, 6 Jan. 1680.
75. John Napper to Farmers of the Customs, 19 Nov. 1679 (*HMC Ormonde*, ns, v, p. 240); Capt. John Lockhart to Ormond, 22 Nov. 1679 (*HMC Ormonde*, ns, v, pp. 240–1); Ormond to Southwell, 26 Nov. 1679 (BL Add MS 21,484, ff. 54–5); Ormond to Mayor of Waterford, 25 Nov. 1679 (*HMC Ormonde*, ns, v, pp. 242–3); Ormond to Sir Stephen Fox, 26 Nov. 1679 (*HMC Ormonde*, ns, v, p. 243); Ormond to Major Halkett, 2 Dec. 1679 (*HMC Ormonde*, ns, v, pp. 246–7).
76. Ossory to Ormond, 29 Nov. 1679 (*HMC Ormonde*, ns, v, pp. 243–4)
77. *Protestant (Domestick) Intelligence*, 23 Jan. 1680.
78. Information of Jane Palmer, 18 Dec. 1679 (*HMC Rep. 11, app 2*, p. 148); *Domestic Intelligence*, 6 Jan. 1680.
79. Coventry to Ormond, 31 Dec. 1679 (*HMC Ormonde*, ns, v, p. 260).
80. Ranelagh to Conway, 27 Dec. 1679 (*CSPD 1679–80*, pp. 316–18).
81. Ormond to unknown, 27 Jan. 1680 (NLI MS 802, f. 8).
82. Francis Gwyn to Conway, 27 Jan. 1680 (*CSPD 1679–80*, pp. 377–8).
83. Lanesborough to Ossory, 28 Jan. 1680 (*HMC Ormonde*, ns, v, p. 268).
84. Ormond to unknown, 3 Mar. 1680 (NLI MS 802, f. 10).
85. Francis Gwyn to Ormond, 6 Mar. 1680 (*HMC Ormonde*, ns, v, p. 286).
86. Massareene to Conway, 9 Mar. 1680 (*CSPD 1679–80*, p. 414); NAUK PC2/68, 425 (9 Mar. 1679).
87. Ranelagh to Conway, 13 Mar. 1680 (*CSPD 1679–80*, p. 416)
88. Rawdon to Conway, 20 Mar. 1680 (*CSPD 1679–80*, pp. 419–20); Charles II to Ormond, 22 Mar. 1680 (*CSPD 1679–80*, p. 421).
89. *London Gazette*, 11–15 Dec. 1679.
90. Burke, *Irish priests in the Penal times*, p. 80.
91. Plunkett to Tanari, 17 Jan. 1680 (Hanly, *Plunkett letters*, pp. 539–44).
92. Tanari to Secretariate of State, 20 Jan. 1680 (*Nunziatura di Fiandri*, ii, p. 74).
93. Plunkett to Tanari, 19 Jan. 1680 (Hanly, *Plunkett letters*, pp. 544–6); same to same, 24 June 1680 (Hanly, *Plunkett letters*, pp. 547–8).
94. Ormond to unknown, 13 Jan. 1680 (Bodl., Carte MS 146, pp. 239–41).
95. NAUK PC 2/68, 382 (6 Feb. 1680).
96. NAUK PC 2/68, 398 (20 Feb. 1680).

97. 'Instructions for A.B. (Egan alias Fitzgerald)', 19 Feb. 1680 (*CSPD, 1679–80*, pp. 394–5); Shannon to Sunderland, 10 Apr. 1680 (*CSPD, 1679–80*, p. 435).
98. K.H.D. Haley, *The First Earl of Shaftesbury* (Oxford, 1968), pp. 539, 570–1; Doyle, 'Ormond', pp. 46, 128.
99. *Protestant (Domestick) Intelligence*, 23 Mar. 1680; Newsletter to Christopher Bowman, 25 Mar. 1680 (*CSPD, 1679–80*, pp. 423–4); *The True News: or, Mercurius Anglicus*, 24–8 Mar. 1680.
100. *The Protestant (Domestick) Intelligence, or, News Both from City and Country*. 2 Apr. 1680; 6 Apr. 1680.
101. Coventry to Ormond, 21 Feb. 1680 (*HMC Ormonde*, ns, v, p. 278).
102. Ormond to unknown, 9 Mar. 1680 (Bodl., Carte MS 146, p. 248).
103. Haley, *Shaftesbury*, pp. 566–70.
104. Coventry to Ormond, 2 Apr. 1680 (*HMC Ormonde*, ns., v, p. 295).
105. Haley, *Shaftesbury*, p. 570.
106. 'The information of William Hetherington of Ganderstown in the county of Louth', 23 Mar. 1680 (NAUK, Shaftesbury Papers 30/24/50 f. 163).
107. NAUK PC 2/68, 454 (24 Mar. 1680). A list of members of the Irish Privy Council (presumably written before Orrery's death in October 1679) contained in Shaftesbury's papers assessed their level of zeal for Protestantism. Orrery, Conway, Hans Hamilton, Henry Ingoldsby and Theophilus Jones were all assumed to be 'zealous', whilst Granard, Henry Jones and Massareene were deemed 'very zealous': NAUK, Shaftesbury papers 30/24/50 f. 163.
108. *Protestant (Domestick) Intelligence*, 2 Apr. 1680; 6 Apr. 1680; Newsletter to Christopher Bowman, 30 Mar. 1680 (*CSPD, 1679–80*, pp. 426–7).
109. Francis Gwyn to Ormond, 3 Apr. 1680 (*HMC Ormonde*, ns, v, pp. 296–7).
110. Folger, Newdigate Newsletters: MS L.C. 919–20 (1–3 April 1680).
111. Massareene to Conway, 23 Mar. 1680 (*CSPD 1679–80*, pp. 421–2).
112. Ossory to Ormond, 6 Apr. 1680 (*HMC Rep. 7, app.*, p. 738).
113. Ibid., 10 Apr. 1680 (*HMC Rep. 7, app.*, p. 738).
114. Ormond to Ossory, 10 Apr. 1680 (*HMC Ormonde*, ns, v, pp. 298–9).
115. Ibid., 12 Apr. 1680 (*HMC Ormonde*, ns, v, pp. 302–3).
116. Ormond to Coventry, 10 Apr. 1680 (*HMC Ormonde*, ns, v, pp. 299–300).
117. Daniel Hignott to Sir John Perceval, 23 Apr. 1680 (*HMC Egmont*, ii, p. 94); Éamonn Ó Ciardha, 'Toryism and Rappareeism in county Armagh in the late seventeenth century' in A.J Hughes and William Nolan (eds), *Armagh: History & Society: Interdisciplinary Essays on the History of an Irish County* (Dublin, 2001).
118. Steele, *Proclamations*, ii, p. 116.
119. Ormond to Ossory, 27 Apr. 1680 (*HMC Ormonde*, ns, v, pp. 312–13).
120. Ormond to unknown, 12 Apr. 1680 (Bodl., Carte MS 146, pp. 255–6); Ormond to Sunderland, 23 Nov. 1680 (*HMC Ormonde*, ns, v, p. 500); Breandán Ó Buachalla (ed.), *Nua-Dhuanaire, Cuid II* (Dublin, 1976), pp. 55–6.

121. P.G. Murray, 'A previously unnoticed letter of Oliver Plunkett' in *Seanchas Ard Mhacha*, 8 (1975–76), pp. 23–33.
122. Ormond to Ossory, 27 Apr. 1680 (*HMC Ormonde*, ns, v, pp. 312–13).
123. Ossory to Ormond, 30 Apr. 1680 (*HMC Rep. 7, app.*, p. 738).
124. Tanari to Secretariate of State, 27 Apr. 1680 (*Nunziatura di Fiandra*, ii, p. 75).
125. Walter Love, 'Civil War in Ireland: Appearances in three centuries of historical writing', *Emory University Quarterly*, 22 (1966), pp. 57–72; T.C. Barnard, 'The uses of 23 October 1641 and Irish Protestant celebrations'; Aidan Clarke, 'The 1641 rebellion and anti-popery in Ireland' in Brian MacCuarta (ed.) *Ulster 1641: Aspects of the Rising* (2nd ed., Belfast, 1997), pp. 139–57; Iain Donovan, 'Bloody news from Ireland': The pamphlet literature of the Irish massacres of the 1640s' (M.Litt, Trinity College, Dublin, 1995); Shagan, 'Constructing discord'; Noonan, 'The cruell pressure of an enraged, barbarous people'; Tom O'Gorman, '"Occurrences from Ireland': Contemporary pamphlet reactions to the Confederate war, 1641–1649"' (M.Litt, University College Dublin, 1999); Joseph Cope, 'Fashioning victims: Dr Henry Jones and the plight of Irish Protestants, 1642', *Historical Research* 74 (2001), pp. 370–91.
126. Francis Gwyn to Ormond, 23 Mar. 1680 (*HMC Ormonde*, ns, v, p. 422).
127. William Ellis to Cyril Wyche, 17 Mar. 1680 (NAI Wyche Papers, 1/1/33).
128. Conway to Sir Edward Harley, 10 Apr. 1680 (*HMC Rep. 14, app. 2*, p. 365).
129. Ormond to Wyche, 14 Apr. 1680 (NLI MS 803 f. 34); Ormond to Ossory, 14 Apr. 1680 (*HMC Ormonde*, ns, v, p. 303).
130. Anonymous, 10 Apr. 1680 (*HMC Ormonde*, ns, v, p. 302).
131. Ormond to Coventry, 14 Apr. 1680 (*HMC Ormonde*, ns, v, pp. 304–5).
132. NAUK PC/2/68, 474 (14 Apr. 1680); Ormond to unknown, 17 Apr. 1680 (Bodl., Carte MS 146, pp. 260–1); Ormond to Ossory, 19 April 1680 (*HMC Ormonde*, ns, v, p. 308).
133. Ormond to unknown, 22 Apr. 1680 (Bodl., Carte MS 146, pp. 262–4).
134. Ibid., 1 May 1680 (Bodl., Carte MS 146, p. 267).
135. Secretary Jenkins to Sunderland, 7 May 1680 (*CSPD 1679–80*, p. 467).
136. Jenkins to Sunderland, 7 May 1680 (*CSPD, 1679–80*, p. 467).
137. Francis Gwyn to Ormond, 8 May 1680 (*HMC Ormonde*, ns, v, pp. 314–15).
138. *The True News: or, Mercurius Anglicus*, 12–15 May 1680.
139. Haley, *Shaftesbury*, p. 575.
140. Ossory to Ormond, 8 May 1680 (*HMC Ormonde*, ns, v, p. 315).
141. Doyle, 'Ormond', pp. 134–40.
142. Jenkins to Ormond, 14 May 1680 (*CSPD, 1679–80*, pp. 478–9; NAUK PC 2/68/510–11); *London Gazette*, 13–17 May 1680.
143. Ossory to Ormond, 21 May 1680 (*HMC Ormonde*, ns, v, 324).
144. *The Narrative of Mr John Fitzgerald, Late of the Order of St. Francis in the Kingdom of Ireland* (London, 1681). The frontispiece of this work claimed that it contained 'several things relating to the Irish plot, managed by Plunkett'. However, the text itself dealt with ostensible attempts to undermine the credibility of Oates and Tonge in which at least one dubious Irishman was involved: but it made no reference

to any 'Irish Plot', or indeed to Fitzgerald's own attempts to provide evidence to prove its existence.
145. NAUK, Shaftesbury papers 30/24/50, f. 163.
146. Ormond to Ossory, 25 May 1680 (*HMC Ormonde*, ns, v, p. 327).
147. Ormond to Jenkins, 23 May 1680 (*CSPD, 1679–80*, p. 491); NAUK PC 2/68, 530–1 (26 May 1680).
148. MacMoyer to Hetherington, 1 June 1680 (Bodl., Carte MS 39, f. 140); Ó Fiaich, 'The fall and return of John MacMoyer', passim.
149. 'News from Brussels', 8 June 1680 (*Nunziatura di Fiandri*, ii, 76).
150. Jones to Mansell, 1 June 1680 (Bodl., Carte MS 39, ff. 142–3).
151. Mansell to Jones, 15 June 1680 (Bodl., Carte MS 39, ff. 146–7).
152. Jones to Mansell, 3 July 1680 (Bodl., Carte MS 39, f. 154v); MacMoyer to Hetherington, 2 July 1680 (Bodl., Carte MS 39, ff. 154r–55).
153. Jones to Mansell, 10 July 1680 (Bodl., Carte MS 243, f. 477).
154. Ormond to Southwell, 11 Nov. 1679 (V & A, F.47.A.40, f. 69). Copies of the various testimonies relating to the accusations against Tyrone are retained in Jones' papers: TCD MS 844, ff. 233–8.
155. Ossory to unknown, 20 July 1680 (Bodl., Carte MS 39, f. 164).
156. NAUK PC 2/69, 43 (21 July 1680); Francis Gwyn to Ormond, 24 July 1680 (*HMC Ormonde*, ns., v, pp. 352–3).
157. Ormond to Jenkins, 16 May 1680 (*CSPD 1679–80*, p. 482).
158. Ormond to unknown, *c*. July 1680 (Bodl., Carte MS 146, pp. 286–92).
159. Netterville to Longford, *c*. July 1680 (*HMC Ormonde*, ns, v, pp. 350–1).
160. Ormond to Cork, 24 July 1680 (*HMC Ormonde*, ns, v, p. 353).
161. Sunderland to Lord President of Council, 28 July 1680 (*CSPD, 1679–80*, p. 577).
162. King to Lord Lieutenant, 3 July 1680 (*CSPD, 1679–80*, p. 538).
163. Lords of Council to Lord Lieutenant, 13 Aug. 1680 (*CSPD, 1679–80*, p. 603); NAUK PC2/69, 69 (13 Aug. 1680).
164. 'Two papers brought by Lord Granard', 5 Aug. 1680 (*CSPD, 1679–80*, pp. 589–91).
165. Francis Gwyn to Ormond, 14 Aug. 1680 (*HMC Ormonde*, ns, v, pp. 379–81).
166. NAUK PC2/69, 72–3 (18 Aug. 1680).
167. Longford to Ormond, 17 Aug. 1680 (*HMC Ormonde*, ns, v, pp. 381–4).
168. Shaen to Privy Council, 18 Aug. 1680 (*CSPD 1679–80*, pp. 611–15).
169. Jenkins to Ormond, 21 Aug. 1680 (*HMC Ormonde*, ns, v, p. 386).
170. Longford to Ormond, 21 Aug. 1680 (*HMC Ormonde*, ns, v, pp. 388–91).
171. Ormond to Arlington, 23 Aug. 1680 (*HMC Ormonde*, ns, v, p. 392).
172. BL Add MS 28,930, f. 157.
173. Gwyn to Ormond, 24 Aug. 1680 (*HMC Ormonde*, ns, v, pp. 393–4).
174. Longford to Ormond, 24 Aug. 1680 (*HMC Ormonde*, ns, v, pp. 394–7).
175. Ormond to Longford, 25 Aug. 1680 (*HMC Ormonde*, ns, v, p. 398).
176. Gilbert MS 207, ff. 13–14.
177. Egan, 'Finance and the government of Ireland', ii, pp. 112–17.
178. Longford to Ormond, 31 Aug. 1680 (*HMC Ormonde*, ns, v, p. 403).
179. R. Mulyse to Sir John Ellis, 3 Sept. 1680 (BL Add MS 28,875, f. 124)

180. Ormond to Jenkins, 1 Sept. 1680 (*CSPD, 1680–1*, pp. 1–2).
181. Ormond to Coventry, 1 Sept. 1680 (*HMC Ormonde*, ns, v, p. 404).
182. Ormond to Thomas Sheridan, 1 Sept. 1680 (*HMC Ormonde*, ns, v, pp. 408–9).
183. Boyle to Ormond, 4 Sept. 1680 (*HMC Ormonde*, ns, v, p. 413).
184. Ormond to Wyche, 25 Sept. 1680 (*HMC Ormonde*, ns, v, pp. 433–4).
185. Newsletter to Roger Garstell, 25 Sept. 1680 (*CSPD, 1680–81*, pp. 39–40).
186. Folger, Newdigate Newsletters: MS L.C. 978 (31 Aug. 1680).
187. Longford to Ormond, 5 Oct. 1680 (*HMC Ormonde*, ns, v, pp. 439–40); BL Add MS 28,875, f. 134.
188. Bishop of Exeter to Sancroft, 11 Oct. 1680 (Charles McNeill (ed.), *The Tanner Letters* (Dublin, 1943) p. 429).
189. John Odell to Gerald Fitzgerald, 11 Oct. 1680 (*HMC Ormonde*, ns, v, pp. 444–5).
190. 'Examination of David Nash before Lord Lieutenant and Privy Council', 16 Oct. 1680 (*HMC Ormonde*, ns, v, pp. 452–4).
191. Arran to Ormond, 9 Nov. 1680 (*HMC Ormonde*, ns, v, pp. 483–4).
192. Longford to Ormond, 30 Oct. 1680 (*HMC Ormonde*, ns, v, pp. 467–8).
193. Ormond to Burlington, 31 Oct. 1680 (*HMC Ormonde*, ns, v, pp. 470–1).
194. Ormond to Conway, 1 Nov. 1680 (*HMC Ormonde*, ns, v, pp. 471–2).
195. Ormond to Arran, 7 Nov. 1680 (*HMC Ormonde*, ns, v, p. 483).
196. Jenkins to Sidney Godolphin, 17 Sept. 1680 (*CSPD, 1680–1*, pp. 23–4); Longford to Ormond, 18 Sept. 1680 (*HMC Ormonde*, ns, v, pp. 427–32)
197. Jenkins to Godolphin, 29 Sept. 1680 (*CSPD, 1680–1*, p. 31).
198. NAUK PC2/69, 109 (22 Sept. 1680).
199. Longford to Ormond, 28 Sept. 1680 (*HMC Ormonde*, ns, v, p. 438).
200. Jenkins to Godolphin, 28 Sept. 1680 (*CSPD, 1680–1*, pp. 42–3).
201. Sunderland to Ormond, 6 Oct. 1680 (*CSPD, 1680–1*, p. 54); NAUK PC2/69, 117 (1 Oct. 1680). For Geogheghan see Burke, *Irish Priests in the Penal Times*, pp. 71–3. There was also a 'Dalton' mentioned as a witness, but this also seems to have a pseudonym attributed to Geoghegan. It seems likely that these were the same individual, but this remains unresolved: 'Conspiracy in Ireland', 8 Nov. 1680 (*HMC Rep. 11, app. 2*, pp. 146–7).
202. 'Newsletter to Roger Garstell', 16 Oct. 1680 (*CSPD, 1680–1*, pp. 61–2).
203. Sunderland to Ormond, 6 Oct. 1680 (*CSPD, 1680–1*, p. 54); Ormond to Sunderland, 17 Oct. 1680 (*HMC Ormonde*, ns, v, pp. 454–5); NAUK PC2/69, 135 (27 Oct. 1680).
204. Jenkins to Ormond, 23 Oct. 1680 (*CSPD 1680–1*, p. 68).
205. Orrery to Dowager Countess of Orrery, 22 Oct. 1680 (*Orrery papers*, p. 237).
206. Benson to Sir John Ellis, 19 Oct 1680 (BL Add MS 28,875, f. 143).
207. *Lords jn.*, xiii, p. 619.
208. 'A new narrative of the Popish Plot' (1680) in Walter Scott (ed.), *A Collection of Scarce and Valuable Tracts Belonging to the Late Lord Somors* (13 vols, London, 1809–15), viii, 63–4.
209. *Parl. Hist.*, iv, col. 1166–7.

210. Francis Gwyn to Ormond, 26 Oct. 1680 (*H.M.C. Ormonde*, new ser., v, pp. 460–1); NAUK PC2/69, 135 (27 Oct. 1680); *Lords jn.*, xiii, pp. 622, 629.
211. *Lord jn.*, xiii, p. 626; NAUK PC2/69, 136 (29 Oct. 1680).
212. Unknown to Sir John Ellis, 2 Nov. 1680 (BL Add MS 28,875, f. 146).

4 Irish Evidence, November 1680

1. *Burnet's History of My Own Time*, ii, pp. 291–2. For Kenyon, the informers were 'a parade of loathsome Irish...they were all "wogs" (*The Popish Plot*, p. 204), whereas Jones observed that 'the witnesses who came over from Ireland were despised bog-trotters and thoroughly contemptible in their characters' (*The First Whigs*, p. 187).
2. *Burnet's History of My Own Time*, ii, p. 292.
3. *Parl. Hist.*, iv, col. 1182.
4. *Lords jn.*, xiii, p. 633.
5. Ibid., pp. 634–8.
6. Ibid., p. 635. On the suggestions of Charles I's alleged involvement in the rebellion, see Michael Perceval-Maxwell, *The Outbreak of the Irish Rebellion of 1641* (Dublin, 1994), pp. 218–19; Canny, *Making Ireland British*, pp. 517–18.
7. *Lords jn.*, xiii, p. 635.
8. Ibid.
9. John J. Hanly, 'Saint Oliver Plunkett 1625–1681' in Hughes and Nolan (eds.), *Armagh*, p. 449.
10. *Lords jn.*, xiii, p. 636.
11. Ibid., p. 637.
12. For MacMoyer's career, see Ó Fiaich, 'The fall and return of John Mac-Moyer.' For his previous allegations against Plunkett, see *HMC Rep. 6, app.*, p. 744.
13. *Lords jn.*, xiii, p. 638.
14. Ibid., pp. 642–3.
15. Ibid., p. 638.
16. 'Examination of Hubert Boark', 18 Mar. 1679 (BL, Add MS 37,772, f. 5); 'Examination of Rt. Hon. Richard, earl of Tyrone', 20 Mar. 1679 (BL Add MS 37,772, f. 6).
17. *Lords jn.*, xiii, pp. 639–41.
18. F.E. Ball, *The Judges in Ireland, 1221–1921* (2 vols, London, 1926), ii, p. 290.
19. *Lords jn.*, xiii, p. 644.
20. Ibid., pp. 644–7.
21. Ibid., p. 645; Report on petition of John Fitzgerald, 31 Mar. 1680 (*CSPD, 1679–80*, p. 427).
22. *Lords jn.*, xiii, p. 647.
23. Ibid., pp. 647–8.
24. Ibid., p. 648.

25. Ibid., pp. 650–2.
26. Ibid., p. 650.
27. Ibid., p. 651.
28. *A Full and True Relation of a New Hellish Popish Plot in Ireland, carried on by the Papists in the Province of Munster* (London, 1679).
29. Harold Love, 'The look of news: Popish Plot narratives, 1678–80' in John Barnard and D.F. McKenzies (eds.) with Maureen Bell, *The Cambridge History of the Book in Britain, vol iv: 1557–1695* (Cambridge, 2002), p. 653.
30. Love, 'The look of news', p. 655.
31. James Carrol, *A Narrative of the Popish Plot in Ireland, for the Murdering the Protestants There* (London, 1681), A 3.
32. Hugh Fenning, 'Sir Cyril Wyche and the Popish Plot, 1678–80' in *Seanchas Ard Mhacha*, 19 (2003), pp. 53–62.
33. *The Present State and Condition of Ireland, but More Especially the Province of Ulster, Humbly Represented to the Kingdom of England by Edmund Murphy* (London, 1681); *Lords jn.*, xiii, p. 709; 'Conspiracy in Ireland', 8 Nov. 1680 (*HMC Rep. 11, app. 2*, p. 168).
34. Raymond Gillespie, 'The transformation of the borderlands, 1600–1700' in Raymond Gillespie and Harold O'Sullivan (eds.) *The Borderlands* (Belfast, 1989), pp. 75–92; Harold O'Sullivan, 'Land confiscation and plantation in County Armagh during the English Commonwealth and Restoration periods, 1650 to 1680' in Hughes and Nolan (eds.), *Armagh*, pp. 333–80.
35. Éamonn Ó Ciardha, 'Toryism and Rappareeism in County Armagh in the late seventeenth century' in Hughes and Nolan (eds.), *Armagh*, pp. 381–412.
36. The following paragraphs summarise the account in *The Present State and Condition of Ireland*.
37. *The Present State and Condition of Ireland*, p. 26.
38. Cited in John J. Hanly, 'Saint Oliver Plunkett 1625–1681' in Hughes and Nolan (eds.), *Armagh*, p. 421.
39. Donnchadh MacPhóil, 'Blessed Oliver Plunkett and the Tories', *Seanchas Ard Mhacha*, 3 (1959), pp. 251–60; P.G. Murray, 'A previously unnoticed letter of Oliver Plunkett.'
40. Plunkett to Tanari, 30 Aug. 1678 (Hanly, *Plunkett letters*, pp. 513–19).
41. P.F. Moran, *Memoirs of the Most Rev. Oliver Plunkett* (Dublin, 1861), p. 302; Curtayne, *The Trial of Oliver Plunkett*, p. 121.
42. *A Narrative of the Late Popish Plot in Ireland, for the Subjugating Thereof to the French King* (London, 1680).
43. *A Narrative of the Late Popish Plot in Ireland*, p. 25.
44. Ibid., p. 26.
45. 'Examination of Eustace Comyn', 28 Sept. 1678 (*CSPD, 1678–79*, p. 254).
46. Ormond to Ossory, 10 Apr. 1680 (*HMC Ormonde*, ns, v, pp. 298–9).
47. Wyche to Ormond, 18 Sept. 1680 (*HMC Ormonde*, ns, v, pp. 426–32).
48. Longford to Ormond, 2 Nov. 1680 (*HMC Ormonde*, ns, pp. 474–5).
49. The original testimonies of Boark and MacNamara were substantively reproduced in *A Narrative of the Late Popish Plot in Ireland*. Eustace Comyn's

testimony was printed as *The Information of Eustace Comyn* (London, 1680). Expanded versions were published as *The Information of Hubert Boark Gent. Touching the Popish Plot in Ireland, Carried on by the Conspiricies of the Earl of Tyrone* (London, 1680); *The Information of John MacNamara, Gent. Touching the Popish Plot in Ireland* (London, 1680). These latter two adopted a very similar title and format; both were published by Randolph Taylor of London.
50. *The Information of Hubert Boark*, p. 2.
51. *The Information of John MacNamara*, pp. 1, 3, 16.
52. Ibid., pp. 8–13.
53. Ibid., p. 22.
54. Ibid., p. 20.
55. Ibid., p. 21.
56. *A Narrative of the Late Popish Plot in Ireland*, pp. 1–6, 10–13.
57. Ibid., A1.
58. Ibid., A2.
59. Ibid., pp. 28–9.
60. Ibid., pp. 7–10, 14–24.
61. Ibid., p. 24.
62. Orrery to Michael Boyle, 16 Sept. 1679 (*HMC Ormonde*, ns, v, pp. 206–7); *The Irish Evidence Convicted by Their Own Oaths* (London, 1682), p. 8.
63. Ormond to Southwell, 8 Nov. 1679 (V & A, F.47.A.40, ff. 65–6).
64. Ibid., 11 Nov. 1679 (V & A, F.47.A.40, f. 69).
65. NAUK PC 2/68, 530–1 (nd); *London Gazette*, 13–17 May 1680; Jenkins to Lord Lieutenant, 14 May 1680 (*CSPD. 1679–80*, pp. 478–9); Ormond to Jenkins, 16 June 1680 (*CSPD, 1679–80*, pp. 516–17).
66. Donough Leyne to 'Capt. Drury', 29 Oct. 1680 (*HMC Ormonde*, ns, v, pp. 463–5).
67. Longford to Ormond, 6 Nov. 1680 (*HMC Ormonde*, ns, v, pp. 479–81).
68. *Lords jn*, xiii, pp. 644–7.
69. Arran to Ormond, 6 Nov. 1680 (*HMC Ormonde*, ns, v, pp. 477–8); *Lords Journal*, xiii, p. 680; *A Narrative of the Irish Popish Plot, for the Betraying that Kingdom into the Hands of the French, Massacring All English Protestants There, and Utter Subversion of the Government and Protestant-Religion; as the Same was Successively Carryed on from the Year 1662. Given in to Both Houses of Parliament by David Fitzgerald Esq.* (London, 1680).
70. *A Narrative of the Irish Popish Plot*, p. 1.
71. Ibid., p. 3.
72. Ibid., p. 4.
73. Ibid.
74. Ibid., p. 5.
75. Ibid., p. 6.
76. Ibid., p. 8.
77. Ibid.
78. Ibid., pp. 10–11.
79. Ibid., pp. 13–22.
80. Ibid., pp. 14, 16.

81. Ibid., p. 15.
82. Ibid., p. 24.
83. Ibid., pp. 24–35.
84. Ibid., p. 25. Contemporary exaggerations of the death toll from 1641 are discussed in Donovan, 'Bloody news from Ireland', pp. 28–39.
85. *A Narrative of the Irish Popish Plot*, pp. 34–5.
86. Ibid., p. 26.
87. Ibid., pp. 27–8, 29–30.
88. Ibid., p. 26.
89. Ibid., p. 7.
90. J.F. Bosher, 'The Franco-Catholic Danger, 1660–1715', *History*, 79 (1994), 5–30; Harris, *Restoration*, pp. 164–5.

5 The Decline of the Irish Plot and the Road to the 'Tory Revenge', November 1680–July 1681

1. *Lords jn.*, xiii, pp. 652–4.
2. Undated petition (Hanly, *Plunkett Letters*, p. 551).
3. *Lords jn.*, xiii, pp. 658–9; 'Draft entry of statement made by Capt. Richardson', 10 Nov. 1680 (*HMC Rep. 11, app. 2*, pp. 169).
4. 'Conspiracy in Ireland', 8–10 Nov. 1680 (*HMC Rep. 11, app. 2*, pp. 146–7, 194).
5. NAUK PC 2/69, 149 (14 Nov. 1680).
6. Arran to Ormond, 6 Nov. 1680 (*HMC Ormonde*, ns, v, pp. 477–8).
7. *Parl. Hist.*, iv, col. 1205.
8. Knights, *Politics and Opinion in Crisis*, pp. 29–54.
9. Robert Willman, 'The origins of "Whig" and "Tory" in English political language', *Historical Journal*, 22 (1974), pp. 247–64.
10. Knights, *Politics and Opinion in Crisis*, p. 5.
11. Kenyon, *The Popish Plot*, pp. 180, 200–1.
12. Miller, *Popery and Politics in England*, pp. 175–6.
13. Tim Harris, *London Crowds in the Reign of Charles II* (Cambridge, 1987); Knights, *Politics and Opinion in Crisis*, pp. 153–347.
14. Miller, *Popery and Politics in England*, pp. 169–70.
15. Joad Raymond, *Pamphlets and Pamphleteering in Early Modern Britain* (Cambridge, 2003), 164, fig. 1, pp. 337–40.
16. The exception is *The Several Informations of John Mac-Namarra, Maurice Fitzgerald, and James Nash* (Dublin, 1681).
17. James Kelly, 'Political publishing, 1550–1700' in Raymond Gillespie and Andrew Hadfield (eds.), *The Oxford History of the Irish Book, Volume III: The Irish Book in English, 1559–1800* (Oxford, 2006), pp. 206–8.
18. Peter Lake and Steve Pincus, 'Rethinking the public sphere in early modern england', *Journal of British Studies*, 45 (2006), pp. 270–92.
19. John Miller, 'Public opinion in Charles II's England', *History*, 80 (1995), pp. 359–81; Tim Harris, 'Understanding popular politics in Restoration Britain' in Alan Houston & Steve Pincus (eds.), *A Nation Transformed:*

England after the Restoration (Cambridge, 2001), pp. 125–53; Lake and Pincus, 'Rethinking the Public Sphere', p. 288.
20. Harris, 'Understanding popular politics', pp. 142–3.
21. [William Petty] *The Politician Discovered* (London, 1681), pp. 7–10.
22. Carrol, *A Narrative of the Popish Plot in Ireland*, p. 1. This is summarized in John Brady, 'Some Connacht links to the Popish Plot', ii, *Journal of the Galway Archaeological and Historical Society*, 28 (1958–1959), pp. 18–22.
23. 'Account of James Carroll', 8 June 1681 (Charles McNeill (ed.), *The Tanner Letters* (Dublin, 1943), pp. 444–5); Carrol, *A Narrative of the Popish Plot in Ireland*, A3.
24. Carrol, *A Narrative of the Popish Plot in Ireland*, p. 12.
25. *An Account of the Bloody Massacre in Ireland*, p. 8.
26. Samuel Clarke, *A Generall Martyrologie, Containing a Collection of All the Greatest Persecutions Which Have Befallen the Church of Christ, from the Creation to Our Present Time* (London, 1651), pp. 347–63.
27. *A Brief Account of the Several Plots, Conspiracies and Hellish Attempts of the Bloody-Minded Papists...* (London, 1679), pp. 10–13, 29.
28. *A Brief Narrative of the Several Popish Treasons and Cruelties against the Protestants in England, France, and Ireland* (London, [1678]), p. 1.
29. *A Brief Narrative of the Several Popish Treasons and Cruelties*, pp. 4–5.
30. Ibid., p. 5.
31. Love, 'Civil War in Ireland', pp. 58, 64–7.
32. Edmund Borlase, *The History of the Execrable Irish Rebellion Trac'd from Many Preceding Acts to the Grand Eruption the 23 of October 1641* (London, 1680).
33. BL Sloane MS 1,008, f. 197.
34. Royce McGillivray, 'Edmund Borlase, Historian of the Irish rebellion', *Studia Hibernica*, 11 (1969), p. 89.
35. BL Sloane MS 1,008, f. 199.
36. John Tillotson to Borlase, 2 Sept. 1679 (BL Sloane MS 1,008, f. 210).
37. Dudley Loftus to Borlase, 25 Oct. 1679 (BL Sloane MS 1,008, f. 226).
38. McGillivray, 'Edmund Borlase', pp. 89–91.
39. BL Stowe MS 82, f. 1. This is an annotated edition of the original printed text.
40. BL Stowe MS 82, ff. 52, 63, 68.
41. *A Collection of Certain Horrid Murthers in Several Counties of Ireland. Committed since the 23 of Oct. 1641* (London, 1679), A2r–A3v.
42. *A Collection of Certain Horrid Murthers in Several Counties of Ireland*, A3v.
43. Harris, *Restoration*, pp. 150–3.
44. Steven Pincus, 'The English debate over universal monarchy' in John Robertson (ed.), *A Union for Empire: Political Thought and the British Union of 1707* (Cambridge, 1995), pp. 37–62.
45. Bosher, 'Franco-Catholic Danger', pp. 8–21.
46. Jonathan Scott, 'England's troubles: Exhuming the Popish Plot' in Tim Harris, Mark Goldie and Jonathan Scott (eds.), *The Politics of Religion in Restoration England* (Oxford, 1990), p. 123.
47. *A Narrative of the Irish Popish Plot*, p. 5.

48. *The Character of a Tory* (London, 1681), p. 1.
49. Steele, *Proclamations*, ii, p. 116.
50. Arran to Ormond, 6 Nov. 1680 (*HMC Ormonde*, ns, v, pp. 477–8); Longford to Ormond, 6 Nov. 1680 (*HMC Ormonde*, ns, v, pp. 479–81).
51. Longford to Ormond, 16 Nov. 1680 (*HMC Ormonde*, ns, v, pp. 490–1).
52. Ormond to Sunderland, 7 Nov. 1680 (*HMC Ormonde*, ns, v, pp. 481–2); Ormond to unknown, 7 Nov. 1680 (Bodl., Carte MS 146, pp. 301–3).
53. Gilbert MS 109, p. 14. Connor Maguire, Baron Enniskillen, was tried in London in 1645 for his part in the 1641 rebellion: Alan Orr, *Treason and the State: Law, Politics and Ideology in the English Civil War* (Cambridge, 2002), pp. 141–70.
54. *Commons jn.*, ix, pp. 651–2.
55. Ibid.; *Lords jn*, xiii, p. 664.
56. King to Ormond, 16 Nov. 1680 (*CSPD 1680–81*, p. 86).
57. *Commons jn.*, ix, pp. 665–7; *Parl. Hist.*, iv, col. 1218; Charles McNeill (ed.), 'Report on manuscripts in the Bodleian Library, Oxford', *Analecta Hibernica*, 2 (1931), pp. 10–11.
58. *Commons jn.*, ix, pp. 656, 658.
59. Quoted in Miller, *Popery and Politics in England*, p. 75.
60. *London Gazette*, 25–9 Nov. 1680.
61. *Lords jn.*, xiii, p. 694.
62. Steele, *Proclamations*, ii, p. 116.
63. John Jephson to Archbishop of Tuam, 29 Nov. 1680 (*CSPD 1680–81*, p. 94).
64. Hetherington to John Jackson, 30 Nov. 1680 (Bodl., Carte MS 39, f. 223).
65. *Commons jn.*, ix, p. 670.
66. Unknown to Shaftesbury, 30 Nov. 1680 (NAUK, Shaftesbury papers 30/24/50, ff. 167–8).
67. 'Articles against the Duke of Ormond', 4 Dec. 1680 (*CSPD 1680–81*, p. 98).
68. Arran to Ormond, 20 Nov. 1680 (*HMC Ormonde*, ns, v, p. 494).
69. Longford to Ormond, 4 Dec. 1680 (*HMC Ormonde*, ns, v, pp. 520–1).
70. Arran to Ormond, 4 Dec. 1680 (*HMC Ormonde*, ns, v, pp. 519–20).
71. Ormond to Arran, 13 Dec. 1680 (*HMC Ormonde*, ns, v, pp. 523–4).
72. John Vesey to Ormond, 17 Dec. 1680 (*HMC Ormonde*, ns, v, p. 526).
73. Henry Jones to Francis and Deborah Annesley, 2 Nov. 1680 (*HMC Ormonde*, ns, v, pp. 473–4). This episode is discussed in J.P. Prendergast, *Ireland from the Restoration to the Revolution, 1660 to 1690* (London, 1887), pp. 112–22.
74. Hans Hamilton to Ormond, 18 Dec. 1680 (*HMC Ormonde*, ns, v, pp. 530–1).
75. Deborah Annesley to Mrs. Katherine O'Hanlon, 7 Dec. 1680 (*HMC Ormonde*, ns, v, p. 535).
76. Francis Annesley to Mrs. Katherine O'Hanlon, 9 Dec. 1680 (*HMC Ormonde*, ns, v, p. 536).
77. Sir John Davys to Ormond, 18 Dec. 1680 (*HMC Ormonde*, ns, v, pp. 526–7).
78. Ormond to Arran, 1 Jan. 1681 (*HMC Ormonde*, ns, v, pp. 543–4).
79. Ibid., 29 Dec. 1680 (*HMC Ormonde*, ns, v, pp. 538–40).

80. Eustace Comyn to Richard Denison, 1 Jan. 1681 (*HMC Ormonde*, ns, v, p. 541).
81. 'Conspiracy in Ireland', 29 Nov. 1680 (*HMC Rep. 11, app. 2*, pp. 218–20); Sunderland to Ormond, 30 Nov. 1680 (*CSPD., 1680–81*, p. 96).
82. *State trials*, vii, col. 1319.
83. Ibid., col. 1323.
84. Ibid.
85. Ibid., col. 1327.
86. *Lords jn.*, xiii, p. 703.
87. Ibid., pp. 709, 715.
88. 'Motion...for Murphy to print his examination', 9 Dec. 1680 (*HMC Rep. 11, app. 2*, p. 169).
89. *Parl. Hist.*, iv, col. 1246; Grey, *Debates*, viii, p. 163.
90. *Commons jn.*, ix, p.695.
91. Knights, *Politics and Opinion in Crisis*, pp. 87–9.
92. 'Information of James Geogheghan', 4 Jan. 1681 (Bodl., Carte MS 39 f. 234).
93. Ormond to Arran, 29 Dec. 1680 (*HMC Ormonde*, ns, v, p. 540); Burke, *Irish Priests in the Penal Times*, pp. 71–3.
94. Lord Lieutenant and Council to Sunderland, 8 Jan. 1681 (Bodl., Carte MS 39, ff. 238–9); NAUK PC 2/69, 198 (20 Jan. 1681).
95. Orrery to Dowager Countess, 7 Jan. 1681 (*Orrery papers*, p. 240).
96. *The True Protestant Mercury: or, Occurences Forein and Domestick*, 1–3 Jan. 1681.
97. *The Several Informations of John Mac-Namarra, Maurice Fitzgerald, and James Nash*, p. 10; *Lords jn.*, xiii, pp. 731–3.
98. *Lords jn.*, xiii, pp. 729, 739.
99. *Parl. Hist.*, iv, col. 1278; *Parliamentary Debates*, ii, 38–45.
100. *Parliamentary Debates*, ii, pp. 42–3.
101. *Lords jn.*, xiii, p. 733; *The Several Informations of John Mac-Namarra, Maurice Fitzgerald, and James Nash*, p. 15.
102. *The True Protestant Mercury*, 8–11 Jan. 1681.
103. *Protestant (Domestick) Intelligence*, 14 Jan. 1681.
104. Newsletter, 13 Jan. 1681 (*HMC Rep. 14, app. 4*, pp. 124–5).
105. *London Gazette*, 27–30 Dec. 1680.
106. *The True Protestant mercury*, 15–8 Jan. 1681.
107. Arran to Ormond, 11 Jan. 1681 (*H.M.C. Ormonde*, new ser., v, pp. 550–1).
108. Ormond to John Davys, 15 Jan. 1681 (*HMC Ormonde*, ns, v, p. 553).
109. Unknown to King, 14/24 Jan. 1681 (*CSPD 1680–81*, pp. 133–5); *Protestant (Domestick) Intelligence*, 18 Jan. 1681.
110. John Nisbit to Secretary Gascoyne, 22 Feb. 1681 (*CSPD 1680–81*, p. 180).
111. King to Ormond, 18 Jan. 1681 (*CSPD 1680–81*, p. 138).
112. Ormond to Massareene, 15 Feb. 1681 (*HMC Rep. 7, app*, p. 747).
113. NAUK PC 2/69, 214 (16 Feb. 1681).
114. Egan,'Finance and the government of Ireland', ii, p. 118.
115. Gilbert (ed.), *Calendar of Ancient Records of Dublin*, v, pp. 201–3.
116. Leoline Jenkins to Ormond, 5 Feb. 1681 (*CSPD 1680–81*, p. 155).

117. 'Information of James Gardner', 4 Feb. 1681 (*HMC Rep 7, app*, p. 747); 'Information of John Red', 5 Feb. 1681 (*HMC Rep. 7, app*, pp. 746–7); Ormond to Massareene, 15 Feb. 1680 (*HMC Ormonde*, ns, v, pp. 583–4).
118. Arran to Ormond, 15 Feb. 1680 (*HMC Ormonde*, ns, v, pp. 581–2).
119. Ormond to Jenkins, 19 Feb. 1681 (*CSPD 1680–81*, pp. 176–7).
120. Longford to Jenkins, 26 Feb. 1681 (*CSPD 1680–81*, pp. 186–7).
121. 'Extract of a letter', 27 Feb. 1681 (*CSPD 1680–81*, p. 188).
122. Ormond to Arran, 19 Feb. 1681 (*HMC Rep. 7 app*, p. 743).
123. Anglesey to Borlase, 17 April 1680 (BL Sloane MS 1,008, f. 262).
124. Angelsey diary, 4 July 1679 (BL Add MS 18,730, f. 2).
125. BL Add MS 18,370, f. 65.
126. BL Add Ms 4,816, ff. 15, 20–4; Herbert Wood, 'Memorandum on the Earl of Anglesey's notes for a history of Ireland', *Analecta Hibernica*, 12 (1943), pp. 175–6.
127. BL Sloane MS 1,015, f. 7.
128. BL Sloane MS 1,015, f. 8.
129. Ormond to Wyche, 1 Mar. 1681 (NLI MS 803, f. 33); Ormond to Capt. Mathew, 5 Mar. 1681 (*HMC Rep. 7, app*, p. 744).
130. The dispute is discussed in Michael Perceval-Maxwell, 'The Anglesey-Ormond-Castlehaven dispute: Taking sides about Ireland in England' in Vincent P. Carey and Ute Lotz-Heumann (eds.), *Taking sides? Colonial and Confessional Mentalities in Early Modern Ireland* (Dublin, 2003), pp. 213–30; idem, 'Sir Robert Southwell and the duke of Ormond's reflections on the 1640s' in Mícheál Ó Siochrú (ed.), *Kingdoms in Crisis: Ireland in the 1640s* (Dublin, 2001), pp. 229–47.
131. NAUK PC 2/69, 191 (21 Jan. 1681).
132. NAUK PC 2/69, 194 (26 Jan. 1681).
133. John Davys to Ormond, 8 Jan. 1681 (*HMC Ormonde*, ns, v, pp. 546–7).
134. *The True Protestant Mercury*, 1–5 Feb. 1681.
135. Ibid., 29 Jan–1 Feb. 1681.
136. Newsletter to Roger Garstell, 29 Jan. 1681 (*CSPD, 1680–81*, pp. 150–1); NAUK PC 2/69, 206 (4 Feb. 1681).
137. *The True Protestant Mercury*, 22–25 Jan. 1681.
138. NAUK PC 2/69, 204 (2 Feb. 1681); 207 (4 Feb. 1681).
139. *A True and Brief Account of the Proceedings between Mr David Fitzgerald and William Hetherington, before his Majesty in Councel on Friday the 11th of February 1680/81* (London, 1681).
140. *A True and Brief Account of the Proceedings*, p. 2.
141. Ibid., p. 4.
142. NAUK PC 2/69, 211 (11 Feb. 1681).
143. NAUK PC 2/69, 217 (16 Feb. 1681).
144. NAUK PC 2/69, 217 (16 Feb. 1681); NAUK PC 2/69, 221 (23 Feb. 1681).
145. NAUK PC 2/69, 226 (25 Feb. 1681).
146. *Protestant (Domestick) Intelligence*, 21 Jan. 1681; 18 Feb. 1681.
147. Ibid., 25 Jan. 1681.
148. Ibid., 18 Feb. 1681.
149. Francis Gwyn to Ormond, 26 Feb. 1681 (*HMC Rep. 7, app.*, p. 744).

150. NAUK PC 2/69, 231 (2 Mar. 1681).
151. NAUK PC 2/69, 246 (11 Mar. 1681).
152. *Lords jn.*, xiii, p. 748; 'Conspiracy in Ireland', 22 Mar. 1681 (*HMC Rep. 11, app. 2*, p. 270)
153. NAUK PC 2/69, 224 (25 Feb. 1681).
154. John C. MacErlean (ed.), *Duanaire Dháibhidh Uí Bhruadair : The Poems of David O Bruadair* (3 vols, London, 1910–13), ii, pp. 218–19.
155. *Lords jn.*, xiii, pp. 750–1; 'Conspiracy in Ireland', 23 Mar. 1681 (*HMC Rep. 11, app. 2*, pp. 270–1).
156. Grey, *Debates*, viii, p. 336.
157. The text is reproduced in *State trials*, viii, col. 357–61.
158. 'News from Brussels', 22 Mar. 1681 (*Nunziatura di Fiandra*, ii, pp. 77–8).
159. 'Popish Plot', 26 Mar. 1681 (*HMC Rep. 11, app. 2*, p. 273).
160. *Protestant (Domestick) Intelligence*, 129 Mar. 1681.
161. 'The humble petition of the Lord Viscount Clare', 1 Mar. 1681 (*HMC Rep. 7, app*, p. 744).
162. Clare to Essex, 7 Mar. 1681 (*CSPD 1680–81*, pp. 201–2).
163. Ormond to Arran, 11 Feb. 1681 (*HMC Ormonde*, ns, v, pp. 576–8).
164. Clare to Essex, 7 Mar. 1681 (*CSPD 1680–81*, pp. 201–2).
165. Conway to Ormond, 25 Mar. 1681 (*HMC Ormonde*, ns, vi, pp. 1–2).
166. *The True Protestant Mercury*, 26–30 Mar. 1681.
167. RIA MS 675, f. 109. I would like to thank Breandán Ó Buachalla for bringing this to my attention.
168. RIA MS 675, f. 111.
169. RIA MS 675, f. 132.
170. Ormond to Jenkins, 'St Davids Day' (*CSPD 1680–81*, pp. 191–2).
171. Order in Council, 9 Mar. 1681 (*CSPD 1680–81*, p. 206); 'Information of William [Dongie], 22 Mar. 1680 (Bodl., Carte MS 39, f. 226).
172. 'Conspiracy in Ireland', 30 Mar.–2 Apr. 1681 (*HMC Rep. 11, app 2*, pp. 273–4).
173. Ormond to Jenkins, 31 Mar. 1681 (*CSPD 1680–81*, p. 227).
174. Ormond to Arran, 31 Mar. 1681 (*HMC Ormonde*, ns, vi, pp. 23–4).
175. NAUK PC 2/69, 256 (6 Apr. 1681).
176. Ormond to Arran, 9 Apr. 1681 (*HMC Ormonde*, ns, vi, pp. 28–9).
177. Arran to Ormond, 9 Apr. 1681 (*HMC Ormonde*, ns, vi, pp. 30–1).
178. [Walsh] to Charles II, n.d. (Bodl., Carte MS 214, ff. 12–13)
179. *A True Discovery of the Irish Popish Plot, Made by Maurice Fitz-Gerald* (London, 1681), np.
180. *Protestant (Domestick) Intelligence*, 5 Apr. 1681.
181. Ibid., 8 Apr. 1681.
182. 'News from Ghent', 9 May 1681 (*Nunziatura di Fiandri*, ii, p. 79).
183. NAUK PC 2/69, 258 (6 Apr. 1681); NAUK PC 2/69, 265 (13 Apr. 1681).
184. Arran to Ormond, 30 Apr. 1681 (*HMC Ormonde*, ns, vi, p. 48).
185. *Count Hanlan's Downfall, or a True and Exact Account of the Killing That Arch Traytor and Tory Redmon O'Hanlan* (Dublin, 1681), p. 5.
186. *Count Hanlan's Downfall*, p. 6.
187. Ibid., p. 7.

188. Carpenter (ed), *Verse in English from Tudor and Stuart Ireland*, p. 457.
189. 'Examination of John Rouse, 9 July 1681' in Joseph George Muddiman, 'Depositions about the Popish Plot (from the Shaftesbury Papers, bundle 43), *Notes and Queries*, 147 (1924), pp. 185–6.
190. Information 'found among John Moyer's papers', Bodl., Carte MS 39, f. 100. This was apparently delivered to the committee investigating the Irish Plot on 28 Dec. 1680.
191. Warcup to Jenkins, 15 Apr. 1681 (*CSPD, 1680–81*, pp. 240–1).
192. NAUK PC 2/69, 270 (15 Apr. 1681); NAUK PC 2/69, 277 (22 Apr. 1681).
193. 'Petition of Viscount Clare', 22 Apr. 1681 (*HMC Ormonde*, ns, vi, pp. 38–9).
194. Ormond to Arran, 4 May 1681 (*HMC Ormonde*, ns, vi, pp. 57–8).
195. *Irelands Sad Lamentation: Discovering its Present Danger, in Some Remarkable Passages Which Have Happened since the Discovery of the Horrid Popish Plot* (London, 1680/81).
196. *Irelands Sad Lamentation* [p. 1].
197. Ibid. [p. 2].
198. 'Act of Lord Mayor and Corporation of Dublin', 14 May 1681 (*CSPD 1680–81*, p. 281); Gilbert (ed.), *Calendar of Ancient Records of Dublin*, v, pp. 216–17.
199. Ormond to Jenkins, 21 May 1681 (*CSPD 1680–81*, pp. 290–1).
200. Ormond to York, 27 May 1681 (Carte, *Ormond*, v, p. 162).
201. *The True Protestant Mercury*, 11–15 June 1681.
202. Henry Boyle to Dowager Countess, 24 May 1681 (*Orrery papers*, p. 247).
203. Owen Callaghan to Owen Callaghan, 17 May 1681 (*CSPD 1680–81*, p. 286); 'Account of Justice John Keating and Edward Herbert', 5 Aug. 1681 (Bodl., Carte MS 39, ff. 364–5).
204. 'Information of Owen O'Callaghan', 14 May 1681 (*CSPD, 1680–81*, pp. 276–7).
205. Arran to Ormond, 17 May 1681 (*HMC Ormonde*, ns, vi, pp. 64–5); *The True Protestant Mercury*, 21–5 May 1681.
206. 'Information of Eustace Comyn', 3 June 1681 (*CSPD, 1680–81*, pp. 303–4).
207. Cibo to Tanari, 14 Dec 1681 (*Nunziatura di Fiandri*, viii, pp. 91–2).
208. Tanari to Secretariate of State, 17 May 1681 (*Nunziatura di Fiandri*, ii, p. 68).
209. *State Trials*, viii, col. 342, 344.
210. *Burnet's History of My Own Time*, ii, p. 292.
211. Anonymous newsletter, 11 June 1681 (Bodl., Carte MS 72, f. 526).
212. *State trials*, viii, col. 447–500; *The Tryal and Condemnation of Dr Oliver Plunkett Titular Primaye of Ireland, for High-Treason* (Dublin, 1681).
213. Anonymous newsletter, 11 June 1681 (Bodl., Carte MS 72, f. 526).
214. Ibid. (Bodl., Carte MS 72, f. 527r).
215. *London Gazette*, 13–16 June 1681.
216. NAUK PC 2/69, 301 (16 June 1681). The witnesses in question were: John MacMoyer, Hugh Duffy, John McClave, Florence Weyer, Hugh Handland (*sic*), Cornelius McGiver, Bryan O'Quinn, Henry O'Neale, Phelim O'Neale, Owen O'Neale, and Owen Murphy.

217. NAUK PC 2/69, 302 (16 June 1681). The remaining seven accused were: Robert Ely, John Butler, Paul Strange, John Shorthall, 'Minister 'Laurence Sullivan, and William Finch.
218. NAUK PC 2/69, 309 (23 June 1681).
219. 'Petition of Oliver Plunkett', 10 June 1681 (*CSPD., 1680–81,* pp. 313–14).
220. Plunkett to Charles II, *c*.17 June 1681 (*CSPD, 1680–81*, pp. 317–18).
221. NAUK PC 2/69, 306 (23 June 1681).
222. 'Report by Sir Roger Sawyer', 23 June 1681 (*CSPD, 1680–81*, pp. 326–7).
223. Brady, 'Oliver Plunkett and the Popish Plot', ii, p. 354.
224. Haley, *Shaftesbury*, p. 571; Jones, *The First Whigs*, p 187; *Burnet's History of My Own Time*, ii, p. 292.
225. Tanari to Secretariate of State, 28 June 1681 (*Nunziatura di Fiandri*, ii, p. 68).
226. *London Gazette*, 30 June–4 July 1681.
227. *The Last Speech and Confession of Oliver Plunkett . . . and Also of Edward Fitz-Harris: at Their Execution at Tyburn* (London, 1681); *The True Protestant Mercury*, 29 June–2 July 1681.
228. Miller, *Popery and Politics in England*, p. 190; Ronald Hutton, *Charles II: King of England, Scotland and Ireland* (Oxford, 1989), pp. 407–8.

Conclusion

1. Arran to Ormond, 2 July 1681 (*HMC Ormonde*, ns, vi, p. 89).
2. Knights, *Politics and Opinion in Crisis*, pp. 258–305.
3. Grey, *Debates*, vii, p. 91.
4. Ormond to Hans Hamilton, 14 July 1681 (*HMC Ormonde*, ns, vi, p. 99).
5. Ormond to the King, 23 July 1681 (*HMC Ormonde*, ns, vi, pp. 104–5).

Aftermath, 1681–1691

1. *The Honesty and True Zeal of the Kings Witnesses Justified and Vindicated* (London, 1681).
2. *Mr Smyth's Discovery of the Popish Sham-Plot in Ireland* (London, 1681); *News from Ireland, Touching the Damnable Design of the Papists in the Kingdom to Forge a Sham-Plott upon the Presbyterians* (London, 1682).
3. [William Hetherington] *The Irish Evidence, Convicted by Their Own Oaths* (London, 1682).
4. NAUK PC 2/69, 332 (28 July 1681).
5. NAUK PC 2/69, 364 (5 Oct. 1681).
6. NAUK PC 2/69, 374 (19 Oct. 1681); Tanari to Secretariate of State, 17 Oct. 1681 (*Nunziatura di Fiandra*, ii, p. 88); same to same, 3 Apr. 1682 (*Nunziatura di Fiandra*, ii, p. 89).
7. Massareene to Rawdon, 1 June 1681 (*Rawdon papers*, pp. 267–9).
8. NAUK PC 2/69, 377 (21 Oct. 1681). Those accused were: Lt. Col. Richard Stephenson, Oliver Stephenson, John MacNamara, Daniel MacNamara,

John Boark, Capt John Purdon, William Boarke, and John Power; NAUK PC 2/69, 387 (4 Nov. 1681).
9. Haley, *Shaftesbury*, p. 679.
10. 'News from Brussels', 5 Dec. 1681 (*Nunziatura di Fiandra*, ii, p. 88).
11. 'Account of John Fitzgerald', 30 Jan. 1682 (*CSPD, 1682*, pp. 46–7).
12. NAUK PC 2/69, 449 (8 Feb. 1682).
13. NAUK PC 2/69, 463 (13 Feb. 1682).
14. 'News from Brussels', 15 May 1682 (*Nunziatura di Fiandra*, ii, pp. 89–90).
15. MacErlean (ed.), *Duanaire Dháibhidh Uí Bhruadair*, ii, pp. 264–88.
16. Ibid., iii, pp. 12–23.
17. Tanari to Secretariate of State, 9 Oct. 1682 (*Nunziatura di Fiandra*, ii, p. 91).
18. NAUK PC 2/69, 641 (28 Feb. 1683).
19. Gilbert (ed.), *Calendar of Ancient Records of Dublin*, v, pp. 232–4.
20. The petitioning campaign is discussed in Harris, *Restoration*, pp. 390–5.
21. Cited in Carpenter (ed.), *Verse in English from Tudor and Stuart Ireland*, p. 494.
22. S. W. Singer (ed.), *The Correspondence of Henry Hyde, Earl of Clarendon* (2 vols, London, 1828). i, pp. 207, 208–9.
23. BL Add MS 72,881, ff. 23–6.
24. RIA, MS 24. G. 2, f. 1.
25. *Calendar of Clarendon State Papers*, v, p. 657.
26. Patrick Melvin (ed.), 'Sir Paul Rycaut's memoranda and letters from Ireland, 1686–1687', *Analecta Hibernica*, 27 (1972), pp. 156–8.
27. *A True Discovery of the Private League, Between the Late King James (Since His Coming from Ireland) and the K. of France: Shewing Their Design to Destroy all the Protestants in Europe* (London, 1690), np.
28. Edward MacLysaght (ed.), 'Report on documents relating to the wardenship of Galway', *Analecta Hibernica*, 14 (1944), pp. 149–50.
29. MacLysaght, (ed.), 'Report on documents relating to the wardenship of Galway', pp. 150–1.
30. William King, *The State of the Protestants in Ireland Under the Late King James's government* (4th ed., London, 1692), p. 100.
31. *Calendar of Clarendon State Papers*, v, p. 688.
32. *A Short View of the Methods Made Use of in Ireland for the Subversion and Destruction of the Protestant Religion and Interest in That Kingdom* (London, 1689), p. 2.
33. *A Short View of the Methods Made Use of in Ireland for the Subversion and Destruction of the Protestant Religion and Interest in That Kingdom*, p. 11.
34. *Reasons for His Majesties Issuing a General Pardon to the Rebels of Ireland* (London, 1689), np.
35. *The History of the Wars In Ireland, Between Their Majesties Army, and the Forces of the Late King James* (London, 1690), p. 93.
36. *A True Representation to the King and People of England; How Matters Were Carried on All Along in Ireland by the Late King James* (London, 1689), A2.
37. Raymond Gillespie, 'The Irish Protestants and James II, 1688–90', *Irish Historical Studies*, 38 (1992), pp. 124–33.

38. *An Account of the Present, Miserable State Of Affairs in Ireland* (London?, 1689), np.
39. *A Letter from a Gentleman in Ireland to His Friend in London, upon Occasion Of a Pamphlet Entitled a Vindication of the Present Government of Ireland...under Tyrconnel* (Dublin, 1688), np; *An Account of a Late, Horrid and Bloody Massacre in Ireland...Procured and Carry'd on by the L. Tyrconnell* (London?, 1689); *The Present Dangerous Conditions of the Protestants in Ireland* (London, 1689); *The Sad Estate and Condition of Ireland* (London, 1689); *The Sad and Lamentable condition of the Protestants in Ireland* (London, 1689).
40. *A Confession of Faith of the Roman Catholics of Ireland* (London, 1689); *Tyrconnel's Letter to the French King from Ireland* (London, 1690).
41. *The Sad and Lamentable Condition of the Protestants of Ireland* (London, 1689), p. 6.
42. *Dublin Intelligence*, 21–8 Oct. 1690.
43. *An Account of the Late Barbarous Proceedings of the Earl of Tyrconnel* (London, 1689); *A Brief and Modest Representation of the Present State & Condition of Ireland* (London, 1689).
44. *A Letter from Monsieur Tyrconnel...to the Late Queen* (London, 1690), p. 4.
45. William King, *The State of the Protestants in Ireland Under the Late King James Government* (4th ed., London, 1692), p. 22.
46. S.J. Connolly, 'The defence of Protestant Ireland, 1660–1760' in Thomas Bartlett and Keith Jeffery (eds.), *A Military History of Ireland* (Cambridge, 1996), p. 236. This argument is reiterated in the same authors *Religion, Law and Power*.
47. *A Sermon Preached to the Protestants of Ireland in the City of London...by Richard, Lord Bishop of Killala* (London, 1691).
48. Brendan Bradshaw, 'Ambiguous allegiances: Early modern Ireland', *The Irish Review*, 33 (Spring 2005), pp. 110–17.
49. Charles O'Kelly, *Macariae excidium, or the Destruction of Cyprus*, J.C. O'Callaghan (ed.) (Dublin, 1850), pp. 13–15.
50. NLI MS 476, 'A light to the blind', f. 275.
51. NLI MS 476, 'A light to the blind', f. 277
52. NLI MS 476, 'A light to the blind', ff. 282–83; Patrick Kelly, 'A light to the blind': The voice of the dispossessed elite in the generation after the defeat at Limerick', *Irish Historical Studies*, 24 (1985), p. 448.

Index

America, 13
Amsterdam, 156
Anglesey, Arthur Annesley, earl of, 75, 103, 110, 134–5
Anglo-Dutch War (1672–4), 29
Annesley, Deborah, 127
Annesley, Francis, 127
Antrim, county, 51, 71
Armagh, county, 1, 11, 12, 23, 32, 80, 85, 106–8, 126, 128
army, in Ireland, 25, 31, 43, 45, 51, 90, 91, 123, 124, 132, 141
Arran, Richard Butler, earl of, 41, 43, 53, 56, 58, 63, 95, 120, 122, 126, 132, 142, 143, 145, 146, 147, 151
Aston, Walter, lord Aston, 50

Baker, Henry, 88, 100, 107
Barnard, Toby, 15, 18
Battye, Jerome, 138
Beckett, J.C., 2
Bedloe, William, 49
Berkeley, John, baron Berkeley of Stratton, 23, 108
Birch, John, 38, 99
Blood's plot (1663), 46, 77
Borlase, Edward, 120–1, 134, 135
Boyle, Michael, Church of Ireland archbishop of Dublin, 40, 44, 53, 55, 56, 62, 88, 93, 95, 109, 120, 137, 145, 157
Bradley, William, 102, 109, 130
Brennan, John, Catholic archbishop of Cashel, 71, 72, 103, 109, 110, 128
Brittas, Theobald Burke, lord, 73, 78, 79, 99, 102, 109, 138, 159
Brookes, William, 49
Brussels, 115

Burnet, Gilbert, 50, 99, 147, 149
Butler, Pierce, 49
'Byrne', 53

Callaghan, James, 137
Cameronians, 154
Capel, Henry, 82, 97
Care, Henry, 124
Carrickfergus, county Antrim, 78, 103, 159
Carroll, James, 118–19, 148
Carte, Thomas, 2
Cashel, county Tipperary, 128
Castlehaven, James Touchet, earl of, 134–5
Catherine of Braganza, queen of England, Ireland and Scotland, 48, 137, 138, 146
Charles I, king of England, Ireland and Scotland, 12
Charles II, king of England, Ireland and Scotland, 1, 5, 6, 7, 8, 11, 18, 21, 22, 24, 25, 26, 29, 30, 39, 42, 47, 48, 53, 54, 56, 64, 65, 68, 69, 70, 72, 77, 81, 83, 84, 85, 90, 92, 93, 99, 100, 114, 115, 121, 123, 129, 130, 132, 138, 139, 140, 142, 145, 149, 152, 155, 156, 158, 159, 161, 162
Charles Fort, Kinsale, 39
Clancarty, Eleanor McCarthy *née* Butler, lady, 127
Clanricarde, William Burke, earl of, 119, 125
Clare, county, 139, 158
Clare, Daniel O'Brien, viscount, 140, 141, 145, 146
Clarendon, Henry Hyde, earl of, 159, 161
Coleman, Edward, 6, 7, 29, 47

Confederate Catholics, 17, 26, 38, 122, 134, 135
Connacht, 25, 35, 81, 125, 126
Conway, Edward, viscount Conway, 71, 84
Cork, county, 30, 38, 39, 44, 55, 60–1, 78, 97, 125, 134, 136, 141, 146, 159
Cork, Richard Boyle, first earl of, 24, 38, 73
Covenanters, 66
Coventry, Henry, 31, 32, 41, 48, 49, 57, 69, 80, 92, 149
Cox, Richard, 60–1
Creagh, Peter, Catholic archbishop of Cork and Cloyne, 86, 103, 113
Crew, James, 116
Cromwell, Oliver, 17, 38, 57

Dancer, John, 61
Daniell, John, 101
Davis, William, 72, 146
Davys, Sir John, 95, 101, 102, 127, 129, 132, 136, 146, 148, 157
Dennis, Bernard, 128, 137, 157
Derry, county, 133, 159
Dingle, county Kerry, 159
dissenters, 57, 66
  see also non-conformists, presbyterians
Donegal, county, 132, 141
Dongan, Thomas, 39
Dorset, 57, 111
Down, county, 144
Downey, Murtagh, 130, 131, 157
Downpatrick, county Down, 144
Drogheda, county Louth, 159
Drumclog, 66
Dublin, city and county, 4, 11, 20, 26, 28, 32, 33, 34, 40, 42, 46, 53, 55, 56, 58, 59, 60, 62, 67, 68, 70, 71, 73, 76, 77, 78, 84, 85, 88, 89, 93, 98, 101, 102, 103, 106, 108, 117, 118, 121, 122, 125, 126, 127, 131, 136, 144, 145, 148, 151, 159
  castle, 11, 33, 53, 60, 68, 78
  corporation, 43, 133, 146, 158
Duffy, Hugh, 137, 148, 149
Dugdale, Stephen, 49, 50, 128
Dundalk, county Louth, 80, 85, 88, 89, 101, 106, 107, 115
Dunmanway, county Cork, 134
Dutch, 6, 29, 68, 112, 121, 124
  see also Netherlands

'Egan', 78
elections
  England, 7, 70, 72
  Ireland, 77
Elizabeth I, queen of England, 9
Essex, Arthur Capel, earl of, 20, 22–5, 34, 53, 59, 62, 64, 65, 68, 76, 78, 80, 81, 82, 83, 85, 86, 87, 88, 92, 106, 110, 111, 119, 121, 129, 130, 140, 145, 149, 156, 162
Everard, Edmund, 47, 48, 139, 147
'Evers', 49
Exclusion crisis (1679–81), 1, 3, 5, 7–8, 10, 31, 57, 84, 103, 104, 116, 117, 150, 151, 153

finances, Ireland, 27, 55, 58, 66, 73, 92, 133
  see also revenue, Ireland
Finan, Daniel, 137
Fitzgerald, James Fitzmaurice, 11
Fitzgerald, John, 130, 138, 143
Fitzgerald, John, informer, 79, 86, 102, 125, 157
Fitzgerald, Maurice, 130, 143, 149, 157
Fitzgerald, 'Mr', 40, 79
Fitzharris, Edmund, 139, 147, 148, 149, 150, 151
Fitzpatrick, John, 62, 63, 72, 78, 145
Fleming, Patrick, 82, 100, 144
Fogarty, 'Doctor', 28, 102
Foley, Paul, 129
Forristal, Marcus, Catholic archbishop of Kildare, 157

Foxe, John, 9, 13
France, 6, 11, 13, 14, 22, 30, 33, 34, 35, 46, 48, 50, 53, 57, 60, 68, 83, 93, 95, 97, 100, 103, 112, 113, 115, 118, 121, 124, 125, 128, 139, 140, 141, 160
  see also French
French, 8, 28, 29, 30, 34, 35, 36, 38, 39, 40, 42, 43, 48, 49, 50, 54, 55, 56, 57, 59, 61, 64, 68, 72, 73, 74, 79, 80, 83, 89, 93, 100, 101, 102, 103, 104, 105, 109, 110, 111, 112, 113, 114, 116, 118, 121, 124, 127, 128, 131, 133, 136, 138, 140, 147, 148, 149, 152, 160, 161, 162, 163
French, Martin, 35, 47
French, Nicholas, Catholic archbishop of Ferns, 19, 25, 26, 160

Galway, city and county, 35, 47, 69, 118, 124, 125, 132, 159, 161
Geogheghan, James, 96, 130, 143
'Glorious Revolution' (1688), 165
Godfrey, Edmund Bury, 6, 28, 33, 48, 49, 60, 162
Granard, Arthur Forbes, earl of, 73, 90, 91–2, 133
Greene, [Robert], 49
Gunpowder plot (1605), 10, 37, 65, 118, 136

Haley, K.H.D., 86
Halifax, William Savile, marquis of, 64
Hamilton, Hans, 87, 126, 127
Harley, Edward, 153
Harris, Walter, 34
Henry II, king of England, 93
Hetherington, William, 80, 85, 86, 87, 88, 98, 100, 106, 108, 115, 116, 124–5, 136, 137, 138, 142, 143, 144, 146, 147, 148, 149, 156
Hyde, Laurence, 92

informers, 4, 35, 49, 65, 75, 77, 78, 79, 81, 85, 86, 87, 88, 89, 94, 96, 98, 99–115 *passim*, 116, 117, 118, 122, 123, 124, 126, 127, 129, 130, 131, 136, 137, 138, 139, 140, 142, 144, 151, 153, 156, 157, 158, 160, 163
  see also witnesses
Ingoldsby, Henry, 85, 86
Irish council, 44, 60, 65, 70, 83, 87, 96, 101, 111, 125, 126
'Irish plot', 38, 44, 47, 49, 50, 52, 54, 56, 66–98 *passim*, 99, 106, 108, 111, 116–18, 122, 124, 125, 129, 130, 131, 132, 136, 137, 138, 139, 142, 143, 144, 145, 146, 148, 149, 151, 153, 154, 158
Ivie, Edward, 111, 157

James I, king of England, Ireland and Scotland, 10
Jephson, John, 46, 124
Jesuits, 10, 11, 28, 31, 40, 46, 50, 52, 58, 61, 66, 69, 71, 74, 163
Jones, Henry, Church of Ireland archbishop of Meath, 14–18, 20, 56, 64, 88, 96, 106, 111, 126, 139, 154

Keating, John, 102
Kelley, Dominick, 49
Kilkenny, city and county, 51, 94
King, William, Church of Ireland archbishop of Derry, 161, 164
Kinsale, county Cork, 39, 40, 61, 91, 124, 132, 159

Lacy, Pierce, 73, 78, 102, 103, 109, 113, 130, 138, 139, 143, 159
Lake, Peter, 10
Lavallyan, Patrick, 73, 74, 110, 125, 127, 128, 141
legislation
  England, 7, 8, 55
  Ireland, 32, 62, 63, 76, 80, 89, 90, 91, 92, 93, 153
Leitrim, county, 71

Lestrange, Roger, 121
Lisburn, 60, 73, 82
London, *passim*
Longford, Francis Aungier, earl of, 41, 58, 70, 77, 95, 122, 123, 126
Louis XIV, king of France, 6, 11, 45, 48, 54, 114, 121
Lucas, William, 144
Lynch, James, Catholic archbishop of Galway, 28, 35, 47, 103, 113, 128
Lynch, John, 18
Lyne, Donough, 94

'Mac-Carte', Daniel, 72
'MacLegh', John, 148
MacMoyer, John, 85, 87, 88, 89, 101, 137, 138, 148
Maginn, Ronan, 100
Malet, John, 45
Mansell, Roderick, 88
Marvell, Andrew, 36
Mary I, queen of England, 9
Massareene, John Skeffington, viscount, 132, 157
Maynard, John, 60, 139
Mayo, county, 146
McCarthy, Justin, 38, 39, 48
McKenna, James, 115
Meagher, Keadagh, 103
Meath, county, 20, 23, 33, 71, 82, 108
Middlesex, 97, 138, 144
Milton, Anthony, 10
Mirandel, 69
Monaghan, county, 82
Monmouth, James Scott, duke of, 48, 64, 66, 68, 75, 148, 165
Mountgarret, Richard Butler, viscount, 35, 68
Mullingar, county Westmeath, 130
Munster, 30, 38–40, 41, 42, 44, 55, 61, 64, 84, 85, 102, 111, 113, 126, 133, 134, 158, 163
Murphy, Edmund, 80, 81, 85, 86, 87, 88, 89, 98, 100–1, 102, 106–8, 115, 116, 123, 126, 127, 128, 129, 137, 148, 158
Murphy, Owen, 126, 128, 157

Naas, county Kildare, 42
Nash, David, 94
Nash, James, 130, 131
Netherlands, 13
Netterville, James, 49
Nijmegan, treaty of (1678), 54
Nine Years War (1594–1603), 11
non-conformists, 70
  see also dissenters, presbyterians

Oates, Titus, 5, 6, 28, 29, 31, 35, 45, 46, 47, 48, 49, 52, 56, 59, 61, 66, 69, 71, 72, 74, 96, 98, 102, 109, 117, 123, 127, 128, 132, 136, 140, 141, 151, 157, 159, 165
Ó Bruadair, Dáibhidh, 138–9, 158
O'Callaghan, Owen, 146, 157
O'Daly, John, 30
Odell, John, 94
O'Hanlon, Art, 144
O'Hanlon, Leighlin, 127
O'Hanlon, Redmond, 71, 82, 107–8, 126, 127, 129, 143–4
O'Kearney, Denis, 73
O'Moloney, John, Catholic archbishop of Killaloe, 86, 103, 113
O'Murphy, Cormucke Raver, 107–8
O'Neale, Neil, 148
O'Neill, Sir Phelim, 11, 12
Ormond, James Butler, first duke of, 2, 3, 4, 17, 25–7, 28–47 *passim*, 49, 53–98 *passim*, 101, 102, 103, 105, 106, 109, 111, 116, 120–8, 130, 132–5, 137, 140–6, 144, 148, 151, 152, 153, 154, 156, 157, 158, 159
Orrery, Roger Boyle, first earl of, 38–47 *passim*, 53–4, 61, 64, 68, 73, 74, 75, 77, 79, 85, 87, 92, 154
Orrery, Roger Boyle, second earl of, 97, 130

Osborne, Thomas, earl of Danby, 56
Ossory, Thomas Butler, earl of, 41, 56, 57, 58, 59, 63, 73, 80, 81, 83, 86, 88, 91, 126
Otway, Thomas, Church of Ireland archbishop of Killala, 25
Oxford, 4, 116, 135, 139

Painstown, county Meath, 71
Paris, 9, 53, 69, 97
parliament, England, 1, 6–8, 10, 14, 15, 17, 33, 34, 37, 38, 43, 45, 53, 55, 56, 57, 59–60, 61, 62, 63, 64, 65, 66, 68, 69, 70, 72–3, 93, 95, 96, 97, 99, 103, 104, 109, 110, 111, 116, 117, 120, 121, 127, 128, 129–30, 131, 132, 135, 136, 139–40, 143, 145, 146, 147
  House of Commons, 23, 38, 48, 60, 97, 99, 116, 123, 124, 125, 129, 131, 139, 153
  House of Lords, 6, 34, 40, 47, 48, 49, 57, 58, 59, 61, 62, 70, 75, 88, 94, 97, 98, 99, 102, 104, 106, 109, 111, 112, 115, 116, 122, 123, 126, 128, 129, 130, 131, 153
parliament, Ireland, 19, 24, 27, 31, 34, 53, 55, 58, 62, 63, 68, 70, 71, 74, 75, 76, 77, 78, 80, 83, 89, 90, 91, 92, 93, 97, 98, 126, 132, 142, 146, 152, 153, 154, 159, 162
Pepys, Samuel, 61
Petty, William, 19, 20, 21, 60, 63–4, 81, 118, 159–60
Philip II, king of Spain, 9
Piedmont, 122
Plunkett, Nicholas, 165
Plunkett, Oliver, Catholic archbishop of Armagh, 1, 23, 32, 37, 65, 74, 78, 80, 81, 82, 83, 85, 86, 87, 88, 89, 97, 98, 99, 100, 101, 103, 106, 107, 108, 109, 110, 115, 116, 118, 123, 124, 128, 134, 143, 144, 147, 148, 149, 151, 153, 155, 156, 157, 158
Poland, 121
Pope, Innocent XI, 20, 46, 49, 50, 59, 60, 103, 128, 136, 141, 147
Pope, Pius V, 9
Portadown, county Armagh, 51
Portsmouth, Louise Kéroualle, duchess of, 42
Portugal, 121
Portumna, county Galway, 118
'Poyning's law', 32, 63
Poyntzpass, county Armagh, 107
Prance, Miles, 48
presbyterians, 19, 24, 25, 26, 61, 65, 66–7, 73, 90, 110, 116, 132, 141, 154, 156
  See also dissenters; non-conformists
Privy Council, England, 5, 7, 32, 37, 41, 43, 53, 58, 62, 68, 75, 77, 78, 79, 80, 83, 86, 88, 89, 90, 91, 95, 97, 111, 130, 133, 136, 137, 138, 141, 143, 148, 153, 157, 158
proclamations, 34, 36, 37, 40, 44, 45, 49, 58, 59, 60, 65, 67, 72, 82, 100, 122, 124, 140, 146, 147

Queen's County, 35, 125, 141

Ranelagh, Katherine Jones, *née* Boyle, lady, 64
Ranelagh, Richard Jones, earl of, 24–5, 31, 32, 53, 55, 58, 64, 65, 67, 69, 70, 71, 75, 76, 77, 89, 90, 91, 92, 142, 152
Rawdon, George, 71, 77
rebellion (1641), 3, 9, 11–17, 18–19, 20, 21, 25, 37, 50–2, 65, 67, 83, 84, 100, 105, 111, 114, 118–23, 134, 136, 152, 160, 161, 162, 163, 164
recusants, 10, 37, 86
remonstrance (1661), 31, 32
revenue, Ireland, 24, 27, 58, 67, 70, 83, 90, 92, 106, 154
  see also finances, Ireland

Rome, 8, 20, 23, 132
Roscommon, county, 24, 146

St Bartholomew's Day Massacre (1572), 9, 13, 53
St Omer, 5
St Patrick's Cathedral, Dublin, 121
Samson, Thomas, 95, 102, 109, 110, 111, 123, 125, 129, 138, 148
Scotland, 2, 4, 6, 8, 14, 21, 22, 23, 30, 38, 48, 56, 57, 64, 66–7, 72, 73, 146, 154, 159
Shadwell, Thomas, 47
Shaen, James, 92–3
Shaftesbury, Anthony Ashley Cooper, earl of, 57, 58, 59, 62, 63, 68, 75, 80, 81, 83, 84, 86, 87, 88, 89, 94, 95, 96, 98, 99, 106, 110, 111, 119, 125, 128, 137, 140, 143, 144, 145, 150, 151, 154, 156, 157
Shannon, river, 39, 110, 113, 140
Sharp, James, Church of Scotland archbishop of St Andrews, 66
Sligo, town and county, 35, 51, 79, 159
Smith, John, 88, 108, 109
Solemn league and covenant, 132
Southwark, 28, 97
Southwell, Robert, 2, 22, 30, 41, 44, 45, 63, 64, 111, 155, 159
Southwell, Thomas, 82, 104, 111, 113, 138, 142
Spain, 9, 14, 34, 47, 97, 100, 115, 140
Spanish Armada (1588), 9, 118
Stuart, Mary, 6
Sunderland, Robert Spenser, earl of, 79

Talbot, Peter, Catholic archbishop of Dublin, 28, 31, 32–3, 44, 45, 46, 48, 49, 60, 69, 124, 125
Talbot, Richard, 32, 33, 35, 45, 48, 68, 103, 125, 145, 158, 163
Tangiers, 90, 91, 123, 132, 141

Tarbert, county Kerry, 113
Temple, John, 15–17, 21, 50, 51, 92, 120, 135, 162
Temple, William, 21, 92
Thirty Years War (1618–48), 11
Tillotson, John, 120
Tipperary, county, 128
Tixell, 50
Tonge, Israel, 5, 158
tory/tories
  English political interest, 116, 122, 146, 158
  in Ireland, 59, 71, 82, 101, 107–8
Tralee, county Kerry, 159
Treasury, England, 59, 65, 92, 124, 133
Trim, county Meath, 103, 109, 126
Trinity College, Dublin, 106
Tyburn, 90, 149
Tyrell, Patrick, Catholic archbishop of Clogher, 100, 124
Tyrone, county, 11
Tyrone, Richard Power, earl of, 74, 75, 76, 78, 79, 81, 84, 88, 95, 96, 98, 99, 101, 102, 103, 109, 110, 111, 123, 128, 129, 131, 135, 138, 145, 157

Ulster, 11, 12, 21, 23, 56, 66–7, 69, 70, 71, 73, 81, 82, 88, 100, 103, 106, 108, 132

Vatican, 78, 85
Vernon, George, 116
Vesey, John, Church of Ireland archbishop of Tuam, 126
Villiers, Edward, 102
Virginia, north America, 94

Wadding, Luke, Catholic archbishop of Ferns, 34, 52
Wakeman, George, 7, 69, 117
Walsh, Robert, 48
Warcup, Edmund, 144, 158
Ware, James, 88
Ware, Robert, 88

Waterford, town and county, 37, 40, 76, 77, 84, 101, 102, 109, 110, 159
Wentworth, Thomas, earl of Strafford, 25
Westminster, 38, 97, 144
Weyer, Florence, 144, 148
whig, 8, 20, 49, 56, 57, 62, 72, 79, 83, 86, 88, 89, 96, 108, 110, 116, 117, 122, 124, 131, 132, 137, 139, 140, 142, 145, 146, 149, 153, 156
Wicklow, county, 34
Williamite war (1689–91), 160, 161
William of Orange, 6, 160, 164
Williamson, Joseph, 38, 39
Windsor, 72
Winnington, Francis, 129
witnesses, 119, 125, 128, 129, 143, 146, 147, 148, 149
see also informers
Wyche, Cyril, 41, 46, 57

York, James Stuart, duke of, 1, 5–8, 29, 32, 39, 48, 56, 57, 59, 61, 65, 72, 74, 80, 83, 84, 93, 100, 103, 110, 113, 121, 137, 138, 146, 147, 148, 149, 156, 161, 162, 165
Youghal, county Cork, 76, 125, 133, 141, 159